THE PUBLIC MINISTRY OF CHRIST

by

William Garden Blaikie

D.D., LL.D.

WIPF & STOCK · Eugene, Oregon

Wipf and Stock Publishers
199 W 8th Ave, Suite 3
Eugene, OR 97401

The Public Ministry of Christ
By Blaikie, William Garden
ISBN 13: 978-1-55635-744-2
ISBN 10: 1-55635-774-3
Publication date 12/3/2007
Previously published by James Nisbet & Co., 1883

PREFACE.

THE present volume bears on a department of the life of our Lord to which, amid all that has been written lately, very little attention has been given I trust therefore it will be found to supply a want, and will prove useful not only to ministers of the Gospel, but to all who take part in Christian service.

A considerable portion of the volume has formed part of the author's lectures on Homiletical and Pastoral Theology, delivered to the students of the New College, Edinburgh. Coming in as that subject does at the very close of a four years' theological course, my aim there is not so much to impart knowledge, as to communicate to the students a tone and practical impulse. For this purpose one of the best means is the study of the Public Ministry and Pastoral Methods of our Lord. I have found the subject grow in my hands from year to year, till it has come to be out of proportion to the other parts of the course; and though the present volume has a measure of completeness, I know well that there are many other parts of the life of Christ that may yield similar lessons.

This volume is in some sense a sequel to my book, "For the Work of the Ministry: a Manual of Homiletical and Pastoral Theology." On another side it has a connection with my "Glimpses of the Inner Life of our Lord." May the three prove a threefold cord, each adding to the effect of the other two, and all contributing, under the Divine blessing, to build up the kingdom of God.

CONTENTS.

Chap.		Page
I.	Our Lord's Ministry as an Example,	1
II.	Preparation for His Ministry,	21
III.	Inner Spirit of His Ministry,	39
IV.	Outer Features of His Ministry,	59
V.	Beginning of His Judæan Ministry,	77
VI.	Beginning of His Galilean Ministry,	95
VII.	His Work as a Teacher,	113
VIII.	Elements of Impression in His Teaching—I. Internal,	134
IX.	Elements of Impression in His Teaching—II. Structural,	155
X.	Elements of Impression in His Teaching—III. Illustration,	174
XI.	Parabolic Discourses,	186
XII.	Public Discourses—Sermon on the Mount,	203
XIII.	The College of the Twelve,	220
XIV.	Dealings with the Apostles,	238
XV.	Dealings with Different Classes—I. Outside the Kingdom,	256
XVI.	Dealings with Different Classes—II. On the Borders of the Kingdom,	275
XVII.	Dealings with Different Classes—III. Inside the Kingdom,	293
XVIII.	His Farewell,	313
XIX.	His Re-appearance,	333

CHAPTER I.

HIS MINISTRY AS AN EXAMPLE.

Is it a bootless, perhaps a presumptuous task, for those who are left to build up the Kingdom of Christ in this world to try to trace out the Master's ways of working, and find footprints in which they may follow? Are the natural and the supernatural, the human and the divine in Christ's earthly ministry blended too closely for us to disentangle them, so as to make good use of what alone belongs to us? Is it only with vague, admiring wonder that we can gaze on that career which was the turning-point of the world's history, the great crisis of the Kingdom of God? Is the ministry of our Lord to be classed with the blue sky, or the rainbow, or the starry heavens, or other wonderful works of God, —things that are not only too high for us, but in every sense beyond our power to imitate, much more to equal?

This position has been held by some, and notably by one of the most reverent of German theologians —Carl Immanuel Nitzsch. In his judgment, our blessed Lord, from His altogether unparalleled personality, and from His unique relation to the Kingdom of God, stands beyond the sphere of our imitation, and can in no sense be treated as a homiletical model. But in opposition to this, it has been forcibly urged that inasmuch as He, the Incarnate Word, Son of God and Son of Man as He was in a sense wholly unique, nevertheless appeared also as a prophet in Israel and went about on earth in the garb of a teacher, there is nothing to hinder us, as disciples in the first instance, and as preachers and teachers next, to sit at His feet and learn of Him.[1] If the example of Christ were wholly inapplicable to us as His public servants, it could hardly be suitable to us as His personal followers. Yet nothing is more certain, or more readily accepted by the Christian conscience in reference to our ordinary life, than that He hath left us an example that we should follow His steps. If the example be so binding in the one sphere, it must surely have some power in the other.

But besides this, many weighty considerations show why the servants of Christ, to the very end of the dispensation, should give earnest heed to His ways and example as a minister.

1. First, Our Lord said to the Father: "As thou hast sent me into the world, even so have I also sent them into the world" (John xvii. 18). And after His resurrection He said to the Apostles: "As the Father hath sent me, even so send I you" (John xx. 21.) The Apostles in their work for the world bore the same relation to Christ as Christ bore to the Father. When Jesus left the world, they remained to continue the work. And when they left the world they committed the things that they

[1] Van Oosterzee, *Practical Theology*, p. 71.

had heard to faithful men who should be able to teach others also. In Christ's hands, no doubt, the work was done very differently from the way in which it was done or can be done in any other. But it is the same work, and as far as the case admits, it is to be done in the same way. The fact that we are sent into the world to continue in certain respects the work which He began should constrain us to look carefully to His ways of doing it. This is the true apostolical succession. What is any amount of laying on of hands, or any mechanical chain that can be conceived, compared to the succession that inherits the true spirit and holy methods of the Master?

2. Again, we are taught that, in doing His work, Christ took upon Him the form of a servant. Though He was "in the form of God, and thought it not robbery to be equal with God, he made himself of no reputation, and took upon him the form of a servant, and was made in the likeness of men." The self-emptying of Christ is one of the deep things which we can never fully comprehend. But we can understand how it brings Him as a Minister nearer to ourselves, and more within the scope of our imitation. He freely placed Himself under conditions many of which were the same as ours. Not only did He work with a body subject to weariness, hunger, and thirst, and with a soul keenly alive to reproach, to contradiction, to treachery, and all kinds of evil treatment, but the spirit of subjection to another ruled His whole life, and the sense of dependence on another for daily strength and succour showed itself continually, especially

in His habit of incessant prayer. " In all things it behoved him to be made like unto his brethren."

Of the working of this servant-feeling in Jesus we have some beautiful glimpses in the Old Testament, and especially in one very remarkable Messianic passage,—the fiftieth chapter of Isaiah. Nothing could be more beautiful than the spirit of subjection there expressed; it reminds us of little Samuel as he seemed to hear the voice of Eli. "The Lord God hath given me the tongue of the learned, that I should know how to speak a word in season to him that is weary; he wakeneth morning by morning, he wakeneth mine ear to hear as the learned." Not only is Messiah's capacity for instructing the gift of God, but the daily bread which he is to serve out; morning by morning Jehovah wakens him to receive the lessons which He is to impart during each day.

3. Hence, thirdly, when we proceed to the more minute examination of our Lord's ministry, we are surprised to find how near it seems to lie to us. Viewing it as an example, we find that it is not so hopelessly beyond our imitation as we might have expected it to be. The supernatural halo that encompasses the prophets—Moses or Isaiah, for example—undoubtedly affects their influence as examples, because it sets their ministry in another plane from ours. In the case of Jesus there is so much more of the supernatural than in the prophets that we might have expected a still greater gulf between His ministry and our own. No doubt, in one sense, the gulf is infinitely wide, yet, in a human sense, Christ appears to walk by our side. Strange to say, He is more of a companion among us than Moses or

Isaiah. In His relation to the twelve He is seen in a more familiar light than they. It is in their intercourse with their friends that men reveal themselves most. It was Christ's pleasure to treat His Apostles not as servants but as friends. This gives us a wonderful insight into the natural life, so to speak, and the social nature of Jesus. It makes Him appear so brotherly, so thoroughly one of ourselves, that it seems just what ought to be that we should live as He lived, and serve as He served.

Yet we must remark, and with deepest reverence, that with all His naturalness and social likeness to us, and with all His participation in the infirmities of our nature, He never shows kinship with us in our sins. It is a strange yet common experience, that out of some of the very blunders of great and good men and of their failings in duty there springs up a fellow-feeling between them and ordinary mortals, otherwise hardly possible. How often do we feel that one touch of fallen nature makes us kin! When Moses strikes the rock, when Elijah flies to the desert, when Jonah takes his passage in the ship, when Jeremiah pleads his youth, when Paul and Barnabas fall out about Mark, we feel that they were men of like passions with ourselves, and possibly, for this very reason, we appreciate more highly the noble service which, despite their infirmities, they were able to render. We see them not as mere lay-figures, invested by fanciful writers with every imaginable excellence, and quite beyond the sphere of humanity,—of the order of angels rather than men; but of flesh and blood like ourselves, not without hasty tempers and carnal fears, hearts that could be moved by temptation, and consciences that could be paralysed for a time by sin.

But there is nothing of this kind in our blessed Lord. He never falls, never slips, never sins. It is very remarkable that in spite of this we should feel so near to Him. That it should be so, is due to the intensity of His love, the depth of His humility, and the fulness of His humanity. He touches us so closely at all points where contact is possible that for the time we are hardly conscious of the points where the distance is so great that contact is not possible. The woman that washed Christ's feet with her tears was separated from Him morally by a whole universe, but compassion drew His heart into closest contact with hers. As two houses that are connected by a mutual gable on one side, may be said on the other side to be separated by the whole circumference of the globe, so Christ in His humanity could come into closest intimacy even with those from whom in a higher sense He was separated by infinity. In His dealings with His disciples, His gentleness, His forbearance, His consideration broke down every barrier to loving and confidential intercourse. As we study His life and ministry we come under the influence of the same attractive power. Not as individuals merely, but as workers together with Christ, we are constrained to draw near; like Mary, we sit at His feet, and learn of Him who is meek and lowly in heart.

4. But if we would perceive more clearly in what respects our Lord's ministry is an example to us, it

will be useful to break up His work into its constituent parts, and consider His offices as prophet, priest, and king.

Of the three, that of priest is the most beyond us, and that of prophet comes nearest to us, while that of king, immeasurably above us in one sense, is yet brought near to us in another. In His glorious work of reconciling God and man by the sacrifice of the cross, we know that we can have not the vestige of a share. In the majesty of His royal power, in the charm of His miraculous works, in the sublime authority that by a word ruled the waves and scattered devils, that by a mere exercise of will controlled the forces of disease, and made even death and the grave surrender their victims, Jesus stands immeasurably above us. It is as a teacher that we may follow Him most fully. We may take up the truths which He revealed and communicate them to others. We may study and in a sense follow His method of getting into the human heart. We may go forth by the footsteps of His flock, and feed our kids beside the Great Shepherd's tent. But even as a teacher He occupies heights that we can never reach. Never man spake as this man. No eye ever penetrated like His into the ways of God, and no tongue ever taught such lessons of truth and life. We are dazzled by His person as the first disciples were: "We beheld His glory, the glory as of the only begotten of the Father, full of grace and truth."

Besides this, we may also enter in some measure into His kingly office. Our work in the ministry is much more than the mere teacher's. We fail wholly unless we persuade as well as teach. As teachers we need the prophetic gift, but as persuaders we must be kings. And the power which we need for this kingly function is likewise communicable, and may be enjoyed by those who earnestly seek it. "Ye shall receive power after that the Holy Ghost is come upon you." It is given to earnest men, in conjunction with the Spirit of God, to wield the sceptre of spiritual influence. It is not only in the world to come but in a sense in this world too that the promise is fulfilled—"To him that overcometh will I grant to sit with me on my throne." Even now we may adore Him who hath made us kings and priests to God. It is but seldom, and in the infancy of His Church, that the power of wielding the forces of nature supernaturally, and turning them to the purposes of the gospel, has been given to His servants; but no faithful minister has ever been left without power in the realm of spirit,— without the power that controls the movements of the human soul, and turns it to God. To enjoy this power of turning hearts to God should be the supreme ambition of the Christian minister; to exercise it his supreme delight. A ministry pitched on any lower key is defective in its highest element, and unworthy of the true servant of Jesus Christ.

It being thus clear that Christian ministers are not merely at liberty but are bound to follow Christ by continuing according to their gifts the work which He began, and, as far as may be, the methods which He practised, we have next to inquire, What was our Lord's own conception of that work—the work for which He came into the world, and for which He lived, died, and rose again? The more definitely we apprehend His work as He viewed it, the more clearly shall we see what is incumbent on those who follow Him.

1. As it presented itself in its broadest aspect to the mind of Christ, His work was that of the Old Testament Messiah. He found innumerable things written in the law, and in the prophets, and in the psalms, concerning Himself. In the main, the work of the Messiah was to be a work of restoration. A great quarrel had to be settled, a rebellion had to be quelled, a ruin had to be built up, a kingdom had to be established, disorder and misery had to be replaced by peace, prosperity, and all manner of blessing. "In thee and in thy seed shall all the families of the earth be blessed." It was not a work that was to carry blessing to one nation only, but to all the world. This is the most outstanding idea of His work that our Lord would gather from the Old Testament. He was to scatter blessing far and near. The eyes of the blind were to be opened, and the ears of the deaf unstopped. The lame man was to leap as a hart, and the tongue of the dumb was to sing. The Spirit of the Lord God was to be upon Him, because the Lord anointed Him to preach glad tidings to the meek. He sent Him to bind up the broken-hearted, to proclaim liberty to the captives, and the opening of the prison to them that were bound.

Thus the most prominent feature of Messiah's work was to be that of benediction. Men were to be blessed in Him; all nations were to call Him blessed. Now, for a work of this kind the appropriate spirit was that of cheerfulness and radiant love. And, corresponding to this conception of the Messiah's work, this was Christ's prevailing spirit. Although to qualify Him for spreading these blessings among sinners, it behoved Him to suffer much, He did not allow this necessity to interfere with the habitual serenity and cheerfulness of His spirit. Essentially He was a bringer of good news to men; and not His tongue only, but His eyes, His face, His whole appearance and manner, habitually preached this gospel. For the most part, Jesus hid His troubles from the world. Only three of the chosen twelve were allowed to go with Him to Gethsemane, where waves of such dreadful anguish were to go Him.

It is in the same serene and cheerful spirit that the work of the gospel is to be conducted still. Whatever sorrows, public or private, the ministers of Christ have to bear, it becomes them like Him to bear them in secret, to hide them as far as possible from the world, and even from the Church. Men of sorrowful spirit and gloomy countenance are not the men to proclaim good news, or win mankind to belief in them. Even experienced Christians do not like a lugubrious minister, and to children and the ignorant he is positively repulsive. The great evangelists of the Church have usually been men of radiant nature, realising the blessedness of the Gospel, and showing its influence in their happy looks and cheerful tones. No doubt there are many things, both in their own hearts and in the world around them, fitted to depress God's servants. But if our Lord could for the most part hide His sorrows from the world, so may they. If in His ordinary intercourse with men He could maintain the cheerful tone that became the bearer of good tidings, so may they. The words of the fiftieth chapter of Isaiah are the Master's words to all His servants: "Who is among you that feareth the LORD, that obeyeth the voice of his servant, that walketh in darkness and hath no light; *let him trust in the name of the LORD, and stay upon his God.*"

But on the very surface of the Old Testament it was not less clearly revealed that the career of Messiah, while it would be one of beneficence, would likewise be one of terrible conflict. He would not be suffered to shed His blessings quietly on the world as the summer sun sheds his beams on the earth. Deadly opposition would meet Him at every point. The prophecy in Eden would come true—the serpent would bruise His heel. Psalms like the second reveal confederate hosts striving to break His bands asunder, and cast away His cords. In Isaiah, He is brought as a lamb to the slaughter, and as a sheep before her shearers is dumb. Terrible wails rise from His lips in psalms like the twenty-second and the sixty-ninth. From the very beginning, Christ must have been conscious that His public life would be a continuous battle. It was not only the cold worldliness and wickedness of the human heart He would have to encounter, but all the active forces of evil. Satan, His personal foe, would be laying snares for Him at every point. Men and devils, clergy and laity, Pharisees and Sadducees, scribes and lawyers, would be found bending their utmost energies on every side to crush Him.

Ere He entered on His public work, He must have gathered all this from the Old Testament pictures of Messiah. Usually beneficence commends itself; philanthropy is popular and carries all before it; but it was not to do so in the case of Christ. Supreme beneficence was to be met by supreme malevolence. It is wonderful that all this should have failed to discompose His spirit, to drive serenity from His heart, or cheerfulness from His face. But, from the beginning He must have been bracing Himself for these conflicts—acting out the prophetic resolution —"The Lord God will help me, therefore shall I not be confounded; therefore have I set my face like a flint, and I know that I shall not be ashamed" (Isa. l. 7).

Here then was Christ's conception of His work, as derived from the Hebrew Scriptures—a blessed work of restoration to be carried on against the fiercest assaults of all the powers of darkness. Few things could be more difficult. Benevolence does not readily harmonise with fighting, and fighting does not foster benevolence. Yet in Jesus the benevolent spirit remains unchilled by all the machinations of evil with which He has to contend. And the spirit of high resolve and fearless exposure to assault acquires strength and firmness from the feeling that it is demanded by the loving errand on which He has come. Jesus is at once the lion and the lamb. But His courage is in vital connection with His compassion. He is rooted and built up in love. Nothing higher can be proposed for the imitation of His servants. We have to combine the attitude of the warrior and the spirit of the lover. The spirit of love must dominate our whole procedure, and reign unchilled in all our conflicts for truth, meekness, and righteousness.

2. A more definite view of the purpose for which Christ felt that He had come may be obtained from studying His sayings that begin with the formula: "The Son of man is come," or "I am come." "The Son of man is come to seek and to save that which is lost." "I am not come to call the righteous, but sinners to repentance." "I am come that they might have life, and that they might have it more abundantly." "I am come a light into the world that whoso believeth on me should not abide in darkness." "The Son of man came not to be ministered unto but to minister, and to give his life a ransom for many." Life, light, repentance, renewal, salvation, are among the blessings which Christ has come to bestow. The reference is very plain in such passages to the needy condition of men, as Christ finds them. They are not righteous but sinful; not whole but sick; not penitent but hardened; not seeing but blind; not living but dead. For all these wants Christ has to furnish the supply. To remove their guilt, He gives His life a ransom; to remove their sickness, He sends His word and heals them; to soften their hard hearts He gives them by His Spirit the new heart and the right spirit; for sight He anoints their eyes with the eye-salve of the gospel; and for life He calls to them, as He called in the graveyard of Bethany: "Lazarus, come forth."

But where are these and all similar blessings to be found? It was Christ's clear and emphatic teaching that all are stored in His own person. Why was He so eager that men should believe on Him? Not, certainly, for any personal reason; but mainly because these blessings were in Him, and unless men believed on Him they could not obtain them. "This is the record, that God hath given to us eternal life, and this life is in his Son." It is obvious, however, that Christ's servants are in a very different relation to these blessings from that in which Christ stood to them Himself. We are not priests. Our Master has not handed over to us the store of grace, nor given us the right to dole it out as we may think right, to those who come to us seeking the heavenly gift. The Church is not a reservoir, filled with the merit of Christ, at the disposal of the priest for such as he may deem worthy to receive it. This dogma is a frightful perversion of the truth. What then? The work of Christ, by which the fountain of life was opened, has to be carried out by His ministers still. The Church has to turn to account the glorious merit of Christ, and get men to share it. How is this to be done? In the first place, she must enlighten men in the knowledge of Christ; and in the next place, get them drawn into personal union with Him. She must first show them how it hath pleased the Father that in Him all fulness should dwell; and next, urge them in the strength of God to the act of faith—to that personal committal of themselves as sinners to Him, and that personal acceptance of Him as a Saviour for them, through which all His blessings come. We must seek that all our teaching and all our ordinances may become channels by which the grace of the Lord Jesus Christ may flow to men. As Jesus sought to draw men to Himself, we must seek to send them to Him. The sense of His supreme and infinite value must be at the heart of all we do. It is a good sign of a ministry when it begins with a profound sense of the truth that from Him all saving blessing comes, when Jesus appears like the Sun in the firmament, the one great source of blessing to sinful men.

3. A third element of our Lord's conception of His work on earth is obtained from His references to "the kingdom" which He came to set up. In forms very manifold He dwelt on this idea. His ministry in Galilee began with the call: "Repent, for the kingdom of heaven is at hand." In the Sermon on the Mount, the manifesto of the kingdom, He proclaimed the duty of seeking first the kingdom of God and His righteousness, and He protested that the righteousness of the Scribes and Pharisees did not come up to the standard of that kingdom. To Nicodemus he taught, "Except a man be born again, he cannot see the kingdom of God." The gospel which He is said to have preached is called "the gospel of the kingdom" (Matt. iv. 23). Many of the parables indicated resemblances in earthly things to features of the kingdom. When Jesus was asked by Pilate, Art thou a king then? He owned it; but His kingdom, He said, was not of this world. It is thus obvious that the establishment of a very glorious kingdom was to be the result of His earthly work. Not that this was to be accomplished at once. Only when the Son of Man should come in His glory and all the angels with Him

would His people, in the fullest sense, inherit the kingdom prepared for them from the foundation of the world.

Meanwhile, men were to be invited into the kingdom, prepared for it, and in a sense incorporated with it. They were to receive its righteousness, to be taught its laws, to acquire its spirit, to be trained to its service, and all this through being first brought into a right relation and attitude to its Head. To lay the foundations of this kingdom, overcome its enemies, transform men and women of the fallen race of Adam into its willing and loyal subjects, and finally complete it in its purity and glory, were constantly referred to as among the purposes for which Jesus was manifested among men.

Let us try to get a more definite understanding of what this implied. Let us take the expression, "Jesus went about preaching *the gospel of the kingdom*" (Matt. ix. 35). This is a more complete and a more significant phrase than merely preaching the gospel. The good news which Christ preached found its highest and fullest development in the idea of the kingdom. The phrase goes further than the angels' song—"Glory to God in the highest, on earth peace, good-will to men." That proclamation did not necessarily imply more than an economy of blessing to individual men. But the idea of Christ's kingdom is that of a *community*, of which the members, besides being blessed by Him individually, are placed in new relations to one another, out of which spring numberless developments of interest and sympathy, of character and enjoyment, of activity and progress, greatly amplifying their life and service, and replenishing all with a manifold glory. In the kingdom, purer affections and sympathies bind husband and wife, parent and child, master and servant, subject and ruler, friends and neighbours. In the kingdom, the common worship and active service of God give rise to new relations greatly increasing the interest, the enjoyment, and the profitableness of life. Hearts are drawn to one another in united worship and work for the Lord. Sympathy is drawn out toward the whole world, and efforts are called forth for its highest good. In the common business of life, selfishness gives place to brotherly interest and regard. The greatest happiness of the greatest number is raised from a mere philosophical formula into a high principle of life.

All this, and far more than this, was embraced in Christ's idea of the kingdom. Human life is but a poor thing in its mere individuality. It is in its social relations and bearings that its full capacity is found, both of action and of enjoyment. To develop these relations to the full, Godward and manward both, and make all of them means of high benefit and pure enjoyment in all their multifarious bearings, is embraced in the plan. But such a consummation is not the achievement of a day. The movement towards it goes on, sometimes more actively, sometimes more languidly. Sanballat the Horonite and Tobiah the Ammonite are continually obstructing it. Indifference often reigns within— while the bridegroom tarries, the virgins slumber and sleep. But the setting up of this kingdom of

Christ in all its glory is the great certainty of the future. And we who are called to continue His work should often have this consummation in our view. The fact that nothing short of this is the goal of our enterprise should draw out our energies to the very utmost. In so vast a work we ought to seek the co-operation of numberless fellow-workers. What a reproof does this grand view of Christ's administer to our low aims, our feeble purposes, and indolent endeavours! How should the fact that this enterprise is committed to us throw us on the infinite power and resources of our Great Master!

4. One other remark is essential to a right understanding of Christ's conception of His work among men. We have spoken of His idea of the kingdom, and the vastness of the transformation of human society which it involves. The manner in which this kingdom was to be established must have been a matter of great importance. Did Christ give any instructions as to the way of setting it up? It is said to be a characteristic of the greatest minds that while the schemes they form are vast and comprehensive, they are marked at the same time by great attention to details. No scheme could have been vaster than that of Christ's kingdom, yet the working of it out was to be matter of minute detail. Each soul must see the Divine light, must respond to the Divine voice. The building up of a coral island, through particle after particle secreted by the insect, is hardly a minuter operation than the building up of the kingdom of Christ by detailed dealings with individual souls. It has often been remarked

that compared with other ministries that of Christ was not remarkably fruitful in conversions. If the crowds that followed the Baptist gathered also round Christ, it was not to manifest the same tokens of wholesale impression, or even to give the same evidence of a desire to be changed. But this very fact fixes our view the more on those dealings *with individuals* which formed so marked a feature of Christ's ministry. He showed no morbid desire to be followed by crowds. In instructing Nicodemus in the doctrine of regeneration and redemption, or the woman of Samaria in the gift of living water and the duty of spiritual worship, He showed himself as ready to take pains with His one hearer, and as much pleased with the result, as if thousands had been hanging on His lips.

In this way He taught us that the building up of His kingdom must depend on individual conviction and individual faith. It was not by royal edicts like those of Hezekiah and Josiah, requiring the people to do this or that in the worship of God, on pain of civil penalties, that the masses were to be converted; but by very earnest work in the case of individuals, whose example and influence might thereafter spread to the many. Let a spiritual movement be once started on the basis of individual conviction and faith, and it may thereafter spread fast enough with all safety among the masses. This indeed was the character of the movement on the day of Pentecost. Thousands were embraced in that revolution, but in every case there was individual conviction and individual faith. Each heart was drawn to the Saviour by the pressure of its own necessities and ardent cravings; a living faith in Him brought its peace and life.

If we are to be fellow-workers with Christ, we must go to work in a similar way. No process under the sun can supply the place of individual conviction and personal union to Christ. There may be temptations to us to get masses of men drawn by some means or other within the pale of the visible Church, and some may mistake this for success. In the middle ages kings would sometimes determine for their people that they should become Christian, and hordes of ignorant and godless men would pass nominally by baptism into the Christian Church. In modern times it has often been thought a great benefit to have some strong social power on the side of Christianity, in order to draw to it many that would otherwise pass it by. But too often these methods have only discredited Christ's own way of building up His Church—by personal conviction. His method is slow and laborious; it demands much consecration, patience, and prayer; but it is the only method that truly effects the great end. The cause of Christian progress has often been kept back by methods that promise a large agglomeration of adherents, but dispense with the one indispensable element. The Church, and every separate section of it, has always been most powerful when Christ's own way has been followed, and His ministers have burned with the desire to make His Church a community of living men and women, who have "been pricked in their hearts," and in their earnestness have asked, "Men and brethren, what shall we do?"

CHAPTER II.

PREPARATION FOR HIS MINISTRY.

THAT our Lord should have been trained for His work at such a place as Nazareth is certainly a thing unlooked for. "My ways are not your ways, neither are your thoughts my thoughts, saith the Lord." If we desired a more than usually striking illustration of these words, might we not find it in the fact that the place selected for the Incarnate Son of God to prepare for His unexampled work was a village proverbial for its roughness and wickedness? Besides the proverb (which spoke volumes), "Can any good thing come out of Nazareth?" we have in illustration of the character of the place the incident that occurred in our Lord's early ministry, when the people dragged Him to the brow of the hill intending to hurl Him over the precipice. Who could have supposed that among so rude and wicked a people the gentlest and tenderest heart the world ever knew should have attained its strength and beauty—that amid the pestilential atmosphere of such a place the Rose of Sharon should have become so fragrant, and the lily of the valleys so sweet? Even in the carpenter's home, if we except Mary and her husband,

Jesus could not have found much that was congenial. He seems to have made no impression on the outer world. No curiosity was raised as to His future career. Till about the time of the crucifixion even His brethren did not believe on Him. We may fancy Him indeed often sitting with His mother reading the Scriptures and speaking of the things of the kingdom of God; but we have no evidence that He ever roamed the hills with a single like-minded companion, or knew the joy of friendship and spiritual fellowship with any one of the same years and occupation as Himself.

It must have been mainly in solitude, therefore, that He pursued His studies for the ministry during His curriculum of thirty years. He had three principal text-books—all of which He mastered thoroughly—the Old Testament, the book of nature, and the human heart. Many things in His life show how thoroughly He penetrated to the very heart and core of the first. The book of nature was interesting chiefly for the analogies which it presented to the operations of God in a higher and more spiritual sphere. The third book—the human heart—must have been a painful but very interesting study. In this department of theological learning He was like a physician studying disease, studying every form and phase of morbid action, that He might the better know how to deal with it. And the rough, unrestrained boors of Nazareth would present him with ample material for this study. Not that the morbid aspects of the human heart would engross all His attention. He would study the openings to the soul of man, the ways of entering it, and interesting it, and moulding it, and turning it. He would become acquainted with its various moods, sometimes cheerful, sometimes dark; in times of prosperity and in days of trouble; now tempted on this side and now on that; now drinking greedily from worldly cisterns, now disgusted and yearning for something better. He would observe how the children of this world were in their generation wiser than the children of light; yet how, all through, human nature had always one dark feature—resistance to the will of God. He would understand the difficulty of the task of the prophets as they struggled against this desperate tendency—a task which, after all, but dimly foreshadowed that which He had himself undertaken. For the most part things in Nazareth were the exact opposite of His model. Possibly His first great Galilean discourse—the Sermon on the Mount—was just Nazareth reversed—Nazareth the negative, and the sermon the positive. But the apprehension of what ought to be was the easiest part of His task. How to make His ideal a reality, how to establish a real kingdom after His pattern, that was an undertaking which required all the wisdom and power of heaven—*hic labor, hoc opus est.*

Where are we to date the conscious commencement of Christ's ministry? How was it that He grew in wisdom, and in favour with God and man? In dealing with such questions we are met by insuperable barriers. Few things are more wonderful than the silence of the Gospels respecting the infancy and youth of Jesus. If there were no other way to refute the mythical theory of the Gospels, their silence as to the infancy would be enough. When, at a later period in the history of the Church, men's imaginations did take a licence, and did surround the life with the creations of fancy, it was chiefly to the infancy that these myths were attached. It is very notable how rigidly the four Evangelists confined themselves to the public life. They felt that their business lay with that portion of time which was embraced between the baptism by John and the day when He was taken up. Whatever may be recorded of earlier occurrences is recorded either as showing the fulfilment of Scripture, or as bearing on the public life of Jesus. So completely have the details of His boyhood been passed over, that we cannot but conclude that there was a Divine purpose in the silence. The whole subject is so mysterious,—the development of the finite human nature in personal union with the infinite Divine nature,—that if details had been given they might have left a wrong impression. One of the most remarkable things about the life of Christ, as presented in the Gospels, is, that while we see the human in every act and word, we are never allowed to lose sight of the Divine. Possibly this effect might not have been so complete had details of His childhood been given. At all events, it has pleased God, when He brings His Son fully before the world, to introduce Him in the maturity of His manhood, in the fulness of His supernatural power, and with the fullest consciousness of His work as Messiah.

It may be noted, however, that the few things that are recorded of the early life of Christ, between

His infancy and His public entrance on His work, bear solely on His preparation for His ministry. Three facts are preserved to us: first, the incident with the doctors in the temple, and especially His reply to His mother's question; next, His being subject to His parents during His residence with them at Nazareth; and lastly, his presenting Himself to the Baptist, and insisting on His being baptized by him, notwithstanding the remonstrance of John.

These three facts throw an interesting light on *the discipline of subjection* which our Lord came under, and the variety and completeness of that discipline. We read, that "though he was a Son, yet learned he obedience by the things which he suffered;" and the Garden of Gethsemane, and other scenes of His public life, show to what an unprecedented length that habit of obedience was carried. In His answer to His mother in the Temple we see the spirit of subjection to the *will of His heavenly Father:* "I must be about my Father's business." In His obedience to Joseph and Mary at Nazareth, the discipline of subjection to *lawful human authority;* and in His answer to John, "Suffer it to be so now, for thus it becometh us to fulfil all righteousness," the discipline of subjection *to the requirements of His official position,* as the Righteous One, or representative of righteousness, standing in the room of the unrighteous. In this habit of our Lord's soul—His subjection to law, His self-restraint, His holy self-surrender—there is much, if I mistake not, that has special application to those preparing for His public service.

1. "Wist ye not that I must be about my Father's business?" We are not disposed to alter the translation, ἐν τοῖς τοῦ Πατρός μου, as the revised version does, "I must be in my Father's house." It is not usual to denote a house by the plural article, nor is it by any means so self-evident that He behoved to be *in the house*, as that He behoved to be *about the business* of His Father. The question has been asked, Did these words of the child indicate a full consciousness of His Messiahship and acquaintance with its obligations? In reply, it has commonly been held, that while His eager questioning of the doctors would seem to denote a human soul seeking more light, and not therefore fully cognisant of the reality, His words clearly imply two things—consciousness of a peculiar relation to God, "my Father;" and consciousness of a profound obligation arising from that relation, "I must be about my Father's business."

The recurrence of that formula, δεῖ, I must (it must), on many occasions of His public ministry, in connection with Messianic obligations, would seem to denote that already these obligations had begun to be apprehended. Already this child of twelve has come to see that His life must be a life of complete consecration. It is interesting to observe that it is the sterner view of duty that seems to influence the child—*I must*. In other parts of Scripture we have indications that this was not His only view; that doing God's will was a joy to Him; that His soul was in such harmony with the Father, that the irksome view of duty was swallowed up by the element of enjoyment which duty brings to a holy nature : "I delight to do thy will, O my God." But, strange to say, at the early age of twelve we find Him rather girding Himself for what is trying and irksome to human nature; bringing his young soul to face it; setting Himself to it, as He afterwards set His face steadfastly to go up to Jerusalem; like one breasting a hill or buffeting the waves. Surely in this the lesson for us is too obvious to escape notice. Be it a young minister, or a young person in any sphere, nothing is more salutary or more promising than this early grappling with labour; no flinching, but the stern, steady "I MUST" of duty.[1]

2. Next we have our Lord's subjection to His parents—the discipline of subordination to lawful human authority. He went down to Nazareth, and was subject to them. This, in any circumstances, would be an instructive fact in the life of Christ; but it has special significance side by side with the statement of His consecration to the work and will of His heavenly Father. In Him duty to the heavenly does not crush out duty to the earthly. A great obligation does not overlay a small. The divine is not allowed to eclipse the human. It is not merely in the august presence of the Eternal Father that the spirit of self is humbled. It is humbled in the presence of earthly relations, to whom it is fit and proper that He should give up His will, even though He has more wisdom than they. It is often a mark

---

[1] See *Glimpses of the Inner Life of our Lord* (chaps. i. and ii. "His Devotion to the Father's Work." "His Delight in the Father's Will").

of human infirmity that the self-control which is exercised on great occasions, under the conscious overawing presence of God, is lost on little occasions, in the presence of men, and especially in the presence of one's family. In the case of Jesus, we see not only self-control, but self-subjection carried out uniformly on all occasions. No doubt the conditions were very favourable. Such a mother as Mary, and such a step-father as Joseph, might well engage His obedience.

3. The same spirit of subjection is seen in His answer to John, when John shrank from baptizing Him. The incident is full of manifold beauty. The meeting of the law and the gospel is singularly graceful. As has been said, in presence of Jesus the reprover of the Sanhedrim and of Herod lost his dauntless bearing. For the first time, probably, that voice faltered, as it said, "I have need to be baptized of thee, and comest thou to me?" Thus the splendour of the New Testament broke forth from the verge of the Old. But the sternness of the Old Testament flashed across the dawn of the New, when Christ said, "Suffer it to be so now; for thus it becometh us to fulfil all righteousness." There is here the quintessence of courtesy. Each honours what was characteristic of the other. John honours the grace embodied in Jesus; Jesus honours the righteousness represented by John. The soul of chivalry and the soul of duty embrace each other.

But what we have chiefly to do with, in this incident, is the evidence of the spirit of subjection in Jesus to the requirements of an official position. The expression, "Thus it becometh us to fulfil all righteousness," is brief and elliptical, but significant. There is an obligation—not expressed by so strong a term as that used in the Temple—δεῖ, I must, because in that case he was dealing with a fact, while in the present he is dealing with a symbol; therefore, πρέπον ἐστί, a milder expression, is employed: "it becometh us." The meaning seems to be, that it was becoming that He should undergo a rite expressive of the duties of the office He had undertaken, in which He must show Himself to be "the Lord our Righteousness." Personally, He was undefiled; and it was not only unnecessary but unbecoming that He should receive the baptism of repentance to the forgiveness of sins. But as the Just who was to stand for the unjust, as the Holy One who was to suffer for the defiled, it became Him to receive the symbol of ablution. It was a token of Christ's subjecting Himself freely and readily to everything implied in His becoming the Champion of Righteousness, and the Substitute of the unrighteous—a sign that He calmly accepted that untold burden of toil, humiliation, and suffering which this relation implied. It is a very noble word with which to begin His public work. It is not the demands of mercy merely He is to fulfil, but the demands of righteousness. Mercy would be lenient, but righteousness is inexorable. The motto of righteousness is, "Verily thou shalt not go hence till thou hast paid the uttermost farthing." Jesus deliberately accepts the condition —"It becometh us to fulfil all righteousness."

In this view of His baptism, the threefold testimony borne to Him, immediately after, is easily understood—the opening of the heavens, the descent of the Holy Ghost, and the voice that proclaimed Him God's beloved Son, in whom He was well pleased. The lesson is now complete. The great business of Christ's preparatory course has been to strengthen and mature the spirit of subjection. When that spirit is ripe, the Holy Ghost comes on Him, in visible form, and a divine testimony is borne to Him from heaven. Having passed through all His trials, He is publicly called to the ministry. How different in His case the discipline of preparation from that of some in whom conceit grows steadily with their years of preparation, ripening at ordination into full-fledged self-sufficiency! Or from the case of others, in whom the completion of preparation marks the climax of a self-seeking spirit, which would have the sun, moon, and eleven stars stand round and do it obeisance! The true spirit is the spirit of subjection; it is to take on us the yoke which Christ took on Him, and learn of Him who was meek and lowly in heart. May this spirit of Jesus be indeed the spirit of every aspirant to the ministry; may it ripen day by day as the close of preparation draws near, and at length be found in such completeness as to be signalised by a descent of the Holy Ghost, and a testimony from heaven that, in Christ, each one is God's beloved son, in whom He is well pleased!

One would have thought that now surely Christ might have begun His work. But no. It seemed good to God to pass Him through yet another ordeal. The thirty years must be followed by the forty days. The long training of the spirit of subjection which has become so ripe must be followed up by a threefold temptation in the wilderness. It is a singular and unexpected occurrence at the very commencement of the ministry. The Spirit that has descended on Him and endued Him with measureless power, does not lead Him to the battlefield, nor to the harvest field, but to the wilderness. He leads Him out, not to attack the enemy, but to sustain the enemy's attacks on Him. There is in this something contrary to our expectations, something we should never have dreamt of, but which we feel has a deep significance, attesting the reality of the narrative. It is vain to represent this as a myth invented by the writer in order that Jesus might appear as great as Moses or Elijah, both of whom had their forty days of fasting. The obvious fact is, that coming in as it does at this particular time in Christ's life, it is a humiliating episode rather than a glorifying one. It is an episode of trial more than triumph. Christ does triumph, but only after a painful encounter. He vindicates His Sonship after being brought into the lowest and most humiliating state of want human beings ever knew. It seemed as if God deemed it right to expose Him to a new ordeal, in order that still further He might learn obedience by the things which He suffered.

Let us try, then, to realise the position of Jesus when, after His baptism, the heavens were opened, the Spirit descended on Him in visible form, and a testimony was borne to Him: "This is my beloved Son, in whom I am well pleased." It was a very glorious position; but if Jesus had been but a man, it would have been full of peril. Let us observe wherein to a mere man the peril lay. First, it was the crowning of a long process—the triumph, openly proclaimed, of a life-long strain, liable therefore to be followed by a reaction, like that which we sometimes see on the part of a student after passing a hard examination, or a young communicant after receiving the communion. Again, Jesus was now invested with new and very remarkable powers. The Holy Spirit came down on Him in a bodily shape, and His Sonship was proclaimed by a voice from heaven. It is likely that this visible descent of the Spirit was the symbol of His investiture with *miraculous powers*, and that He Himself knew the fact. We know that before this He wrought no miracle, in spite of the foolish statements of the Apocryphal Gospels; we know also that immediately after, the tempter addressed Him as one conscious of miraculous powers. Jesus then at this time had just arrived at two remarkable experiences: a strong assurance of God's favour, and the possession of supernatural power. Had He been a mere man, the concurrence of these two things would have been full of peril to Him. It seemed good to God to pass Him through a trial which made it plain that the circumstances that would have proved perilous to others were wholly without hurt to Him.

Let us observe how others have too often been affected, when either they were put in possession of remarkable power, or seemed to receive a strong assurance of God's favour. It is simply a matter of history that few men have been able to wield remarkable power, suddenly acquired, of any kind without danger, and without being corrupted by it. They seem to feel as if ordinary rules were not made for them, as if they were above ordinary restraints, as if they were a law to themselves. Take the case of Saul, so modest before he was on the throne, so wild and reckless after he became conscious of royal power. Take the case of Luther in his conflict with Zwingle, or indeed the case of any church ruler in the hour of unlimited power. Take the case of Henry VIII., or that of the leaders of the French Revolution; or that of Napoleon, who took many a liberty with the moral law, because he was an extraordinary person, and finally divorced Josephine to marry a princess of Austria.

Then again, in the enjoyment of a remarkable sense of the Divine favour, there is another danger for weak mortals. Men who are not hypocrites have been known to presume on their spiritual attainments to play loose with moral restraints, some subtle feeling getting into their minds that their spiritual elevation raised them above the necessity of minding rules and restraints needed for other men. A time of religious awakening often brings such phenomena. Agents that appeared to be eminently blessed have been known to fall into the most deplorable immorality. Others, without tumbling so deep into the mire, have brought much discredit on the cause by crooked, dishonest, untruthful ways. The wonderful revival of religion under Jonathan Edwards, in New England, had its own share of such lamentable blotches. Even in our own day we have seen how little able some men are to bear a popular position, and a high reputation for sanctity. Some have indeed stood it nobly, thanks to the grace of God. But others,—men taken from the plough or the mine, when they have come to hold a whole village in their grasp, when they have been looked up to as oracles, revered as almost angels— have been filled with conceit and spiritual presumption,—the pride that goeth before a fall.

It seemed good to God then, that when invested with special miraculous power, and assured specially of the Divine favour, Christ should be exposed to a fresh ordeal. It was borne in the wilderness, at a distance from those to whom he had been pointed out as the Lamb of God and Lord of the heavenly kingdom, and therefore without the stimulus which their presence would have supplied,—the inducement to sustain before them the lofty reputation which He had just acquired. A temptation in the wilderness, apart from all human observation, is a peculiarly subtle one, being fitted to show whether our habits are the result merely of regard for our character in the sight of men, or of inflexible regard to the will of God.

The ordeal was threefold: first, A temptation to use His power for *self-indulgence*—"command that these stones be made bread;" second, for *self-display*—"cast thyself down;" and third, for unholy *self-advancement*—"all these things will I give thee if thou wilt fall down and worship me." Self-indulgence, springing from the *lust of the flesh;* self-display, springing from the *lust of the eye;* and self-advancement, springing from the *pride of life,* were the three things to which the prince of this world appealed in Christ; but now, as at the end of His public life, it was made apparent that there was no loose joint in His armour: "the prince of this world cometh, but hath nothing in me."

This is not the place for going into Christ's way of dealing with these temptations. His treatment of them showed how carefully He guarded Himself against every abuse of His power, and how resolutely He maintained the spirit of subjection which He had been exercising so long. His purpose was quite resolute to make no use of His supernatural power for merely personal ends. I am not sure but we sometimes feel as if He carried that spirit to a too chivalrous extreme. What harm would there have been in turning a stone into bread? This harm: it would have shown Christ using for personal ends the powers intrusted to Him for the good of others; it would have damaged at the outset the moral meaning of His miracles; instead of symbols of redemption, they would have become manifestations of self-interest; instead of tokens of patient, self-denying charity, they would have been tokens of an impatience that cannot wait till God's time be come. But in point of fact, every one of the devil's temptations was steadily resisted; and Jesus came out of the ordeal greater because He had hid His greatness, more powerful because He had suppressed His power.

I cannot help thinking that the circumstances of young ministers, about to enter on their ministry, present a close analogy to those of Jesus now.

Generally, we may say, there is the temptation connected with the achievement of a purpose for which there has been long training, and, perhaps, much straining too. Then there is the temptation connected with the entrance on a new office, and the exercise of a new power. The temptation is not a gross temptation, and yet, in a subtle way, it may work to very evil results.

1. Thus, entrance on the ministry may prove the occasion of some forms of self-indulgence. Especially, if it should happen that one enters the ministry without a converted heart and sympathetic spirit. The records of our churches contain such miserable cases. Men resorting to false excitement to keep up a work for which they have no heart: and falling from one depth to another, till at last deposition ends their career. It makes one tremble to think how fearful falls of this kind sometimes occur.

But apart from such an extreme, we sometimes see even young ministers, after a brief term of resolute activity, sinking into lazy ways and slack service. There is not much of outward stimulus in their surroundings, and the poor creatures sink into an easy-going, unsystematic, unenergetic life. "O my soul, come not thou into their secret; unto their assembly, mine honour, be not thou united." Bargain for no easy berth; claim no surroundings agreeable to flesh and blood; be ready for such hard service at home and abroad as the Master may point out. For it is written *for you*, Man doth not live by bread alone; not by a good income, superior society, or a numerous and respectable congregation, but by every word that proceedeth out of the mouth of God.

2. Again: the ministry may become the occasion of self-display. Some like to show the world what

they can do—how they can mount on pinnacles of the temple and perform wonderful flights, if not literally, yet figuratively. How sweet to some men are the plaudits of others! But is it not odious for us to be thinking of ourselves in a profession that aims at saving dying souls? Men like Chalmers and M'Cheyne are constantly noting in their diaries what assaults they had from this devil, and how hard they found it to beat him back. The temptation is all the more subtle that there is a legitimate ground for desiring the approval of estimable men. But never for one instant should this be allowed to be the end of our service. Whenever man's approval is sought more than God's, "Get thee behind me, Satan," is the meet word for the temptation.

3. Once more, entrance on the ministry may become the occasion of unholy self-advancement. It may be sought for raising us above our fellows, for procuring for us a deference and a consideration not to be otherwise attained. We may be tempted to use mean arts for succeeding. We may be tempted to become sycophantish to men of influence. I know that such arts are abhorrent to most young men. But the tempter is subtle, and can bide his time. It was when our Lord was hungry that he assailed Him. The time may come when you will be ecclesiastically hungry. You may have failed to get a call within the usual time. You may be left alone, after all your fellows have been called. You may be dissatisfied with your position. Then is the moment when you are liable to be tempted to unholy methods of self-advancement. Then you may be more disposed than you ever were before to

listen to offers of the glory of this world. It is well, at such moments, to realise vividly the presence of God; well to remember from whom such unholy offers usually come; well to say, with holy firmness, "I will worship the Lord my God, and Him only will I serve."

It is not only one of the most beautiful, but one of the most instructive incidents of the temptation that when the devil left Jesus, angels came and ministered unto Him. We accept the fact in all its literalness; while at the same time we recognise in it a symbol of that holy peace and joy which fills the soul after a great struggle, and a great moral victory. Whether angels come literally to comfort all who fight the good fight, we cannot tell; but at least they come figuratively; and words cannot express the beatific feeling that fills the soul. There never was a happier summer than that of 1843 among the outed ministers of Scotland, though it was spent in the wilderness, amid the ruin and desolation of a dismantled Church. But it was peace after a great struggle; it was the angels coming to comfort those who had been signally beaten, but had yet overcome. This peace that passeth all understanding is God's token to him that overcometh; it is the encouragement to persevere when you are hard pressed, when the temptation is strong, and the flesh is weak and weary: for the joy of the victory is in proportion to the hardness of the battle; when the devil leaves, angels come and minister to you.

CHAPTER III.

THE INNER SPIRIT OF HIS MINISTRY.

FROM the moment when Jesus comes before us in His public capacity to the last hour of His life, His mind is entirely occupied with one object—the spiritual enterprise to which He has given Himself up. Nothing else awakens in Him more than a passing interest. Not that He deems other pursuits unworthy of the regard of those who have a calling to them. The use He makes for illustration of the employments of fishermen, vine-dressers, builders, merchants, and the like, shows that He could appreciate these callings, and commend those who pursued them diligently, with due regard to higher things. His allusions to the lilies of the field and the fowls of the air; to the fig-tree when its branch is yet tender; to the appearance of the sky at night and at morning; to the sparrows; to the lightning, and other objects of nature, indicate an eye for natural phenomena as both interesting in themselves, and useful in the analogies and lessons which they suggest. Many other subjects are wholly passed by in our Lord's conversations and discourses, to which we cannot believe Him to have been indifferent. His active interest centres in the building up of the kingdom of God, and all that is not immediately connected therewith seems for the time to be beyond His view.

To understand His relation to these things, we must think of Him as we think of a general in a war crisis, or of a physician in a time of plague, or of any one else who has got in hand some urgent business, and has but a short time to overtake it. A soldier sent to Egypt or India, or other remote country, on momentous duty, and requiring to despatch his business with the utmost rapidity, has to leave behind him a thousand interests, that with more leisure and less urgency might worthily occupy a share of his attention. He may be fond of scientific inquiries, but what can he do in them on the field of battle? He may be greatly attached to his family and friends, but in active service all thought of enjoying domestic life must be abandoned. He may be a devourer of books, but with the duty which he has in hand, general reading is not even to be dreamt of. The same is true of a physician while a plague is raging. It is evident that our Lord regarded His duty as akin to theirs. He had to work while it was called to-day. He knew well that His time was very short. In three or four brief years the whole of the work had to be accomplished for which He came into this world. The foundations had to be laid of the kingdom that can never be moved. A direction had to be given to the thoughts and feelings of men in opposition to all the forces of evil that were to sweep through the world to the end of time. Suffering had to be borne, enemies to be conquered, obedience to be rendered, atonement to be made, everlasting righteousness to be brought in,—in a word, a work had to be completed that, besides its bearing on the glory of God and the salvation of men, would form a new point of departure for the history of the universe, inasmuch as it was the Divine purpose that Jesus Christ, when glorified, should become the pivot, as it were, for the universe to move on, the new centre for all things in heaven and on earth (Eph. i. 10, R.V.)

It was surely fitting that a work so stupendous, and that had to be accomplished so quickly, should fill His soul. Whatever He might think of art or science, philosophy or culture, politics or social progress,—these were not suitable matters to occupy His attention, or to be brought before His disciples during the great crisis of His work. He that was so straitened by His baptism of suffering, till it should be accomplished; that so agonised in Gethsemane under the shadow of His conflict; that even in the less exciting times of His ministry spent nights in prayer for needed strength, could not have allowed other topics to divide His attention while the redemption of a world hung in the balance, and all depended on Him.

The life of our blessed Lord, then, is the very pattern and perfection of consecration. He is the perfect example of the single eye, and, in consequence, of the whole body full of light. He is at the furthest possible remove from all who serve two masters—from the whole tribe of men to whom Bunyan gives his expressive names, Mr. Facing-both-ways, Mr. By-ends, and Mr. Worldly-wise-man. He has no interest but that of the kingdom of God; and for advancing that kingdom He spares no energy that can be brought into play, declines no suffering, grudges no sacrifice, dreads no danger. From whichsoever of the four gospels we derive our impression of His life, the result is the same. He soars high above all vulgar ambitions and personal aims. While in the world, He is not of it. On the men of His time this feature of His life must have made a profound impression. On the men of all time it continues to make the same. It is one of the chief elements of the halo that surrounds His name, and that even from those who are least like Him draws forth the almost involuntary exclamation, "Thou art fairer than the children of men."

This consecration of our Lord to the service of God in the interest of sinful men may be viewed in three lights, according as we direct attention to one or other of the three parties concerned,—God, man, and Christ Himself. In reference to GOD, the Father, Christ became His servant for the work of redemption, and the thoroughness of His consecration appears in His complete surrender of Himself to the Father's will. In reference to MAN, He was moved by a burning desire for his salvation; and the thoroughness of His consecration appears in the unexampled nature of the work undertaken out of compassion and sympathy for him. In reference to HIMSELF, the same appears in the completeness of His self-abnegation, giving up every personal interest and feeling, encountering every danger and suffering, making nothing of Himself, if only He might accomplish the work of deliverance so dear to His soul.

All who have been remarkable for faithful and zealous service in God's cause have been more or less marked by these three qualities. But in human ministries they are seldom blended in tne fittest proportions. In some of the prophets, for example, you find that quality prominent that vindicates the will of God and His claims on His creatures. To men of this type the chief aspect of the world's sin is as insult to God, as rebellion against His will and repudiation of His claims. They are like servants of an injured master, bent on securing for him the honour that he deserves. In their addresses to men a tone of indignant remonstrance marks their words. Pre-eminent as examples of this class are such prophets as Elijah and John the Baptist. Soft raiment is not their apparel, and soft words are not their mode of speech. Their mission is mainly to startle and rouse a careless generation, and demand their homage for the authority of God. "Glory to God in the highest" is the key-note of their song.

Again, there have been servants of God in whom the element of human tenderness predominates. Men like Jeremiah and Hosea have very sensitive hearts, and are profoundly moved by the misery of their brethren. Some of their most touching appeals are inspired by the feeling that their sinful ways are driving men to misery and ruin, and that if they would be saved, if they would be happy, they must return to the Lord. It is the brotherly or human element that is most conspicuous in such men. Entreaty is much more their weapon than rebuke. To lessen the sum of human misery is their ruling passion. "Peace on earth and goodwill to man" is the predominant note in their song.

In both classes the service is accompanied by profound self-abnegation. Personal aims are disregarded. In the case of Elijah and John the Baptist this self-abnegation is carried out into absolute crucifixion to the world. They seem to strip themselves of every human comfort and joy. Those who are more moved by sympathy for their fellows are hardly less conspicuous for their self-denial. The intensity of their brotherly feeling makes it impossible for them to live at ease while their brethren are in misery. Whatever they can do, whatever they can give, whatever they may have to suffer in the cause of their brethren, all is done with a freeness and cordiality that cannot be surpassed.

These three elements of consecration, as we have said, are not always found in due proportions. As in some species of granite you find a preponderance of quartz, in others of felspar, and in others of mica, and only in a few varieties the three elements blended in the best proportion, so in human ministries. No true servant of God, indeed, wants any of the three elements, and in the great Old Testament ministries, while the proportion varies, the combination is ever found. But in some cases, chiefly outside the Bible, we see a tendency to excess in one direction or another, and for want of the balancing element, the result is not so favourable. Where zeal for the honour of God greatly predominates there is sometimes a hardness of manner if not of feeling that causes a recoil to more sympathetic natures. In his eagerness to execute judgment on those who outraged the authority of God, Phinehas seems hardly to remember the misery to which they are doomed. Human sympathy is not his forte. His watchword is, "Let God arise, and let His enemies be scattered." Even where this zeal for God is real—say in a Cromwell—the character that results is often in its severity terrible. But where zeal for God is counterfeited by ecclesiastical or other ambition, and where the place of human sympathy is usurped by a most bitter malignity, the scenes enacted baffle description. Witness the atrocities of Mohammedan massacres, or the cold-blooded horrors of the Inquisition.

On the other hand, if human sympathy be allowed to prevail unduly, there is a tendency to a sentimental compassion, that would separate between sin and the suffering which is its natural consequence. Wrong-doers may become the objects of an interest and even a complacency which are withheld from the struggling and the industrious. It was this excess of compassion for the criminal class, as illustrated in the refined arrangements of our "model prisons," that provoked the ridicule and sarcasm of Mr. Carlyle in his *Latter-Day Pamphlets*. The same tendency may be traced in the disposition of the present day to tone down the sterner features of theology, and especially those which relate to the punishment of sin. Under such influences the whole system of government, human and divine, becomes relaxed and feeble, and the solemn truth which needs to be so well remembered loses all influence—" The soul that sinneth it shall die."

It is the combination of the two elements in due proportion—of regard to God's will and zeal for His glory on the one hand, and sympathy with man and brotherly concern for his sorrows and sufferings on the other, that constitutes the highest type of service, and tends to results the most solid and satisfactory. Where these two features are thus combined, and are accompanied by that personal self-abnegation which always lends so high a charm, a species of excellence is realised to which, however it may condemn themselves, few hearts can withhold the tribute of their admiration.

Now, when we turn our attention to the public service of our blessed Lord, we find it marked by a faultless combination and beautiful proportion of all the three elements. At the very foundation of His human character lay the profoundest reverence for the Father's will, and an indefeasible regard for His rights and claims. Blending with this in beautiful harmony was a very tender spirit of humanity —a heart that bled for every human misery, and panted to relieve it. And in the fulfilment alike of the one feeling and the other—of zeal for God and sympathy for man—there was the most complete renunciation of self in every shape and form; where God's will on the one hand and man's welfare on the other were concerned, self was not for one moment thought of. The whole earthly career of Christ was a career of self-renunciation; but, like a Jungfrau or Matterhorn, rising high above its mountain chain, acts of still loftier self-denial rose above the ordinary level of His life, culminating, to speak paradoxically, in the sacrifice of the Cross and the humiliation of the tomb.

Let us dwell for a little on each of these features of the public service of our Lord.

I. And first, of His high reverence for the will and the claims of the Father. Knowing as we do His supreme Godhead, it is very difficult for us to get into our minds the possibility of His assuming a position of entire subjection to another. But we must remember that the Person of Christ is quite beyond the sphere of our experience, and that what bears upon it can only be matter of revelation and of faith. It is one of the most beautiful features of Christ's human life delineated in Scripture that throughout its whole extent He is seen actuated by the feeling that personally He must be subject to the will of another. He was under the constant sense of that obligation, both in what He did and in what He suffered. "I came down from heaven not to do mine own will, but the will of him that sent me." "My meat is to do the will of him that sent me, and to finish his work." So also with regard to His sufferings. After strong crying and tears in Gethsemane that if it were possible that cup might pass from Him, He becomes thoroughly reconciled by the simple thought that God wills them : "Not my will, but thine be done." Not only is the thought of God's will a support under bodily and mental pain, it is a refuge too under mental perplexity. In itself it could be only profound pain to Christ to think of the hardness of Chorazin and Bethsaida, the impenitence of Capernaum, and, generally, the opposition to the gospel of those whom He calls "the wise and prudent" (Matt. xi. 25). But even in the view of these things He finds a quiet nook where His soul may rest in peace, in the thought of the holy will that ruled over all: "Even so, Father, for so it seemed good in thy sight." In reviewing their public life, there is probably no feature in which even God's best servants find more cause for self-condemnation than their forgetfulness of God's will, both in what they have done and what they have suffered: how striking, in contrast to this, the uniform, profound, uncompromising regard to it by our blessed Lord! At the end of all He could say, without reserve or compunction, "I have finished the work which thou gavest me to do."

And as our Lord thus honoured God's will Himself, so He constantly maintained its claim on others. For men to transgress the commandment of God by their traditions—to neutralise the fifth commandment by the absurdities of Corban—was an outrage on the law of God. To Jesus Christ the moral law contained in the Scriptures was the reflection of the Divine will, the very transcript of God's holy nature; and of all wrong notions of His mission that which He was most eager to explode was, that in reference to that law He had come not to fulfil but to destroy. In His parables He is ever upholding the authority of the Lawgiver, vindicating His sovereignty, His right to do what He will with His own; vindicating His proprietorship, His right to the fruits of the vineyard; vindicating His authority and power as Judge, and the certainty of His punishing the indolent and careless, and rewarding the good and faithful servant. Not only is regard to the will of God an important element of Christian character in Christ's view, but it is the great test by which every life will be tried at the judgment, and the most momentous issues of eternity determined —"Not every one that saith unto me Lord, Lord, shall enter into the kingdom of heaven, but he that doeth the will of my Father which is in heaven." And the element of character that endears men socially to Christ, and that establishes in His society that oneness of spirit and aim which is the joy and charm of family life, is consecration to the will of God: "For whosoever shall do the will of my Father which is in heaven, the same is my mother, and sister, and brother."

Thus, during all His ministry, our Lord was overshadowed by a lofty sense of what was due to the will of the Father; it penetrated His soul to its core, controlled all His actions, influenced all His teaching, and moulded all His aims. In proportion to the depth of this impression was His sense of the evil of sin, His grief for the moral ruin of the world, and His desire to build up a kingdom in truth, righteousness, and love. Of His sense of the evil of sin we have a striking proof in such earnest words as these: "If thy right hand cause thee to stumble, cut it off and cast it from thee." Sin is such an awful thing that even a right hand or a right eye is not too much to lose if the loss should save you from the sin. Yet on every side He sees the traces of sin, and the disorder and misery which are bred of it. A nature less controlled might have abandoned itself to despair in view of such moral confusion and desolation; in the case of our Lord, He is only braced for the efforts and sacrifices necessary for the work of redemption—necessary at once to vindicate the honour of God and the majesty of His law, and to give birth to a regenerated world in which the will of God should rule supreme—the "new heavens and the new earth in which dwelleth righteousness."

II. If the public ministry of our Lord was thus controlled by a supreme regard to the will and glory of God, it was marked, not less conspicuously, by the intensity of his sympathy for man.

It is not enough to say that our Lord's heart was kind and tender. There are many such hearts that are not sympathetic; that pursue calmly the tenor of their own comfortable way, not much disturbed by the troubles and sorrows of their brethren. A sympathetic heart is one that makes the case of another its own; that feels a personal pang at its griefs; that cannot rest till all is done that can be done to allay them; and that freely gives up for this purpose its time, its means, its comforts, and if need be, its very life.

It is said of Jesus Christ, that "Himself took our infirmities and bare our sicknesses" (Matt. viii. 17). He did not view men's troubles afar off, sending from time to time a substantial contribution for their relief, with hearty wishes for their welfare. He went in among them, lived in the midst of them, and burdened Himself with their case. Even their temporal ailments moved His heart to its core; while their spiritual condition, terrible though it was, led to nothing less than His placing Himself in their room, to bear for them all that Divine justice demanded, and by this sacrifice save them from their sins.

The whole miracles of Christ were monuments of sympathy. Every case of disease healed, of devils ejected, of the hungry fed, of the dead raised, was a token of His compassion for the suffering. Such parables as that of the good Samaritan, the prodigal son, the son asking bread of his father, revealed the tenderness of His own heart. It seemed impossible for Him to witness suffering without relieving it. "Come unto me, all ye that labour and are heavy laden, and I will give you rest"—indicated the largeness as well as the tenderness of His heart. Instead of being repelled by the miseries and disorders of the world, Jesus was attracted to them. He flung Himself into the great flood of disorder and suffering to take on Him the burden of stemming it and curing it. He knew that it could not be cured without most grievous suffering on His part; but His intense compassion overcame all dread of suffering, and indeed all thought of Himself. The bright consummation for which His loving heart thirsted must be realised. "For the joy that was set before him, he endured the cross, despising the shame."

III. This calls up the third element of high consecration—self-surrender, readiness for every form of self-denial necessary for the achievement of a great end.

What Jesus did in this respect lies on the very surface of His history. First, there was the self-surrender involved in His incarnation—coming into this disordered world, and becoming a member of our fallen family. Then there was the self-denial of His humble mode of life—without even the comforts of a fixed home—"the foxes have holes, and the birds of the air have nests, but the Son of man hath not where to lay his head." Further, there was the self-denial arising from collisions with opponents, from the contradiction of sinners, from the plots of calumniators, and from the frailties and sins of His disciples. And lastly, there was the mysterious and incomprehensible suffering arising from the relation in which He placed Himself to the Father as the surety and substitute of His people, when, in the strong language of the apostle, He became sin and a curse for them, "that the blessing of Abraham might come on the Gentiles; that they might receive the promise of the Spirit through faith."

Side by side with such acts of self-renunciation, it may seem trivial to refer to the surrender of all those intellectual pursuits and social pleasures in which in other circumstances our Lord might have been pleased to engage. Engrossed as He was with His work, He had no time for foreign travel, or for science, or art, or philosophy, or history, or any branch of literature, or for any of the ordinary recreations or amenities of life. It behoved Him to discard all such things while engaged in laying the foundations of His kingdom. And such things as the pursuit of wealth, or of comfort, or of fame, or applause, or earthly distinction of any kind, were manifestly so entirely absent from His mind that we can hardly fancy them giving Him any trouble, or requiring so much as an effort to brush them completely aside.

Such was the nature of our Lord's consecration to His work. When we think of it deliberately, we cease to wonder that the period of preparation was so long in proportion to the period of active service. We cease to think of thirty years as too long a preparation for a ministry of so remarkable quality. We seem to understand better how the thirty years would be occupied. We fancy the spirit of regard to the will of God, of sympathy for man, and readiness to suffer for him, gaining strength from year to year, under the holy discipline of Nazareth. The silence of that long period becomes sublime when we think of Him, under the guidance of the Father, slowly and steadily maturing the human instrument for its unexampled work—strengthening it at every point where the strain would be greatest, forestalling the pressure and the conflicts of His coming ministry, putting on the whole armour of God that He might be able to withstand in the evil day, and having done all to stand.

We come, too, to understand better another feature of His public life—His continual prayerfulness. Here again is an unexpected feature. Why should the Son of God have needed to pray? "In the beginning was the Word, and the Word was with God, and the Word was God." Had He not all-sufficiency in Himself? Was the fulness of His Divine nature not available to supply all the needs of His human? But here likewise we must bear in mind what has been stated already, that the Person of Christ is beyond our comprehension, and that the actings of His personality must be received by faith. We are taught that the conditions of His earthly life and ministry were such that His supplies needed to be asked from the first Person of the Godhead. In this we find the key to His unwearied prayerfulness. It is not in human nature to hold supplies of Divine strength that last for ever. As the body needs its daily bread, so does the soul. Even the human nature of Jesus needed to be kept up to the mark by constant communications from above. His devotion to the will of God needed to be sustained in strength, where the doing of that will was so difficult as the struggles of Gethsemane showed. His sympathy for man needed nursing and replenishing, when man himself was doing his utmost to extinguish it,—was seeking in every way to compass the ruin of Him who was striving, not less unweariedly, to effect his salvation. It was a strange duel—the Son of God striving to save the sons of men, and these very sons of men striving to destroy the Son of God. His self-renunciation needed daily renewal, for often would the weary body crave rest when duty demanded continued activity; often would the spirit be ready to fail when it was necessary though faint to be still pursuing. To keep up the supply of Divine influence, and have it full and ready for every emergency, was the purpose of Christ in these continual prayers. If duty never seemed to Him too hard; if self-denial never appeared too arduous; if day by day found Him at His post, healing, teaching, journeying, meeting the cavils of His opponents, and trying to put into the crass minds of His followers some spiritual views of the kingdom of God; if the stream of His beautiful life flowed calmly on, spreading purity and blessing on every side, unaffected alike by the heats of summer and the frosts of winter, it was because that habit of prayer to His Father was kept up so constantly: "I have set the Lord always before me: because he is at my right hand, I shall not be moved" (Psalm xvi. 8).

The question cannot but arise in conclusion, Is this consecrated life of Christ's a literal example for His ministers now? Granting that some parts of Christ's work are wholly beyond our sphere, and granting that at the utmost it is but a fraction of what fell to Him that falls to us, are we bound to consecrate ourselves as much as He did, and especially are we called on to renounce all those lawful pursuits and recreations which in His case behoved to be set aside?

One thing is very plain, along the whole line of Christian biography and history, that in proportion to the degree in which men do consecrate themselves to the service of God and their fellows, is the measure of success they are privileged to enjoy. Consecration and spiritual power go together. The great evangelists of the world—men like Paul, Augustine, Columba, in the olden time, men like Wesley, Whitefield, Burns, Moody, in more recent years, have been marked not less for the thoroughness with which they have given themselves to Christ's work than the marvellous results they have been enabled to achieve. Perhaps the greatest snare of the Christian minister is half-heartedness in his service. And the things that he reserves, and in his secret heart is not prepared to give up, are not commonly things conspicuously sinful. They are rather subtle forms of selfishness, subtle cravings of the heart, seldom spoken of to others, and seldom placed distinctly before his own mind. It is hard for him to give up a craving for the good opinion of the world. Undue love of praise, of distinction, of fame, will often, like the dispossessed Canaanites, lurk in their old holds. Love of ease, self-indulgence, leading to indolent habits and very ineffective service, find many a victim, especially in places far removed from the centres of life and influence. It is hard to see how indolent, self-indulgent men can deem themselves servants of Christ. We do not speak of those who enter the priest's office that they may eat a bit of bread,—it is no wonder if the current of their lives becomes carnal, and their alienation from Christ complete. We speak of those who enter the ministry with an honest desire to be useful in the highest of all ways—in turning many to righteousness—but who, being destitute of thorough consecration, fall under lowering influences, are content just to keep things going, and do nothing effectual for building up their Master's kingdom. Place their indolence and self-indulgence alongside Christ's whole-hearted self-surrender, His unwearied devotion of every energy to the good of men and the glory of the

Father, and what trace of resemblance can you find between them?

Ought a Christian minister then to take no interest in anything except the immediate work of his calling? Are literature, art, science, society, general culture, simply snares which it would be his best and wisest course to eschew for ever? In some cases it may be so. Some department of mission or of pastoral work may be so urgent, it may demand such constant attention, it may provide such blessed opportunities for the highest usefulness, that his true course is to give himself wholly to it, to follow Christ exclusively, and let the dead bury their dead. If any true man feels called to this course, let him have all honour for it. Never let his want of literature or culture or art be any reproach, if, like his Master, he has thrown them aside, not because he despises them, but because he feels his work so great, his race so urgent, that he must devote himself to it alone!

For more ordinary men in the ministry the demand of duty may be, not to discard all such things, but to try to use and consecrate them. By God's blessing they may be made helpful in the Lord's work. Genius and all its gifts may be used in the service of Christ for the good of man. Learning may be devoted to the highest uses. Culture may become the handmaid of high Christian usefulness. But the Christian minister must look well to it, that he and all he has *are* truly consecrated to Christ's service. Even good men are so liable to reserve little stores for personal gratification, that there is an imminent danger of self-deceit.

Would only we had a host of truly and thoroughly consecrated ministers! Stagnation would be unknown in the Church; life would spring up even in the most barren desert; the glory of Carmel and Sharon would appear throughout all her borders.

CHAPTER IV.

OUTER FEATURES OF HIS MINISTRY.

THE public ministry of our Lord falls into three main divisions. First, His early ministry in Judæa, of which John only takes any notice, and of which he records but a few incidents. It is plain, however, that our Lord began His work in Jerusalem and the neighbourhood, deeming the ancient capital the right place for Him to present His commission and set up His kingdom; and it was only when John the Baptist was cast into prison, and persecution was manifestly impending on Himself, that "He left Judæa and departed into Galilee" (Matt. iv. 12; John iv. 1-3). Second, His Galilean ministry, occupying probably two years, and embracing three circuits of Galilee, varied by excursions to places more distant, such as the coasts of Tyre and Sidon, and by visits to feasts at Jerusalem. Of this part of His ministry the fullest account is given us by Matthew. Third, the ministry after the transfiguration, when His face was set towards Jerusalem, embracing several tours and detours, on the way and after His arrival there. Of the journey towards Jerusalem we have the fullest account in Luke; while of the events connected with the last days, the narrative of John is the most copious and the most touching.

The whole of this public ministry is commonly believed to have extended to about three years, though opinions have prevailed that it was as short as one year,[1] and also that it was considerably longer than three. It is by studying the references to the feasts, mainly as given in the fourth Gospel, that we arrive at three years, or perhaps a little more, as the true duration of the ministry. In that little space, and mainly in the rough, wild province of Galilee, Jesus did a work which changed for all time the complexion of the world's history, and exalted immeasurably the life and the destinies of men.

Keeping in view, then, the shortness of the time occupied in this unexampled work, we notice—

I. First, *the systematic industry, diligence, and self-command* which characterised our Lord from the beginning to the very end. In regard to the Galilean ministry, we are led to understand that His itineracy there embraced, to say the least, a large proportion of its towns and villages. Even when we make allowance for the freedom with which general expressions like "all" and "whole" are often used in Oriental speech, we must hold that the visits were very comprehensive which Matthew thus characterises:—"Jesus went about all the cities and villages, teaching in their syna-

---

[1] Keim, one of the most recent neological writers on the life of Christ, contends elaborately that the whole public ministry was comprised in one year; but to make out his case he throws overboard the Fourth Gospel.

gogues and preaching the Gospel of the kingdom, and healing every sickness and every disease among the people" (ix. 35). We learn from Josephus that in Galilee there were 204 towns and villages, so that if most of these were embraced in Christ's personal visits, the labour involved must have been very great. The same impression of most abundant labour is derived from the figurative expression of John, that if all the mighty works of Jesus were recorded, the world itself would not be able to contain the books that should be written. Besides making these circuits of Galilee, we read of His visiting the remoter north, at Cæsarea-Philippi, and the remoter north-west, in the coasts of Tyre and Sidon; we know of His passing oftener than once through Samaria; we know too of His being on the east side of Jordan, and coming up from the Jordan valley by Jericho; and we are familiar with His frequent visits to Jerusalem. Strange to say, the only districts of the country where we do not read of His having been during His public ministry are, that classical region of the Old Testament—the tribe of Judah, embracing His own birthplace, Bethlehem, as well as Hebron and Beersheba, the haunts of the patriarchs; and likewise the Shephelah, or maritime plain, embracing the land of the Philistines and the plain of Sharon. But though there be no record of such visits, it does not follow that none took place.

Throughout every part of the wide district which He traversed, He not only preached, and taught, and healed, but He had numberless collisions with opponents; He lived under constant apprehensions of attack, whether by fraud or violence; He carried on the work of instructing and training the apostles, and in their slowness of heart, want of faith, childishness, and paltry strifes, He encountered a serious addition to His burdens, although it would be harsh to suppose that on the whole their company did not afford Him both refreshment and aid. From His nature being so communicative and social, Jesus enjoyed society, and, with all their failings, these rough but honest and warm-hearted fisher-lads must on the whole have been a real acquisition. The strain on the bodily energies in a life involving so much movement and labour must have been very great; still greater must have been the strain on the mind where there was so much excitement, and where interests so serious were at stake. From the fact that the Jews spoke of fifty years as the limit of age which He had not passed, although He might be approaching it (John viii. 56), it is probable that He had acquired that older look which is commonly produced by great mental and bodily strain.

Through all this immense labour our Lord appears to have passed with quite marvellous calmness and self-possession. From the narrative of His life nothing is more remote than the air of bustle or hurry;—there is indeed about it a wonderful aspect as of Oriental calm and leisure. Though we read of His resting through exhaustion at Jacob's well; of His being, with His disciples, so pressed by the multitude, that they had no time so much as to eat bread; of His having to get into a boat to escape the pressure; and of His inviting His disciples to come into a desert place and rest a while, there is no trace of flutter or discomposure; His movements are as orderly and deliberate as if He had enjoyed the most ample leisure.

It is evident that this diligence and industry must have been the effect of a remarkable power of arrangement. It has been remarked that the faculty of order was quite a feature of the Hebrew mind.[1] It was conspicuous in Abraham, Joseph, Moses, Gideon, David, Solomon, Ezra, Nehemiah, and a host of other Hebrews. It is very remarkable in our Lord. We see it in the symmetrical character of His discourses; we see it in the mission of the twelve and of the seventy; we trace it in some of His allusions, as when He supposes a man about to build a tower, sitting down to calculate whether he have enough to finish it, or a king going out to war considering whether his ten thousand are a match for his opponent's twenty; we see it moreover in the miracle of the loaves and fishes, and in the instructions to the two disciples for celebrating the Passover; in a word, we see it in every arrangement of our Lord's public life. That our Lord worked by system, and could not otherwise have got through His work, is plain as noonday to all who know the difference between systematic and random working. It may be thought a mechanical way of work; hours and laws, we may be told, were made for slaves; and it may be extolled as a higher life where one obeys the impulse of the hour, and is free to catch and follow whatever gales of inspiration may at any time come upon one. No doubt, one may be bound by lines too hard and too fast; and for our part we

[1] See Isaac Taylor's *Remarks on Colenso's Strictures on the Pentateuch.*

deem a little elasticity an advantage in any system, —a power of adapting it to emergencies as they arise. But those who are habitually systematic will probably find that they come to be comparatively independent of fitful impulses and inspirations, and that their faculties come to them, to use Milton's phrase, as nimble servitors whenever their aid is sought.

We hold then that we may well claim our Lord as showing the value of system as an aid to the spirit of industry in labour. And partly no doubt through this habit, He was habitually *beforehand* in His work. He was always ready. His discourses have a wonderfully finished air, as if they had been matured before they were spoken. His very answers to casual objectors were marvellously clean-cut and finished. He was never disconcerted or at a loss how to answer or to act. His presence of mind never deserted Him. And what is very remarkable, He never allowed one thing to jostle another in His mind, however full it may have been of projects, and however burdened with anxieties.

This marvellous orderliness and business-like composure come out strikingly in connection with the last scenes of His life. Who can conceive the burden that was then pressing on His soul? Yet nothing could exceed the deliberate forethought and systematic regularity with which everything was planned and arranged. There are instances in private life familiar to us all of dying persons giving minute directions about their funeral, or of persons struck by a sudden calamity, thinking as calmly of the details of necessary business as if

OUTER FEATURES OF HIS MINISTRY. 65

no such blow had fallen. But no instance can approach the case of our Lord. Calmly and minutely He describes to the two disciples the arrangements to be made for keeping the passover. Assembled with the twelve, He deliberately girds Himself, pours water into a basin, washes the feet of the disciples, deals with the objections of Peter, explains the figurative import of the act, and enforces the example which it supplies. With equal calmness, He institutes the holiest of the mysteries of the Christian religion, giving calm utterance to the few but memorable words which were to be repeated on the most solemn occasions in the history of His Church till His second coming, and to be the vehicle of the most profound impressions of salvation through His blood. Then with a courage which none can know who have never needed to break in on the calm peace of a gathering of friends by some appalling announcement, He exposes the treachery of Judas. With equal calmness, He rebukes the confidence of Peter. If any documents in the world bear the stamp of self-possession and repose, it is the farewell address and the intercessory prayer. But the agony in the garden lets us see what a hurricane was raging, and how great was the effort needed to maintain the calm.

On the cross we have renewed evidence both of the conflict and the victory. What a power of thinking of others did He show all through these last scenes! Uttering a discourse so full of consolation; offering such a prayer; healing the ear of Malchus; casting that look of tender rebuke on Peter; bidding the daughters of Jerusalem weep

E

not for Him but for themselves and for their children; praying for His murderers; gladdening the heart of the penitent thief; committing His mother with so simple kindliness to the care of John; and leaving as His last legacy to the faith of His disciples that glorious word, τετέλεσται, It is finished!

In fine: in our Lord's whole demeanour on this memorable occasion we see the triumph of two things;—the power of a well-ordered mind to give its whole attention to the proper business of each moment,—not to let duties or occupations jostle one another, not to let the shadow of the more distant disturb the more immediate; and second, the power of a noble mind to throw off consciousness of itself even when its case might seem all-absorbing; the triumph of a mind, as the hymn puts it,

"At leisure from itself, to soothe and sympathise."

II. Another very prominent feature of our Lord's ministry was its *variety and naturalness of method.*

Speech having been His great instrument of instruction, He made use of it in many forms. Discourses, parables, proverbs, texts of Scripture, conversation, controversy—were among the forms of speech which He addressed to men. The places where He spoke showed a like variety. In the synagogue, in the temple, in the street, on mountains, in plains, in private houses, at the dining-table, at the bedside, at the well-side, at the seaside, by the wayside, from the boat-side, in journeys by land, in journeys by sea, He spoke the word of God. Now He defended Himself from the misrepresentations of opponents, and now He assumed the offensive, and by well-planted blows, exposed their hollowness and hypocrisy. *Semper, ubique, omnibus,* might have been His motto, for the word of God was a burning fire shut up in His bones, and He could not stay.

Here, however, one remarks an apparent exception:—Our Lord *wrote* nothing. There is no evidence of His having ever reduced permanently to writing so much as a single scrap. The only mention of His writing is His writing on the ground when the woman was brought to Him charged with adultery. The Epistle to Abgarus, King of Edessa, mentioned by some early writers, is now universally given up, though learned doctors and even bishops have, in their day, contended for its genuineness. Even if it were otherwise, it is too trifling a production to make any real exception. But though Christ wrote nothing personally, He virtually wrote much. *Qui facit per alterum, facit per se.* His spoken words were destined to be changed into written words. No one who reflects on the extent and exhaustiveness of our Lord's personal labours will wonder that in the brief period of His ministry, He confined Himself to oral teaching. He knew that His life and His work would not want historians, and that trustworthy records would be written, that would carry them down to the end of time. He had marvellous faith in the permanence of His words, though unrecorded and unrevised by Him. Heaven and earth would pass away, but His words, though then unwritten, would not pass away. He could assure His disciples that the loving act of the woman who had anointed Him would be proclaimed wherever His gospel should come.

But amid all His variety of method, He was singularly unconventional. He did not confine Himself to consecrated places, nor canonical hours, nor professional methods. He did not seek the shelter of professional propriety, delivering a serious discourse when it was deemed the right thing to do; and at other times conforming to the spirit of the world, and conducting Himself simply as an agreeable member of worldly society. What He taught in public, He was earnest to impress in private. He was instant in season, out of season. And the state of mind that made Him so was the great secret of His power. Even the world has little respect for the mere professional preacher. One who speaks from his brief is little thought of, compared to one who speaks from his head. And the man that speaks from his head cannot confine himself to mere public occasions—he cannot but speak what he has seen and heard.

No doubt, in a settled state of things, there is something to be said for conventionality. But there is little to be said for the man that can serve his Master only in conventional ways. He is tempted to lose sight of his Master altogether. He is liable to forget the great end at which he ought to aim. To go through the allotted routine of "duty," more or less respectably as he may be able, is his main concern. Whether he may not in this way be wasting half his energies or more, whether by methods more simple, more direct, more Christlike, he might not accomplish much more good, is no question for him. He does the work which he is required to do, and that satisfies his conscience. But does it satisfy his Master? Is there not much for us to think of, and to try to follow in that free, unconventional method of influencing others of which our Lord sets us so bright an example? Have not all great evangelists, all successful ministers, followed it more or less? And in reference to the two ways of work, in these settled times, conventional and unconventional, may not a combination of both be the rule incumbent on us, as if our Master repeated to us His own words, "These ought ye to do, and not to leave the other undone"?

III. Not less remarkable, among the outer features of our Lord's ministry, was its *combination of apparently opposite qualities.*

1. Thus, first, we find it combining quite remarkably the *popular* and the *profound*. The whole style of His ministry was popular—matter, manner, and form. He never spoke as a metaphysician; dealt not in "abstract and concrete," "subjective and objective," "positive and negative," or in any scholastic terms or forms whatever. Yet His teaching was profound in the truest sense and highest degree. It went right to the heart of things, and brought out, clear and strong, their profoundest lessons. One might elaborate the idea of God's fatherhood through philosophical volumes without settling the matter for ever as Jesus did by His happy "how much more:" "If ye that are evil know how to give good gifts unto your children, how much more shall your Father which is in

heaven give the Holy Spirit to them that ask Him?" His allusion to the lilies as they grow brought out the right and privilege of children to repose in the thoughtful care of the great Father, in a way that, instead of bitter anxiety, fills one's life with repose and expectation. "No man can serve two masters" solves a thousand questions of casuistry, as it exposes at the same time a thousand hollow schemes of life where men vainly strive to achieve the impossible. It was in the application of Divine truth to the human heart that Christ showed such profundity—that He so surely and steadily hit the nail upon the head. Other teachers might say on a subject much that was good and true; but Christ brought out its very pith and marrow, presenting it with a clearness that no understanding could refuse, and with a force that no conscience could withstand.

2. Similar to this combination is that of *homeliness* and *sublimity*. The whole tenor of his conversations and discourses was homely; his illustrations were drawn from the commonest sights of earth, and the homeliest occupations of men. The pursuits of the farmer and the fisherman, the builder and the vine-dresser, the shepherd whose sheep had wandered, the woman that had lost her piece of silver, furnished texts for His parables and discourses. Yet with these homely illustrations, to what heights He rose! What glorious truths He brought down from heaven by means of the lost sheep, the lost piece of silver, and the prodigal son! Who would have thought that a poor woman's pleasure in recovering a trifling coin could be allied to feelings that thrill the hearts of

angels, and in some sense refresh the soul of God Himself? Who would have found, in the homely task of the shepherd dividing his sheep from the goats, a picture of that dread scene when small and great shall stand before the great white throne, to receive the deeds done in the body? Or who would have supposed that their treatment of some poor dirty outcast was to be elevated to the level of the King Himself, and to be greeted with that strange announcement, "I was a stranger and ye took me in"? What hands but those of Christ could thus weave the homely and the sublime into the same web?

3. Combination of *earnestness* and *tact*. Usually earnestness is impetuous, rushing at its object; tact is cool and careful, picking its steps with dainty deliberation. But in Christ there was a remarkable combination of both—of the cool head and the burning heart, the calmness of deliberation and the fervour of zeal. His very soul goes out in His lament over Jerusalem : " How often would I have gathered thy children together as a hen gathereth her chickens under her wings, and ye would not!" Yet observe what tact He shows, for example, in His way of approaching the woman of Samaria. The first thing He does is to ask a favour of her— "Give me to drink." What a knowledge of human nature is shown in this! If any one thinks that you are looking down on him, the best way to conciliate him is to ask a small favour of him, for in doing so, you make yourself for the moment his inferior, you show a sense of dependence on him, you pay him a kind of deference that pleases and

thus conciliates him. Have we not seen some rude wild boy of the street pleased when we approached him respectfully, and asked him if he could tell us where a neighbour lived—have we not seen him bound before us to the very top of some high stair, much gratified at being asked to be our guide? Consider, in the like way, our Lord's tact in dealing with Simon the leper. As Simon sees the woman in his house washing Jesus' feet, a little tumult gathers in his breast. Christ does not attack it at once, to show its unreasonableness. He looks inquiringly at His host and says, "Simon, I have somewhat to say unto thee." To what magical secret do these words owe their tranquillising power? To the tact that first asks leave, as it were, to speak, when something like reproof is to be administered. And then to the further exercise of tact that puts the reproof in a parable, and that asks Simon himself to give judgment in the case. In fact, Simon administers his own reproof. Even the subtle power of so small a thing as repeating a person's name in order to make a reproof more tender, does not escape the notice of Jesus: "Martha, Martha, thou art careful and troubled about many things;" "Simon, Simon, Satan hath desired to have you;" "O Jerusalem, Jerusalem, how often would I have gathered thy children together . . . but ye would not."

4. Combination of *faithfulness* and *kindliness*. He could be kind to the sinner while He detested and rebuked his sin. Pharisaism confounded these two things, and vindicated its contemptuous treatment of the sinner on the ground of the vileness of his sin. And there is always some tendency to

this where the besetting sin is of a repulsive and provoking character. In the case of Jesus it is otherwise; He receives the sinner to His heart, and He dies for his sin. This union of faithfulness and kindliness was evinced on many occasions of His earthly life. We see it in the case of the young man who had great possessions, on whom Christ looked with such affection, but to whom He presented a test of such stringent severity, in order to show him that he did not love his neighbour as himself. We see it in the case of the woman with the issue of blood, in whom true faith and gross superstition were so strangely blended; Jesus at once rebuking her superstition and rewarding her faith. We see it in His treatment of publicans and sinners; He did not shrink from being called their Friend, yet every feeling of His soul was against their wickedness, and He never ceased to testify that unless they were converted, they could never see the kingdom of heaven.

5. Combination of *power to enlighten honest inquirers*, and *reprove dishonest cavillers*. The one He advanced to further knowledge of the kingdom of God; the other, incapable through the rebellion of their hearts, of appreciating or even understanding the order of the kingdom, He showed the more clearly to deserve condemnation. This double purpose, as He Himself told His disciples, was the occasion of some of His parables. They presented truth under a veil, sufficiently transparent for the eager heart to penetrate, but not transparent enough for the careless, or for the hostile caviller. There was light enough to attract the honest inquirer, and

dimness enough to scare away the worldly mind. Here, it is plain, our Lord took up ground of His own; so judicial a task is not laid on His followers. Our duty is to make the vision plain to all, that he may run that readeth; it is not for us to determine to whom we shall be the savour of life to life, or to whom the savour of death to death.

6. Combination of *humility* and *majesty*. Is there need for illustration here? The homely, unassuming bearing of our Lord in all the relations of life is one of the great charms of His character. Yet how boundless His claims to honour! "Before Abraham was, I am;" "I and my Father are one;" "He that hath seen me hath seen the Father." With what calm but high dignity, too, did our Lord exercise His powers, and dispense His gifts! "I will, be thou clean;" "Son, thy sins be forgiven thee;" "Lazarus, come forth." With all His homeliness there is a profound sense of His personal dignity, and a sublime consciousness of power. "We were witnesses of his majesty," says Peter, "when we were with him on the mount." Here, too, our glorious Lord stands in a position all His own. We gaze on His person across an infinite gulf. Yet even here the combination has features for our imitation. There is an essential dignity in the office of a Christian minister, not to be sacrificed to the spirit of good-fellowship, or geniality, or jesting. It imposes a certain restraint on our mirthful and frivolous moods. While we follow Christ in being among our people as one that serveth, we are to follow Him in never forgetting our relation to

the kingdom of God. Avoiding the extremes of lordly arrogance and of frivolous familiarity; magnifying our office, yet making ourselves of no reputation—we are to try to combine the spirit of two apparently opposite functions, servants of servants, and ambassadors of the King.

IV. We note a fourth general feature of our Lord's ministry—its *catholicity*. This quality is apparent, not only in the wide-reaching hints and instructions as to the extent of His kingdom which He gave from time to time, but likewise in His bearing toward the different classes of society with whom He came into contact at home. Himself a man of the people, He had all that sympathy with the toiling multitude which gains their affection, and draws their respect and confidence. A son of labour, He could throw out His invitations with the thrilling power of one who understands what weariness means: "Come unto me, all ye that labour and are heavy laden, and I will give you rest." Yet, while full of this fellow-feeling for the children of toil, He had no recoil from the other classes of society, and no want of will to help them, and to bless them when they showed a desire to enjoy His gifts. The nobleman at Cana, the centurion at Capernaum, the Pharisee that entertained Him in his house, Zaccheus the rich publican of Jericho, Nicodemus who came to Him by night, the lawyer who asked what he could do to inherit eternal life, were all regarded by Jesus with interest and affection. Utterly indifferent to their wealth, and having no vestige of desire for any part of it, He simply looked on them as men and brothers, groaning under the curse of Adam, and as much in need as the most miserable outcast, of the grace of God. And thus the ministry of Christ has this feature—it is specially attractive to the burden-bearing mass, but it is not repulsive to any section of the social community. "The common people heard him gladly;" but no class of people as such could find anything to repel them. And, in point of fact, the religion of Christ has never been confined to one class or section. It has sustained its early character throughout. While offering special attractions to the poor, and while finding not only the largest number but the largest proportion of its adherents among them, it has never wanted representatives, and often they have been very noble representatives, from the cultured, the leisurely, the wealthy sections of society. It is a religion alike for sage and savage, for prince and peasant, for barbarian, Scythian, bond and free. And when it reaches its final triumph, the kings of the earth shall be seen bringing their glory and honour into the new Jerusalem. Not only the hereditary or other rulers of this territory or of that, but kings in a higher sense—the kings of intellect, the kings of art, the kings of eloquence, the kings of social influence. Many a voice will blend in that lofty anthem, "Worthy is the Lamb that was slain to receive power, and riches, and wisdom, and strength, and honour, and glory, and blessing."

CHAPTER V.

BEGINNING OF HIS MINISTRY IN JUDÆA.

IT is seldom that searchers for the sources of great rivers find anything there that bears a visible proportion to the grandeur of the stream. The wonderful fountains of Herodotus have been found by no explorer of the Nile. Usually the waters begin to gather in some flat, oozy bed, and the first trickling of the stream can hardly be distinguished. Nevertheless, in a geographical sense, the source of a great river is a phenomenon of deepest interest, for the movement that begins so languidly in the marshy level, gives birth to a current deep and broad, that carries the commerce of kingdoms on its bosom, and on its banks rears cities that hold intercourse with the globe.

When we trace the ministry of Jesus to its beginnings, we may perhaps share the feeling of the explorer, and be somewhat disappointed not to find there anything imposingly great. Our Lord seems to slide gradually into His work rather than at once mount His throne and wield His sceptre. But there is always an interest, though it may be a quiet interest, in the beginning of great undertakings. We naturally look for something characteristic in the first public words and acts of One to whose advent all previous generations looked forward, as all subsequent generations have looked back on it, with such unexampled depth of feeling.

We have seen that our Lord deemed Jerusalem the right place for the commencement of His ministry. It was the City of the Great King. It was the seat of that Temple in regard to which the last of the prophets had said, " The Lord, whom ye seek, shall suddenly come to his temple." There it was certain that His public career would end, and there it was suitable that it should also begin. But He did not at once, after His inauguration at His baptism, turn His face to Jerusalem. He waited till the greatest of the annual feasts should give Him a natural opportunity of going thither. After His temptation in the wilderness, He returned to the scene of John's baptism. There, at Bethabara, beyond Jordan, and therefore outside the more immediately classic land of Israel, His first group of followers were drawn to Him. Next He proceeded to Cana, to a marriage feast to which He had been invited. A few days were then spent at Capernaum. Then came the passover at Jerusalem, and there took place the first public appeal of Jesus to the nation. This was really the commencement of His public ministry. The events at Bethabara and Cana were significant; but they were done somewhat privately. It was at the passover that Jesus first challenged public attention; and no one who bears in mind the significance of the passover can doubt that, of all times and seasons for His manifestation, this was the most becoming.

BEGINNING OF HIS MINISTRY IN JUDÆA.

We propose in this chapter, after glancing at the two events that happened at Bethabara and Cana respectively, to study the beginning of His ministry in Judæa.

At Bethabara five disciples were drawn to Jesus, —Andrew and John, Peter, Philip, and Nathanael.[1] They were not made apostles at this stage, but they became personal believers and followers. All appear previously to have been disciples of John the Baptist. On the day when Jesus returned to John after His temptation, the Baptist pointed Him out as the Lamb of God that taketh away the sin of the world, and gave his reasons for believing Him to be the Son of God. Next day, as Jesus passed, he exclaimed, " Behold the Lamb of God!" To two of His disciples these words were like an electric spark. They followed Jesus, went with Him to His lodging, and spent the rest of the day in His company. We are told that one of the two was Andrew; we infer that the other was John. It is evident from what followed that decisive work was done that day. Andrew and John were filled with a holy enthusiasm. Of the conversation that passed between them and Jesus we have no record. But whatever it was, they became convinced that Jesus was the Son of God, and they hastened to share the discovery with their companions. They had heard the Baptist proclaim this fact, and on this ground they were disposed to believe it. But their intercourse with Jesus evidently turned this disposition into a fixed and firm belief. "We beheld his glory," the apostle says (though not with an exclu-

[1] Possibly also James. See Godet, *in loco.*

sive reference to this occasion), "the glory as of the only begotten of the Father." It was not by any miraculous exercise of power they were convinced, for "the beginning of miracles" took place two days afterwards at Cana. What led them to believe must have been some outbeaming from Christ of the light and love of heaven, something that showed His power to satisfy all the longings of their hearts, and bring them into happy fellowship with the Father. It is very likely that on this occasion Jesus imparted to them some of the truths which He soon after made known to Nicodemus and to the woman of Samaria. He Himself gives us a hint of the line of His communication when He says to Nathanael, "Hereafter ye shall see the heaven open, and the angels of God ascending and descending on the Son of man." As if He had said, I have come to establish a friendly relation between earth and heaven; I have come to heal the breach between man and God; ere long you shall see visible tokens of this reconciliation; you shall see angels of health, and life and forgiveness descending, and angels of gladness and thanksgiving and holy delight ascending on the Son of man.

Now, the full significance of these things cannot be seen unless we bear in mind that they took place at the very scene of the triumph of John the Baptist, and that the five disciples whom Jesus now drew after Him had been disciples of John. It is implied in this that there was something in Jesus far beyond what there was in John. John himself had frankly owned that it was so. And he had pointed to the difference when he styled Jesus "the Lamb of God that taketh away the sin of the world." Jesus was to be a reconciler of man and God. *That* John had never been or professed to be. All that could be said of him was, that he had made men feel the *need* of reconciliation; but the blessing itself, he had always said, must come from another. Now Jesus accepts this view when He tells Nathanael that on His person there will soon be a visible communication between earth and heaven. Thus it appears that on the very first occasion when Jesus speaks of Himself to men, He represents Himself as much more than a moral teacher—much more than John was, much more than any prophet was; nothing less than a Mediator between God and man. It seems plain that it was the apprehension of this truth that filled Andrew and John with such a feeling of satisfaction, and set them to announce the discovery to their companions—to tell them how they had found in Jesus a blessing that John, bright and shining light though he was, could never have bestowed.

This incident in the career of Jesus is to be regarded, we think, as much more important and characteristic than that which took place two days after at Cana of Galilee. There was a marriage there, and Jesus and His disciples were among the guests. It would seem as if the marriage had been that of one of His own followers—(could it have been Peter, or any other of the five?)—because it is difficult otherwise to account for the invitation of "Jesus *and his disciples.*" It was certainly a striking transition so soon after His long fast—after He had been in the wilderness and had experienced the extremity of hunger—that He should be a guest at a wedding festival. His presence on the occasion may well be taken as a proof that so far from frowning, He smiled on marriage, and on the family constitution and relations generally, and also as showing that though there might be suitable occasions for fasting, He held that there were also occasions when feasting was legitimate even for His disciples. If there was a time to mourn, there was also a time to rejoice. This was to be the law of His kingdom. What He said to His mother was an indication that now He had come into a different relation to her from that which had prevailed at Nazareth—that now He was bound by new obligations that must be regarded as more sacred than even her will. The form of the miracle, too, the converting of water into wine, was fitted to symbolise the power of Jesus to sweeten the homely comforts of life—to make "the little that a righteous man hath better than the riches of many wicked." All this is true, and yet it fails to give any peculiar significance to this occurrence, as the first miracle that Jesus ever performed. For in truth, the most of Christ's miracles, unlike this one, were miracles of redemption,—miracles in which some great disorder was removed; they were symbolic of the great work of Christ, in redeeming men from sin and suffering and death. The miracle of Cana was not one of this class, and cannot therefore be ranked among His most glorious and significant works. It has really no distinction except that it was first in order. We are like the traveller here, arriving at the source of a great stream, but not finding anything unusually notable at the spot.

Why, then, is it recorded? Mainly, we believe, that *its effect on the disciples* may be pointed out. "This beginning of miracles did Jesus at Cana of Galilee, and manifested forth his glory; *and his disciples believed on him.*" But did they not believe before? Certainly; they believed in virtue of what they saw and heard at Bethabara. But their faith was not so stable as not to admit of being corroborated. The effect of the miracle was to increase their faith. And thus it was made to appear how the internal and external evidences for Christ work to one another. The right order of things is this: the internal evidence does the work; the external confirms the impression of the internal. First, Christ commends Himself to the soul by His outbeaming grace and glory; then miracles follow, to convince the soul that in its estimate of Him it has made no error, that it has rightly concluded Him to be the Son of God. In the case of the disciples the right order was followed,—first, their souls apprehended His heavenly glory; then their eyes beheld His mighty works. But there were many of Christ's countrymen who could not be impressed with the first mode of proof. In their case the miracles took away all excuse for unbelief, and perhaps awakened a spirit of inquiry, which in some cases led to better results. With the disciples and likeminded persons the order was different: the miracle confirmed and sealed the faith which sprang first from the contemplation of His spiritual glory. And this, we may say, indicates a great peculiarity of the fourth Gospel; in it miracles hold a subordinate place; its great theme is the spiritual glory of the Son of God. The fourth Gospel is not properly a biography; its design is to show how faith in Jesus was produced in some, while unbelief continued in the minds of others; and in particular to show the action of the two kinds of proof, external and internal, on men—the signs and miracles on the one hand, and the inward manifestations of Divine life and power by Jesus on the other.

And now we come to the public commencement of the Judæan ministry,—Christ's visit to Jerusalem at the feast of the Passover. The first incident at Jerusalem is a somewhat unexpected and surprising one—His forcible cleansing of the temple. It has to be specially marked, for it is eminently significant, that the first public act of Jesus, entering the sacred city in His character as Messiah, was to make a whip of small cords and drive the traders from the temple. It seems at the first blush inconsistent with the meek and gentle spirit which was so remarkable in Him; just as the turning of the water into wine seems at first inconsistent with the Christian spirit of self-denial and victory over all carnal delights.

Let us look carefully, then, at the circumstances of the case. It is remarkable that Jesus met with no opposition to His task, though He was but one against scores; a panic seems to have fallen on the traders. He came upon them like that warrior of whom Isaiah asks, "Who is this that cometh from Edom, with dyed garments from Bozrah? this that is glorious in his apparel, travelling in the greatness of his strength?" He came *in propriâ personâ* as the Lord of the Temple, and there was that in the pose of His figure, in the flash of His eye, in the majesty of His march, and the imperial tones of His voice that showed Him to be what He claimed. In regard to the physical violence which He employed, it was by no means inconsistent with the character of one whose great weapons were gentleness and love. There are occasions when physical violence is the irresistible outcome of the holiest and purest spiritual feelings,—the outcome even of the warmest love. In the first of Chrysostom's celebrated Homilies of the Statues, when the whole community of Antioch was petrified by dread of the Emperor's wrath, and when any fresh sin, provoking the wrath of God, seemed to the great preacher like the loosening of an avalanche over the city, he said: "I desire to ask one favour of you all, in return for this my address, which is that you will correct, on my behalf, the blasphemers of this city. And should you hear any one in the public thoroughfare, or in the midst of the forum, blaspheming God, reproach, rebuke him; and should it be necessary to inflict blows, spare not to do so. Smite him on the face; strike his mouth; sanctify thy hand with the blow; and if any should accuse thee, and drag thee to the place of justice, follow them thither; and when the judge on the bench calls thee to account, say boldly that the man blasphemed the King of Angels. . . . Let the Jews and Greeks learn that the Christians are the saviours of the city, that they are its guardians, its patrons, and its teachers." . . .

John Foster tells an anecdote of the devoted Grimshawe, who more than a century ago was incumbent of Haworth, in Yorkshire—a wild sequestered place, famous in our time as the home of the Brontë sisters:—that having been told one winter night that a number of blackguards were disturbing a religious meeting, held in a room at the end of a passage, in order to stop the disturbance, as there were no police, he took the matter into his own hands. Disguising himself in a coarse coat, he went among the ruffians, as if he belonged to the gang, till the door of the place being thrown open, he suddenly, by a desperate effort, forced them all into the meeting-room, and after locking the door, pulled from his pocket a horse-whip, with which he laid on them till his arm was tired; then falling on his knees, he prayed for them with such an awful emphasis on the words hell and damnation, that the wretches were appalled, and the meetings were never disturbed again.[1]

To understand the significance of our Lord's act, we must bear in mind that even then, He was no stranger in the temple. We know not if any tradition lingered of the presentation of the infant child of Mary—if there were still any living echoes of the *nunc dimittis* of Simeon, or the thanksgiving of Anna. But the visit of the child from Nazareth could not have been forgotten among the doctors, more especially as that child probably returned from year to year, and could hardly fail to be an object of interest and curiosity among them.

[1] Contributions to the *Eclectic Review*, i. 505.

But a much more certain and important fact has to be pondered. It was but a few weeks since a deputation of priests and Levites had been sent from Jerusalem to John the Baptist, to ask him who he was (John i. 19). That deputation was at Bethabara when Jesus returned from the temptation. They heard John declare that he was not the Messiah, but that there stood one among them whom they knew not, whose shoe's latchet he was not worthy to unloose. They heard John speak of the descent of the Holy Ghost on Jesus, and as Jesus passed by, they heard him say, "Behold the Lamb of God!" Observe, then, that when Jesus came to Jerusalem, and entered the temple as its Lord, the priests and Levites knew full well what John had testified respecting Him. Thus they had a double reason for receiving Him as their Lord. They had the testimony of John, strong and solemn; and they had the majestic bearing of Jesus Himself, and the striking witness to Him in the crouching attitude and unresisting flight of the sacrilegious wretches who had brought their traffic into the sacred court. But the authorities of the temple did not yield. They would not own Him as their Lord. They demanded, "What sign showest thou unto us, seeing that thou doest these things?" Rejecting the higher evidence, they demanded the lower. Rejecting the spiritual and inward, they asked for the external. Jesus gave them an answer which was at once an enigma and a sublime assertion of supernatural power, "Destroy this temple, and in three days I will raise it up again." But in vain. He was not the kind of Lord they wanted.

They would have nothing of Him. "He came unto his own, and his own received him not."

Two great facts were thus impressed on the mind of Jesus: first, that He was rejected by the spiritual authorities of Jerusalem; and second, that the moral evidence of His heavenly mission went for little—signs and wonders were what men clamoured for. His rejection by the authorities was a significant and painful fact. At the very beginning the door was slammed in His face. His ministry in Jerusalem could never be a general success. But though rejected by the authorities, there was a remnant, an election according to grace, to whom His ministry would prove a blessing. There were units here and there that might be saved. Our Lord, therefore, did not rush from Jerusalem, but laboured on, patiently and diligently, if by any means He might save some.

And as it appeared that the people could not appreciate the higher and more spiritual evidence of His claims, He gave them "signs and wonders." We read (John ii. 23-25), "when Jesus was in Jerusalem at the passover, in the feast day, many believed in his name, when they saw the miracles which he did. But Jesus did not commit himself unto them, because he knew all men, and needed not that any should testify of man: for he knew what was in man." We gather from this, that their faith was not of a very trustworthy character. The faith that rested on signs and wonders was not of the same quality as the faith of those who, with true spiritual insight, beheld His glory, the glory as of the only begotten of the Father. The one faith was no more than a step towards the other. The true faith was that which sprang from conviction of sin, such as John the Baptist had produced,—from an inward sense of need, and an inward apprehension of the power of Jesus to meet their case and bring them to God. Jesus did not despise the lower faith, though He deemed it in itself unsatisfactory. Wherever it existed there was some hope of building on it a higher and more spiritual faith. A noble opportunity to do so occurred immediately in the case of Nicodemus. In dealing with Nicodemus, as we shall see presently, He illustrated in various ways the difference between what we may call a mechanical and a spiritual faith. The lesson for His servants in the ministry is obvious. Call it what we may, we can commit ourselves to the faith of no man whose soul has not been drawn to Christ by the discovery of His spiritual glory, and the apprehension in Him of all the stores of blessing which, as a sinner, he requires.

The precise idea that Nicodemus had of Christ, and that many more in Jerusalem had of Him, may be gathered from his words, "Rabbi, we know that thou art a teacher sent from God; for no man can do those miracles that thou doest except God be with him." There is no evidence here of more than what we have called a mechanical faith. There is no proof that the truth had been apprehended by Nicodemus spiritually, or that he had a due conception of the exalted function which Christ had come to fulfil. He was simply convinced that such supernatural power as He had shown indicated a Divine mission, and being restless and unsatisfied in regard to his state before God, he came to see if He could throw light on his perplexities, and guide his feet into the way of peace. It is evident that as soon as the case was before Him, our Lord judged it a suitable one for more searching and spiritual work;—a case for exciting spiritual desires, and revealing His power to satisfy them, so that faith of the highest order should be the result. At once, therefore, and with an apparent abruptness that amounted to bluntness, our Lord struck a spiritual note. "Verily, verily, I say unto thee, except a man be born again, he cannot see the kingdom of God." The objections of Nicodemus to this doctrine led only to its being more fully and emphatically affirmed. And in fact, as our Lord goes on, He lays down the most vital positions of Christian theology, while at the same time He gives prominence to His own personality, as the author of that salvation which all men require.

What has been called the three Rs—man's ruin by sin, his redemption by Christ, and his regeneration by the Spirit, are set forth very clearly in this conversation with Nicodemus. The three persons in the Trinity, God, the Son, and the Spirit, are severally brought forward. It is indicated that the redemption of man is to be achieved through the Son of man being "lifted up, as Moses lifted up the serpent in the wilderness;" but nothing specific is stated as to what is meant by this "lifting up," because men are not yet prepared to receive the doctrine of Christ's death and crucifixion. In the course of His conversation, our Lord refers repeatedly to the strange and unpopular aspect which His teaching presented. "Art thou a master of Israel, and knowest not these things? ... If I have told you earthly things, *and ye believe not*, how shall ye believe if I tell you heavenly things?" "And this is the condemnation, that light is come into the world, and *men loved darkness rather than light, because their deeds were evil.*" He speaks as one who has been rejected, and who understands the reason why. It is not because He has furnished too little evidence of His claims, but because "he that doeth evil hateth the light, neither cometh to the light, lest his deeds should be reproved." The disorder under which men are labouring hinders them from recognising and welcoming their deliverer. Jesus can now look for nothing but rejection by the mass; and this adds infinitely to the difficulty of His work.

There is every reason to believe that Nicodemus became a true disciple, and that he came to be ranked among those who beheld in Christ the glory as of the only begotten of the Father. Thus, though the rulers as a body rejected Christ, one of them believed. We seem to find here an explanation of that enigmatical prophecy in Isaiah, where the servant of the Lord says, "I have laboured in vain; I have spent my strength for nought and in vain; yet surely my judgment is with the Lord, and my work with my God." With the rulers of the nation he had laboured in vain, and his labour was in vain to the very end of the day; but in individual cases there were tokens that the Lord his God was with him, and that none of his words were falling to the ground. How often is this true of the faithful minister! On the mass he seems to make no impression; but here and there a soul is given him, to cheer his heart and send him on his way rejoicing.

We have no data for determining the length of time spent by our Lord at Jerusalem, but we know that when He left the city He did not leave the district. "He came into the land of Judæa, and there he tarried with his disciples, and baptized" (John iii. 22). It is quite possible that this visit embraced some of the more noted places in that neighbourhood, so celebrated in Old Testament story. At one time He was evidently not far off from John. "John was also baptizing in Œnon, near Salim, because there was much water there; and they came and were baptized." The only place, says Captain Conder, where an Œnon occurs near to a Salim, and where there are copious springs of water, is in a valley at or near the boundary between Judæa and Samaria. The fact of their being so near led to two results. On John's being informed that Jesus was baptizing more disciples than he, he was led to give a very beautiful and instructive testimony to Jesus. The Pharisees, moreover, were informed that Jesus was becoming more popular than John; and as John was shortly after cast into prison by Herod, and it was evident that the Pharisees, being rid of John, would try next to get rid of Jesus, our Lord left Judæa, and directed His steps to Galilee as the future scene of His ministry.

The testimony of John to Jesus was a very remarkable one. It was quite apparent that Jesus was now more popular than John. John accepted this fact with remarkable calmness, and showed that where there was such an infinite difference between the two men, it was only what might be expected that the one should increase and the other decrease. But John, penetrating below the surface, perceived that though Jesus was successful in one sense, He had not succeeded in a sense more profound. No doubt the people were impressed by His miracles, and what we have called a mechanical faith prevailed very generally. But the inner or spiritual faith, the evidence of the only true impression, was but rare. Contrasting himself with Jesus, John spoke of himself as one who had got from God all that he had testified. But Jesus had come from heaven, He was "from above, above all," and had testified that which He had seen as well as heard (iii. 32). Nevertheless, John adds, "no man receiveth his testimony." Apparently popular, He is really rejected. While many believe in His signs and wonders, few apprehend His spiritual doctrine. The faith shown by the multitude was not necessarily a saving faith. John saw very clearly the whole bearings of the case. He apprehended the infinite difference between the change on the five or six disciples who had left him at Bethabara, and probably Nicodemus on the one hand, and the multitude that accepted baptism at the hand of Christ's disciples, on the other. He saw that the kind of popularity which Jesus was enjoying was no test of a satisfactory and abiding impression. Perhaps he could foresee that the amazement of the multitude now would not hinder them from crying out on a future occasion, "Away with him! crucify him!" But all the more because Jesus had been rejected by the rulers, did this noble witness-bearer renew his testimony to Him. Nay, he rises to a higher eminence than ever, and speaks of Jesus with a solemnity which could not be surpassed; for the interests depending on men's reception of Him are interests of overwhelming magnitude: "He that believeth on the Son hath everlasting life; and he that believeth not the Son shall not see life, but the wrath of God abideth on him."

It is a very solemn view that this chapter of our Lord's ministry gives us of the difference between a superficial and a spiritual faith. It shows us how little comparatively is gained when men are attached to Christ merely by the outer attributes of their nature. It is the profound apprehension of His saving qualities, the sense of the guilt and pollution of sin on the one hand, and the power of Christ to redeem us on the other, and the clinging of the soul to Him, as with a death-grip, for these unspeakable blessings, that constitute true discipleship. "Lord, to whom shall we go? Thou hast the words of eternal life."

CHAPTER VI.

BEGINNING OF HIS MINISTRY IN GALILEE.

It must have been with solemn and painful feelings that our Lord turned His back on Jerusalem and Judæa, and sought for a more congenial sphere of labour in the rougher regions of Galilee. His first attempt to gather the children of Jerusalem together, as a hen gathereth her chickens under her wings, had been repulsed. He had been rejected by the rulers in spite alike of the inward manifestations of Divine authority supplied by His life, His spirit, and His lessons, and the external credentials which His miracles afforded. Jerusalem, for a thousand years the city of the Great King, had virtually declared Him an impostor. Such a rebuff at the very outset of His ministry must have been most chilling; yet neither at this time, nor afterwards, did His habitual serenity and cheerfulness forsake Him. Though He did not bid a final farewell to the great centre of religious influence, His visits to it in after days could be only during the brief seasons of the feasts, and even then at great personal hazard, and with the profound conviction that one day, like so many of the prophets before Him, He would be put to death in Jerusalem.

But on His way to Galilee, it was our Lord's lot to meet with a wonderfully refreshing incident. His route lay through Samaria, no longer peopled by the tribe of Ephraim, but by the despised descendants of that mongrel race whom the king of Assyria had brought from the provinces of the East to occupy the homes and lands of the dispossessed sons of Joseph. There were in fact two great encouragements provided for Him in this unpromising field. First, there was the change produced on the woman whom He met at the well, the narrative of which is one of the brightest gems of gospel history. The place of meeting, Jacob's well, was striking, recalling one of the great fathers of the Hebrew race, and the dawn of a history of which much of the past had been so brilliant, though Ichabod was now visible on all sides. There was the condition of Jesus Himself, so thoroughly exhausted in body as to be unable to accompany His disciples into the neighbouring city, yet ready to wake up with youthful animation at the joy of bringing a lost sheep to the fold. There was the repulsive history of the woman —all her life a wanderer from the ways of God, and now so low and so lost that to man her recovery seemed impossible; yet not too deep in the pit to be won back by that Divine grace and love which can prevail when all other reclaiming forces have lost their virtue. There was the graciousness of Christ, breaking through all the barriers of prejudice, and revealing such a tender interest in the woman's soul; and there was His beautiful revelation to her of Divine things, of free grace, and abundant blessing, and His very skilful way of dealing with her,—of preventing her from running off into any sidepath of discussion,—and of guiding her, poor sinner as she was, to the fountain of living waters. The pains that the great Teacher took with this single hearer; the magnificence of the truths which He taught to her all alone; the way in which, while He was dealing with her, the willing spirit overcame all the weakness and weariness of His flesh; and finally, the interest in the welfare of her townspeople that was kindled in her breast, turning her into a missionary, into one who carried the good news of the kingdom to the men of the city,—such things as these are like a burst of sunshine in a gloomy day, and they combine to make the incident at Jacob's well one of the most interesting and beautiful in the whole ministry of our Lord.

The other encouragement which our Lord had in connection with this incident was the effect produced on the men of the city. Evidently they underwent a great spiritual change. Many believed because of the saying of the woman, and having prevailed on Him to spend two days among them, many more believed because of His own word. It is remarkable that we read nothing in this case of signs and wonders. It was the higher evidence that impressed these people. They recognised the divinity of what Jesus taught. And when they declared their faith in Jesus as the Christ, it was not as a temporal prince they honoured Him, but as "the Saviour of the world" (ver. 42). If it be asked, what had Christ taught them that led to this acknowledgment? our answer is, that in all probability it was the substance of what He had taught Nicodemus,—that "God so loved *the world*" (the very expression used by the Samaritans) "that he gave his only begotten Son, that whosoever believeth in him should not perish, but should have everlasting life." Thus we have another proof that from the beginning our Lord assumed much more than the *rôle* of a moral teacher—that from the first He proclaimed the doctrine of salvation. What a blessed encouragement it must have been to Him to be welcomed and honoured by these outcast Samaritans, just after He had been rejected by the rulers of the Jews!—to find congenial hearts in the highways and the hedges, while those for whom the feast was prepared scorned His invitation! In all likelihood it was this same city of the Samaritans that was so impressed and blessed afterwards under the preaching of Philip the evangelist, for both in John iv. 5 and Acts viii. 5 we find the same expression (εἰς πόλιν τῆς Σαμαρείας). And probably John had this remarkable case in view when he wrote—"He came unto his own, and his own received him not. *But as many as received him,* to them" (though not sons by Hebrew descent) "gave he power to become children of God, even to them that believed on his name: which were born, not of blood, nor of the will of the flesh, nor of the will of man, but of God."

It is interesting to remark, too, in our Lord's future career, the feeling which He had for the Samaritans generally. He seems to have recognised a certain kindliness of nature in them, when, in the parable of the Good Samaritan, He made one of them His model philanthropist. Of the ten lepers that were healed, the only one who returned to give thanks was a Samaritan—another proof of warm-heartedness. When a village of Samaritans would not receive Him, and His disciples proposed that He should call down fire from heaven to consume them, He deprecated the proposal with unusual warmth. Their treatment in not receiving Him seems to have been an exception to the ordinary rule. Kindness on the part of an uncouth, rugged people has a very touching effect, as Paul felt at Melita, when "the barbarous people showed no little kindness" to him and his companions. It was strange that, from an excommunicated people like the Samaritans, our Lord should have had a better reception than from either Judea or Galilee. "I am found of them that sought me not; I said, Behold me, behold me, unto a people that was not called by my name."

Leaving Samaria, our Lord entered Galilee. Outwardly His reception was favourable. "When he was come into Galilee, the Galileans received him, having seen all the things that he did at Jerusalem at the feast." It appears from this statement that it was the external rather than the internal evidence that made an impression on the Galileans. In this respect they were behind the Samaritans, but in advance of the rulers at Jerusalem. The Galileans were certainly not a spiritual race. It was the signs and wonders that impressed them—not the holy life of Jesus, or His Divine wisdom and grace. Still it was something that they admitted the authority of the miracles wrought at the feast.

Finding that mighty works were the only way of impressing them, Jesus performed very many such during His subsequent ministry in Galilee. Matthew says that He went about all Galilee, healing all sickness and all manner of disease among the people. The Gospel according to Mark is mainly a record of the mighty works done in Galilee. Jesus did not treat these people otherwise than as they were capable of appreciating. As yet they were open to little more than external influences, and these were brought to bear on them with unsparing hand. But even in Galilee our Lord took pains to show that a faith that rested merely on mighty works, and that recognised no higher ground than these for trusting Christ, was not a faith with which He was satisfied. Two remarkable occasions for showing this presented themselves: one at Cana, and the other at Nazareth.

Cana seems to have been the first place in Galilee to which Jesus went when He came from Judæa, just as it had been on His leaving Bethabara. While He was there, a nobleman or king's officer came to Him from Capernaum, beseeching Him to go down there and heal his son. The reply to this request was striking. Addressing the nobleman, not as an individual, but as a representative of the people of Capernaum, Jesus said, "Except ye (plural, *i.e.* ye people of Capernaum) see signs and wonders, ye will not believe" (John iv. 48). During His temporary residence there (John ii. 12), Jesus had taken the measure of the people of Capernaum. They were not a people easily impressed. They had no sympathy with what was spiritual. They saw no halo of Divinity around His head. Nothing would impress them but signs and wonders. Somewhat tauntingly, Jesus says, "Except ye see signs and wonders ye will not believe." He speaks like one somewhat vexed that as soon as He set foot in Galilee He should be asked to work miracles, rather than to make those revelations of the grace of God which He had been asked for in Samaria and which had been accompanied by such blessed results. There was implied in it a contrast between the spirituality of the Samaritans and the carnality of the Galileans. There was no making any impression on the latter save through mighty works.

The nobleman patiently accepted the reproach, but quickly observing that the answer of Jesus was not a refusal of his request, he pressed it on Him with increased urgency: "Sir, come down ere my child die." Like the Syrophenician mother, who took meekly the comparison that ranked her among the dogs, but still pressed for the blessing, though only as a dog, so the nobleman tacitly admitted that it was as Jesus represented, but nevertheless, O sir, "come down ere my child die." Jesus perceived that a higher faith might spring from that which he had just displayed; and while He refused his request in form, He granted it in spirit. "Go thy way, thy son liveth," was the final answer to the man's request. He taught the man to believe in His word as well as His works; thus laying the foundation of a higher faith, which would find many an opportunity for its exercise when Jesus should go to reside at Capernaum.

One might suppose that such a man as this would

have proved a useful apostle, had Jesus been pleased to call him to be such. But both Nicodemus the ruler at Jerusalem and this nobleman of Capernaum were passed by, and men of humbler rank were chosen. The selection of the men who formed the college of the twelve was not ruled by sheer necessity; it was the result of deliberate choice. It seemed good to Jesus then, as it so often has since, to select His officers from the less favoured orders of society; not that there is any advantage of itself in a humble origin, or a rugged manner, but because those who are most unfurnished with earthly advantages ought the more to appreciate the value and to long for the possession of those higher spiritual gifts by which alone the true kingdom of Christ can be advanced in this world.

The other occasion in His early ministry in Galilee when our Lord showed emphatically the unsatisfactory nature of a faith resting merely on signs and wonders, was when He visited Nazareth and preached in the synagogue there. The precise date of this visit is uncertain, but the early place which the narrative occupies in Luke's Gospel (iv. 16-30) shows that it occurred early, and very probably about this very time.

It is probable that our Lord had been a full year absent from Nazareth. Since He was last there, there had occurred His baptism by John, His temptation in the wilderness, His visit to John at Bethabara, His visits to Cana and Capernaum, the entire time spent in His Judæan ministry, His visit to Samaria, and to Cana, and to other parts of Galilee. Whether Nazareth was taken in ordinary course, or whether a special visit was arranged, we are not told. It could not but be a trying visit, for few tasks are harder than to give God's message to one's own relatives and intimate friends, especially when they are in no mood to receive it. No doubt our Lord settled clearly beforehand what line He would take at Nazareth. Especially He must have settled whether He would endeavour to make an impression by signs and wonders, or whether it would be by the more spiritual course—by setting before them the glorious truths of Divine grace and love, and seeking to bring their souls into sympathy with Himself. It was the latter of these courses that He resolved to take. The selection of this line was in reality a compliment to Nazareth. It implied that it was feasible to expect that an impression would be made on them by the higher class of evidences, that they would recognise the truth of heaven when they heard it, and welcome Him who had come at once to proclaim and apply it.

Entering the synagogue, He stood up, no doubt according to established custom, to take part in the service. The book of the prophet Isaiah was handed to him, and having turned up the 61st chapter, He read the following passage: "The Spirit of the Lord is upon me, because He hath anointed me to preach the gospel to the poor; He hath sent me to heal the broken-hearted, to preach deliverance to the captives, and recovering of sight to the blind, to set at liberty them that are bruised; to preach the acceptable year of the Lord."

Having finished the reading, and given back the book, He sat down; and in expectation of hearing an address, and probably in no little curiosity to know how He would view the passage, "the eyes of all that were in the synagogue were fastened on Him." His commentary was very direct and explicit. Substantially it is contained in the words, "This day is this scripture fulfilled in your ears." It must have been an exposition of the gracious saving purposes for which He had been sent into the world by the Father. It must have been substantially the same view of truth that had captivated Andrew and John and the other disciples at Bethabara, that had more than answered the questions of Nicodemus, that had subdued the woman of Samaria at the well, and that had drawn to Him the inhabitants of the Samaritan city. Probably He discoursed at some length on the ladder now set up between heaven and earth, on which the angels of God were ascending and descending; on the glorious qualities of the water of life; on the errand of salvation on which He had come into the world; on the rest which He offered to the weary, water to the thirsty, healing to the sick, and life to the dead. His lips seem to have dropt as the honeycomb, being steeped in the very odours of heaven, and up to a certain point the audience felt the power and charm of His words. "They bare Him witness," it is said; they responded to Him; they "wondered at the gracious words that proceeded out of His mouth." Now was the critical moment in their state of mind on which the future depended. They were convinced, their understandings were carried, nay, their feelings were touched; but this was not enough. It is the *will* that governs the soul. In the case of the Nazarenes the will was not moved. For all that they had heard of gracious words, for all that they had seen in Christ of a heavenly demeanour, they were not willing to accept Him as the Samaritans had accepted Him. It was their pride that stood in the way. They said, "Is not this Joseph's son?" This remark was one that could have been made only for a particular purpose. It was not put as a question needing an answer. Every one must have known who He was, as well as the people of a village know any one who has lived among them for thirty years. The precise purpose for which the question was put will appear if we fill up the obvious ellipsis with such words as *after all*—"After all, is not this Joseph's son?" It will appear thus that the words were uttered as an excuse for not surrendering themselves to Jesus, and accepting Him as Messiah. Evidently they had felt a strong impulse in that direction, but the impulse is neutralised by the consideration, "Is not this Joseph's son? Why fling ourselves at *his* feet? Why surrender soul, body, and spirit to *him*"? They made the low earthly connection of Jesus a screen, as it were, to cover His Divine glory. The glory was shining through Him, shining through in His gracious words—but they would not see it; they stifled it, as it were, and stifled their own convictions by obtruding the fact that, after all, Jesus was but one of themselves—the son of Joseph the carpenter.

What followed is briefly and elliptically told; but the bearing of it is not difficult to see. The spirit of unbelief must have something to fall back on, by way of apology; and, as on other occasions, it demanded a sign. If this Jesus was something more than Joseph's son, why should He not perform some of His miracles among them? Had He not been performing miracles at Capernaum, and was not the place of His own upbringing more worthy of such a display than Capernaum? If *they* did not quite treat *Him* as he deserved, it was His own fault for not treating *them* as they deserved. Jesus discerned their thoughts without any expression of them in words. They were thinking that the Physician might have healed Himself—that is, healed His own people, His own city. "Whatsoever things we have heard done in Capernaum, that do in thine own city." But it was not the purpose of Jesus to show them signs and wonders. In point of fact He had shown them what was above all signs and wonders. And, in thus declining to use His miraculous power, He had parallel cases, Old Testament precedents, to bear Him out. In the days of the famine, Elijah had wrought no miracle for his own people, they had abundant evidence of his claim without miracles; it was but one pagan widow who got that benefit. Elisha had cured no Israelite leper; one leper only was cured, and he a Syrian. Thus Jesus not only refused to pay them honour, but justified His refusal. He not only withheld a miraculous display, but brought forward for His defence the example of the highest prophets.

We are hardly prepared for the result. But in refusing to acknowledge Him when the evidence of God's presence with Him was so overpowering, they had been guilty of vexing the Holy Spirit, and this prepared the way for a terrible outburst of sin. They were so enraged that they would have dashed Jesus over a precipice had He not miraculously escaped. So there was a miracle, but it was not a miracle of display. Some may think that the fitting thing for Christ to do would have been to let them dash Him over the precipice, then confound their malice by coming quietly and safely to the ground. But Jesus absolutely avoids all self-display. In the spirit of His rebuke to Satan, who would have had Him cast Himself from the pinnacle of the temple, He declines the more ostentatious way of escape. By some quiet means He slips out of their hands, and passes on His way. Once more then He is rejected. His own city are now the rejecters. Again " he came to his own, and his own received him not."

Thus Jesus had been rejected at the two places where He might have looked for the most favourable reception. But there still remained open to Him eastern and northern Galilee. Samaria was not the home of Israelites, and was therefore passed over meanwhile. Eastern Galilee had already yielded Him some good fruit, in the person of the five followers secured at Bethabara, and the other disciples whom He afterwards called to be apostles. To these districts of Galilee, therefore, Jesus now gave His main attention. Among them He itinerated and preached. But He did not preach quite in the same strain as He had preached at Nazareth, or as He had spoken at Bethabara, or at the city of Samaria. We read (Matt. iv. 17) that when He began His ministry in Galilee, His cry was, "Repent, for the kingdom of heaven is at hand." In the same Gospel (iv. 23) we read that "He went about all Galilee, teaching in their synagogues, and preaching the gospel of the kingdom, and healing all manner of sickness, and all manner of disease, among the people." Undoubtedly His chief employments in Galilee were, on the one hand, expounding God's law, and calling men to repentance; and on the other hand, scattering everywhere temporal blessings. Let us glance briefly at these two things.

First, He called men to repentance. And in doing so, He gave them a new idea of the extent to which repentance was needed. He opened up the nature and extent of the Divine claims on them in a way that had never been known. In this point of view, we see a great advance in our Lord's teaching over even the most spiritual of the Old Testament prophets. The prophets had strongly denounced every form of immorality and idolatry; they had shown the need of a new heart, and in some of the Psalms the cry for inward conformity to the law of God had been earnest and vehement. Our Lord's teaching was in the same direction, but it was both more extensive and more intensive. He embraced more fully the whole sphere of human life and duty: duty to God, to our brother, to our neighbour, to our enemies, to our parents, to our children, to our rulers, even to our cattle; thus indicating deep obligations in the whole sphere of human life. Then He penetrated more deeply into the soul, exposing irregularities in thought and feeling; showing sin to lie in every angry thought, in every lustful feeling, and in every idle word; and denouncing everything that lurked in the heart incompatible with the kingdom of God. The true kingdom of God was ruled by a profound inward conformity to the will of God; not merely an outward compliance with what He required, but an inward approval and delight therein. All that was inconsistent with that was sin; the kingdom demanded humiliation and repentance before God; sin must be cast out of the soul that was to inherit the kingdom: "Blessed are the pure in heart: for they shall see God."

But was this really a gospel? Was it not the gospel of impossibility, and therefore the gospel of despair? So it would certainly have been had our Lord stopped here. But in all Christ's preaching, when He demanded repentance and absolute purity of soul, there is an indication that He came not only to proclaim but to furnish the qualities which He so earnestly enforced. As in the case of the man with the withered hand, our Lord not only ordered him to stretch it out, but furnished the power to do so; so, when He enjoined repentance, and a higher righteousness than that of the Scribes and Pharisees, He indicated His willingness to supply the power by which these attainments were to be secured. Is this not the lesson of the beatitudes at the beginning of the Sermon on the Mount? —" Blessed are the poor in spirit : *for theirs is the kingdom of God.*" For men consciously poor and needy there is a glorious provision in the kingdom; the kingdom supplies the power by which they are fitted for it, as the sun supplies to growing trees the luminous element by means of which afterwards, when cut down and turned into fuel, they become light-giving bodies.

This great truth underlay all Christ's teaching in Galilee. He taught men to pray, "Thy will be done on earth, as it is done in heaven;" but this prayer would have been sheer mockery if He had not indicated how power was to be got to do that will of God—"If ye that are evil know how to give good gifts unto your children, how much more shall your Father which is in heaven give the Holy Spirit to them that ask Him?" Any representation of Christ's Galilean ministry which would view it as merely didactic is defective in a most vital element. If that had been all that Christ did, He would only have tantalised men. But there was heart, and hope, and cheerfulness in all His teaching; every willing disciple He took by the hand, and inspired with confidence in His ability to lead him up to the heavenly heights to which He pointed him.

And this readiness of Christ to give as well as to exact in the moral and spiritual sphere is beautifully symbolised by the unstinted abundance of His miracles of mercy as He goes through Galilee. Everywhere He appears with an open hand. He heals the sick, He expels evil spirits, He cleanses lepers, He subdues storms, He conquers the forces of disorder, He even raises the dead. All these acts show what stores of temporal power and blessing are in His person. And very readily they suggest the existence of corresponding spiritual stores. He that is so rich in power to bless the body cannot be helpless when the soul has to be dealt with. He who knows so well and teaches so wisely what the soul ought to be, cannot be at a loss when called in as physician there. And, in point of fact, we find Christ from time to time crossing the line between the temporal and the spiritual. We find Him dealing out at times the blessing of forgiveness. After a time, after the transfiguration which testified that, even though He was to be put to death, He was still the Son of God, we find Him letting His disciples know something of the process by which He was to be qualified to grant forgiveness and all other blessings. He was to suffer and to die. After the resurrection, He explained the necessity for all this, when, beginning at Moses and all the prophets, He expounded to them in all the Scriptures the things concerning Himself.

Thus we come to see how it was that our Lord abstained from preaching in Galilee in the strain in which He had spoken at Bethabara, at Jerusalem to Nicodemus, at the city of Samaria, and at Nazareth. He felt it necessary to go back a little, and prepare men by more elementary lessons, and by more sensible signs, for the full revelation of His gospel. Even when the messengers from the now imprisoned John come to Him in Galilee with their master's question, the evidence to which He points is purely external: "Go and show John again those things which ye do hear and see: the blind receive their sight, and the lame walk; the lepers are cleansed, and the deaf hear; the dead are raised up, and the poor have the gospel preached to them." Why He should have confined Himself to the external proof in dealing with the question of John is one of those difficulties which belong to this incident, and which, from ignorance of John's precise state of mind, it is not likely we shall ever be able to remove. But it illustrates the remark that, in its direct form, the great doctrine of salvation was kept somewhat in abeyance in Galilee, and that the doctrine of His person, and the exposition of the manner in which He was to save men from their sins, belonged more to His Judæan ministry, and to the closing scenes of His earthly life.

All this tracing out of the lines of our Lord's ministry in Galilee and in Judæa is of importance, chiefly as helping us to understand the plan and aim of His public life. That life ceases to be a mere collection of beautiful fragments; it becomes an organised whole, systematically directed, though on somewhat different lines, to the great purpose for which He came into the world. We see how carefully our Lord studied the capacity of His hearers, and adapted His dealings to the nature of the case. "All things to all men" was as much His motto, and within similar limits, as it was the apostle Paul's. And for us there remains the abiding lesson to be patient towards those who are too carnal to apprehend the more spiritual relations of the kingdom, adapting our lessons to their temper and capacity, until, by God's blessing, a spiritual taste is formed in them, and they learn to discern the things of the Spirit of God.

CHAPTER VII.

HIS WORK AS TEACHER.

WHILE we repudiate emphatically the aim of unbelief to reduce Jesus of Nazareth to the position of a mere teacher, we accept cordially its concession that as a teacher His power and His influence were unrivalled. Certainly the Divine Saviour of the world was far more than a teacher; but a teacher, a prophet of the Lord, He undoubtedly was. It is remarkable that even in the earlier days of His public ministry, before He could have acquired the facilities that usually come from experience and practice, His ability as a teacher impressed all kinds of hearers. It was in the earliest days of His Judæan ministry that Nicodemus came to Him, assured that He was a teacher sent from God, and therefore able to solve the great mysteries that seem to have been pressing on him respecting sin and salvation, life and death. It was on occasion of His first visit to Nazareth, not far from the beginning of His public career, that His hearers " wondered at the gracious words that proceeded out of His mouth." It is of His first great public discourse in Galilee that Matthew says : " The people were astonished at his teaching, for he taught them as one having authority, and not as the scribes." It was early in His ministry, too, as we find it recorded in John vii., that the officers sent by the priests and Pharisees to apprehend Him brought back the testimony—"Never man spake like this man." Later on, we find similar testimonies to the remarkable ability and power of His teaching. The common people heard Him gladly. The people pressed on Him to hear the Word of God (Luke v. 1). The publicans and sinners drew near to hear Him (Luke xv. 1). On occasion of His last visit to Jerusalem all the people came early in the morning to the temple for to hear Him (Luke xxi. 38). It was this readiness of the people to hear, and this practice of hearing with interest, that led our Lord to give so many warnings on the insufficiency of mere hearing, as in the parable of the sower, or in the solemn contrast between the house built on the rock and the house built on the sand.

There are two uses to be made of our Lord's qualities as a teacher, and on the first blush it might be supposed that these are inconsistent with one another. The one use may be termed apologetic, and the other homiletic. When we view His teaching *apologetically* we find it far above all mere human teaching, and on this quality we construct an argument for His Divine mission. When we view it *homiletically* we regard it as furnishing an example to us, and we endeavour to bring out the particulars in which the example holds. But is it possible to combine these views? May Christ's teaching be so far above us as to prove that He was far more than a human teacher, and yet so much on the same plane with us as to furnish us with an example? If we exalt it in either aspect, do we not depress it in the other? Must we not say of it as of the baptism of John, that it was either of heaven or of men?

These questions are not difficult to answer. It is in respect of the *source* whence it was derived that the teaching of Christ was so palpably and completely above us. No earthly fountain of wisdom could have furnished it. His countrymen saw this, and wondered, and asked, "From whence hath this man this wisdom?" (Matt. xiii. 54.) From the mind of Christ truth came out not in little sparks but in brilliant flashes; not in drops but in gushing streams. Unlike Socrates and Plato, and the other wise men of the early world, He did not grope and guess, but He walked steadily, fearlessly, erect, through realms of darkness and mystery. He seemed endued with a new spiritual sense. The ways and purposes of God, hidden from our view so far away in the depths, seemed to Him a familiar theme. The phrases that are so often in the mouths of the greatest philosophers about the limitation of our knowledge were never used by Him, except with reference to one thing—a day of which not even the Son knew, but only the Father. He did not, like Newton, compare Himself to a child gathering pebbles on the beach, while the great ocean of truth lay unexplored before Him. He did not, like Butler, speak of the government of God as a scheme imperfectly comprehended. He did not, like Paul, contrast the state in which we see through a glass darkly with the state in which we are to see face to face. Not only did He appear to know certainly all that He did teach, but He appeared also to possess great stores of Divine truth which He kept in reserve. Nor can it be said that in all this He showed a trace of pretentiousness. His lessons have stood the test of eighteen hundred years. All that time it is His torch that has been flaming in the van of the truth-loving host, and guiding their steps towards the land of promise. All that time the great spiritual leaders of the race have owned allegiance to Him. No spiritual Seer has arisen to overtop Him, or to give a new direction to the steps of men bent on learning the ways of God.

The teaching of Christ, therefore, is an impregnable apologetical argument. It shatters the theory that He was merely a young man of remarkable powers who picked up His ideas cleverly among the hills of Nazareth. The judgment of all fair men goes as far at least as that of Nicodemus, that He was "a teacher sent from God."

While the apologetical position is thus secure, the homiletical and pastoral rests on an equally firm foundation. The process by which our Lord obtained His knowledge of Divine things is hid from us; but the knowledge which He did obtain, and the manner in which He made use of that knowledge, are recorded for our instruction in the narratives of the Evangelists. The truths which He imparted are matter of revelation—His method of imparting them is matter of observation. Both these matters are not only legitimate topics for our study as His servants, but if we should fail to study and ponder them, we should be guilty of a great breach of duty. In the present chapter our subject will be chiefly the truths Christ taught; in what is to follow we shall consider the form and method of His teaching. First, What were the great truths which He made it His business to proclaim? Next, What was characteristic of His way of handling them, and of finding an entrance for them into the understanding, the conscience, and the feelings of His hearers?

Before we take up what is ordinarily understood by the *substance* of Christ's teaching, we must fasten attention on a very remarkable feature of it, well fitted to be an introduction to the whole, because it forms a connecting link between the Divine and the human. The feature we refer to is the connection of Christ's teaching with His *person*. His teaching was eminently *personal*, and this not accidentally but essentially. He Himself was the centre of His system. A great purpose of His preaching was to reveal *Himself*, and to induce men to accept Him and use Him in conformity with this manifestation.

But this was very different from what may be called the personality of some men's teaching. Among ordinary teachers, we find great differences in this respect. Some men keep themselves entirely apart from what they speak or write,—they lose themselves in the subject; while other men mix themselves up with it, and, indeed, are hardly capable of viewing it apart from their own experience. We may take the historical books of the Old Testament as samples of writings where the writer is as completely out of sight as he is in the propositions of Euclid. On the other hand, we may take Jeremiah or Ezekiel as samples of writers whose personality runs like a thread through the whole texture of their work. A still more marked instance is that of the apostle Paul, especially in the more important and characteristic of his epistles. There the personal element is so strong and so characteristic that even the modern critical school is compelled to ascribe these epistles [1] to Paul.

In general terms, we should say that Jesus belonged to the latter class of teachers. But on closer examination it is found that the personal element in His teaching was essentially different from the same element in theirs. It was not that He mixed up His own experiences with what He taught on Divine things to His disciples, but that He ever represented His personality as a vital element in His system. For men could not receive His moral teaching to any good purpose unless they received Himself. That which first of all He was ever most eager to press was, that He was the Messiah, the Son of God sent into the world, to guide lost men to salvation, and if they were to be saved, they must become one with Him.

So vital did our Lord deem this, that in the fourth Gospel it is the conspicuous feature throughout. Not that it is absent in the first three: " Come unto ME, all ye who labour and are heavy laden, and I will give you rest,"—is the view presented in the Synoptics of what He is, and of the manner in which men are to be blessed. " All things are delivered unto me of my Father" is the

[1] Romans, 1st and 2d Corinthians, Galatians.

ground on which in these Gospels He rests His claim, and vindicates His invitation. But in the fourth Gospel, His oneness with the Father is proclaimed in ways without number, as well as the fact that by divine ordination His person is the one storehouse of all blessing for the children of men. He is the light of the world, the bread of life, the water of life, the resurrection and the life. And what makes this truth of such boundless importance is, that unless men believe it, and come to Christ for all spiritual blessing, they cannot obtain such blessing. "I am the vine, ye are the branches. Abide in me, and I in you; as the branch cannot bear fruit of itself except it abide in the vine, no more can ye except ye abide in me." "Without me ye can do nothing." Very plainly, Jesus had a consciousness of a relation to God essentially different from that of any prophet, and different from anything ever claimed by any founder of a religious school.

It was from this exalted standpoint that He taught His other lessons. The sceptic may say, "This was a hallucination — but apart from this, His views of truth were very clear, and His lessons remarkably powerful." But let us observe that, apart from supernatural vision, there is but one thing that can give great insight into truth, and great power of imparting it. That one thing is singleness of eye, freedom from prejudice, purity of moral nature, the stillness of the element in which one lives. In nature, no man sees far with a watery eye or in a foggy or tremulous atmosphere. In a stormy day no eye can penetrate to the depths of ocean through foaming waves. So in the spiritual world one's nature must be pure and still, undisturbed by prejudice, unmoved by hallucinations, to see deep into moral and spiritual truth. But if Jesus was under the wildest hallucination as to His own person—if He was mystified by Old Testament ideas of a Messiah, He was under the influence of a disturbing cause that would have dimmed His spiritual eye, and blurred the whole landscape of truth. The sceptical position is the absurd one, that the most prejudiced and mistaken of all teachers was by far the clearest and the best. We must either deny Him all true insight and spiritual power; or acknowledge Him in the personality which He claimed—as the anointed of the Father, containing, in His own person, all the blessings needed for sinful men.

Between the Great Teacher testifying of His own person as the appointed storehouse of all saving blessing, and the teachers whom He now sends to minister to His Church, there is, and can be, in this vital feature, no resemblance. The function of all teachers in respect of this feature is simply that of witnesses. They are not that light, not even a spark of it, but are sent to bear witness of the light. They are sent to proclaim wherever they go, that "it hath pleased the Father that IN HIM should all fulness dwell." Vital union with Christ brings with it pardon, acceptance, holiness, strength, consolation. Nor, apart from this vital union, is there any possible way of obtaining such blessings. As little could you find, apart from the sun, any provision of light and heat, and other solar influences for some planet that had shot away from its orbit and plunged into the abyss, as apart from the person of Christ you can find light and life and power for any sinful soul. Woe be to the minister who does not make the person of Christ the centre of his system, and the fount of all blessing! A gospel resting on any other basis is not Christ's gospel at all.

Passing now to the consideration of what in the more ordinary sense was the matter of our Lord's teaching, we cannot but be struck with its eminently *practical* character. It is not *doctrinaire* teaching; it gives us no theory of the universe; no system either of philosophy or theology; no categorical answers to the questions that had been puzzling inquirers from generation to generation. In form it is very unlike such works as Calvin's *Institutes*, *The Westminster Confession*, Doddridge's *Rise and Progress*, or Boston's *Fourfold State*. It is like clinical teaching, not the teaching of the class; like the teaching of the physician in the hospital, finding there a great number of impotent folk, and trying simply to show how each of them is to be made whole. Jesus finds men sick and dying; He takes them by the hand, raises them up, and leads them back to God. And yet, while Christ's teaching is thus unformal, incidental, and as it were *pro re natâ*, it is wonderfully complete, with reference to its object. He just takes man as he is in all his disorder and misery, and He not only shows how he is to be renewed and restored, but He actually renews and restores him. He establishes for him a communication between heaven and earth, and He brings the one down to the other. His words are not truth merely, they are spirit and life. What a different man the apostle Peter is when he comes, as it were, out of Christ's hands! At first ignorant, self-confident, and unstable as water, he has become spiritually wise, strong through distrust of himself, and firm as a rock in his testimony for truth and duty. It is the spiritual influence of Christ that has changed him; under Christ's influence, that which was born of the flesh has been displaced in Peter by that which is born of the Spirit.

But what, in substance, were the lessons which Christ taught?

I. Let us begin with the great central subject—GOD. It is of Him and of His ways that man needs most to learn. First, Christ taught His righteousness, His claims on man, His intolerance of sin, the certainty and the awfulness of the judgment of sin, especially in the life to come. This view of God underlies all His teaching. Man is a sinner, and needs to be forgiven. God has given him a law, but he has not kept that law. The idea of deserved punishment, the idea of hell as the place of punishment, is conspicuous in all Christ's teaching, and a dark and terrible element of that teaching it is. But further, Christ taught that God had brought in an economy of grace, of which economy He Himself, as we have seen, was the head. The angels' song was a glimpse of the glorious truth which was revealed in its fulness on the cross at Calvary. Man is not left to perish, for God has sent His Son, " that whosoever believeth on him should not perish, but should have everlasting life." Salvation is not of merit, it is of grace. It does not come to the pharisee with all his respectability, but to the publican who smites on his breast and cries, " God be merciful to me a sinner!" Publicans and sinners are not beyond the pale of this dispensation of grace; for Christ came to call not the righteous but sinners to repentance. Yet this grace which reaches the sinner does not break down the claims of law and righteousness; one jot or one tittle shall in no wise pass from the law till all be fulfilled. The Son of man gives His life a ransom for many. The cup in the holy Supper is the new testament in His blood, shed for the remission of the sins of many. The conditions of redemption by Christ are, that the claims of the righteous law shall be implemented to the uttermost, yet the door of mercy is to be thrown open, and publicans and harlots are to be admitted to the blessings of the kingdom.

It was not enough for Christ to teach that God had provided a channel by which His grace might flow to sinners; He showed by emblems of great beauty and power how rich and comprehensive this grace of God is. This is the great lesson of the parable of the Prodigal Son. The compassion of God is not extinguished even by the most unnatural conduct of men. There are yearnings in the Divine bosom toward the most inexcusable and guilty. He teaches us to call Him " Our Father which art in heaven." No doubt this lesson had been taught in the Old Testament. It had been verified in the history of rebellious Israel. It was the lesson of the 103d psalm and other psalms; it was the gospel of Isaiah and the other prophets; it was the very spirit of the whole course of Revelation. What Christ did was to repeat these lessons, but at the same time to give them a new emphasis and pathos. For Jesus not only taught them in words, but exemplified them in His life. Symbolically He showed the mercy which He proclaimed. When He touched and cleansed the leper; when He accepted the homage of the woman that was a sinner, and sent her away forgiven; when He brought salvation to the home of Zaccheus—that publican extortioner; when He prayed for His murderers; when He gave to the wretched thief a pass to Paradise; when he met the persecutor breathing out threatenings and slaughter and turned him into an apostle, He was in all these things at once proclaiming and exemplifying the marvellous riches of the grace of God. Can any one deny that this was the great glory of Christ's teaching—His teaching by life even more than by word? He proclaimed an infinite tenderness in the Divine bosom, but in union with infinite righteousness; an infinite bounty resting on infinite holiness. Boundless mercy, but no trifling with sin: a compassion that trembles at every human sorrow, yet a majesty that upholds the law to its last jot and tittle.

The lesson is all the more striking that it connects itself so closely with the sufferings of Christ. That the most gracious of all beings should also be the deepest sufferer; that He who was ever scattering blessings should be familiar with sorrow like no other sorrow; that He who was "the light of the world" should have been the person to encounter the hour and power of darkness; this is strange indeed. But it makes the lesson that Christ teaches all the more striking: He magnifies the grace that heals all our diseases; but when the instrument of this healing is inquired for, it is seen that it is "*by* His *stripes that we are healed.*"

Equally remarkable was the view which Christ presented of the spirituality of God, and of the fact that our whole bearing toward Him, our obedience, our trust, our worship must be essentially from and by the spirit. Our obedience must be the obedience of willing hearts, free and unconstrained—a surrender of our will to His will; and to help us to realise this we have the prayer, " Thy will be done on earth as it is in heaven." Our religion must be a very trustful religion, a leaning on our Father even in the dark, a happy confiding assurance that if He feeds the ravens He will not leave us to starve, if He clothes the lilies, His children shall not go in rags. And our worship must be a very spiritual worship: its one great rule being that God is a Spirit, and they that worship Him must worship Him in spirit and in truth. No drawing near to Him with the lips while the heart is far from Him; no new moons or appointed feasts while the hands are full of blood. Nothing is more remarkable in what Jesus prescribed as to the worship in His Church than the entire absence of those minute directions which were so conspicuous in the Church of the Old Testament. What confidence He must have had in the infusion into men's hearts of the spirit of worship, and in that spirit clothing itself in suitable forms! Did ever a religion start with so little of form and outward ceremony, with such an absence of that which the human heart substitutes for spiritual service? The fact that in the Church of Rome and elsewhere men have added so much of this kind to the religion of Christ makes its spirituality, as it came from Him, all the more remarkable.

Then, as to the sphere of God's service. Our Lord never taught that the sphere of divine service is apart from everything else, and that the discharge of duties technically religious is what will please God. Nothing was more abhorrent to His mind than that tithes of mint, anise, and cumin could give pleasure to God, when men were outraging the weightier matters—mercy, judgment, and faith. It was absurd to attach a sanctity to the gold of the temple which did not belong to the temple itself. It was horrible to relieve sons from their duty to their parents by the pretext that they were consecrating their money to God. If men were to serve God at all, they were to serve Him all round. It is true that the germs of all this teaching are found in the prophets. What our Lord did was to bring it into a clearer and more striking light—to give it the sort of relief which is given by the stereoscope to the lines of a photograph—to make it start out, vivid, pointed, arresting, on the canvas of Scripture. Whoever ponders Christ's lessons can have no doubt or difficulty on this point—that no service, no offering, no homage can please God which is not the outcome of a loving, loyal heart. And where the heart is loyal, it will try, in everything, to please God.

II. Precisely corresponding to these views of God were the lessons which Christ taught regarding man. As we have seen, He taught his need of reconciliation, of forgiveness, of deliverance from hell, of everlasting life. He taught his need of union to Himself, in order that he might share the blessings which He brought, and live with Him in everlasting rest and glory. He laid great' emphasis on these topics, for He taught a high doctrine on the value of man. Perhaps in analysing His teaching we ought to put His doctrine of the value of man in one of the foremost places. Jesus Christ "brought life and immortality to light." Not a human creature came within His ken whom He did not think of as an immortal being, and whom, in that aspect, He did not regard with profound concern. The Old Testament had dealt with men chiefly in the mass, or if it attached great importance to individuals, it was mostly individuals of high position and influence,—usually kings, holding in their hands the lives of all their people. But in the New Testament and under Christ's teaching, the individual soul rises to sublime importance, and becomes a jewel of incomparable worth. We tremble as we think of its value and its possible destiny. Why might not the woman that was a sinner have been left to end her life as she began it? Why should the thief on the cross have been taken such notice of, and have got such a promise? Of what use was it for Christ to arrest Zaccheus in his covetous life, and compromise His own character in the eyes of the respectable classes by appearing as a friend of publicans and sinners? Because they had immortal souls. It might be but a step for them to the grave; but when they rose again, they that had done good would rise to the resurrection of life, and they that had done evil to the resurrection of condemnation. Men are not dumb driven cattle! It is Christ that has taught us, far beyond any prophet of the old economy, to honour all men because of their immortality, and to hold no labour too great to save a single soul.

The word "soul" indeed got a higher meaning in the lips of Christ. To fear those that killed the body was foolish; but it was a different thing to fear Him who had power over the soul. Nor was the soul merely the part of a man, so to speak, that would survive, the part that would be happy or miserable hereafter. The soul was the man himself, the inner, the essential part of him, that to which everything that was good or valuable in him belonged in this life, as well as in the life to come. His outer man, his wealth, his decorations, his best actions even, were absolutely nothing—had no atom of intrinsic value: his soul was all. What he was in the inner man of the heart was the vital matter; what qualities flourished there; God-like on the one hand, devil-like on the other; born of the Spirit, or born of the flesh. At the core of every man's being was a mysterious something that determined all the rest; if that was right, all was right; if that was perverted, the whole man was in disorder; and as the disorder, if unchanged now, would last for ever, the whole life to come would be wrapt in misery.

Nor could the disorder be removed and the soul

made whole but by the grace of Christ. The cause of the disorder was separation from God; but by Him God came back into the soul and shed over it all His gracious influence. "I am the way, and the truth, and the life; no man cometh unto the Father but by me." "If a man love me, he will keep my words, and my Father will love him, and we will come unto him, and make our abode with him." The soul must be thrown open, and wholly open, to the Divine influence. It must be emptied of the carnal. "Ye cannot serve God and mammon." "Blessed are the poor in spirit: for theirs is the kingdom of heaven." And men must not spend their lives in a hesitating way, as if uncertain whether it be worth while to sacrifice anything for Christ. "If any man will come after me, let him deny himself, and take up his cross, and follow me." We must deny, renounce, empty ourselves. This self-emptying is a very comprehensive process. We must renounce our own righteousness and accept of His; we must renounce our own will, and follow His; we must renounce our own honour, credit, and profit, and be content to serve our King. "He that saveth his life shall lose it, and he that loseth his life shall save it." Selfishness in every form gets a mortal blow from Christ. We are to do our duty, we are to follow our Master, we are to seek the welfare of others, even though personally we should suffer thereby. Is this a hard rule? It was our Master's rule. The disciple is not above his master, nor the servant above his lord. It was a rule that in Christ's own case led to noble and glorious results, and the results cannot be attained by us but by the practice of the rule. The principle of the world is self-indulgence; Christ's is self-denial. It was a bold stroke of policy to substitute self-denial for self-indulgence. Just in proportion as men have really followed Christ has the substitution been effected. And it is from this substitution that all has come that is best and purest in the lives and labours of Christian men.

III. We add a word on what was most characteristic in Christ's teaching as to our bearing towards our fellow-men. It is summed up in the golden rule: "Whatsoever ye would that men should do to you, do ye also to them." When you have to do with other men, put yourself in their place, think how you would have them to act to you, and act you so to them. Here we find another great blow given to selfishness. Moralists, trying to establish morality on an independent basis, have found a great difficulty here. How are men to be induced to think of others and act fairly and kindly by them? Under Christ, all is plain. In Him, men become brethren. Becoming one with Him, they become one with each other. "Being born again, not of corruptible seed, but of incorruptible, by the word of God, which liveth and abideth for ever," they learn to "love one another with a pure heart fervently." It was nothing short of a revolution our Lord effected when He taught—"The princes of the Gentiles exercise dominion over them, . . . but it shall not be so among you: but whosoever will be great among you, let him be your minister; and whosoever will be chief among you, let him be your servant: even as the Son of man came not to be ministered unto, but to minister, and to give his life a ransom for many." It is the servant of all that is greatest of all. The truly successful man is not he that has done most for himself, but he that has done most for others. Real wealth is not measured by the amount of one's property, but by the capacity to use it well. Greatness does not lie in ability to draw everything to one's-self, but in ability to use what one gets for the good of the many. To live for God, and for God's sake to become the servant of others; to soothe the sorrows and lighten the burdens of the oppressed; to make the world's crooked places straight, and its rough places plain; to rescue the perishing; raise the fallen, and cheer the desolate; to do all these offices of love with unwearying patience and self-denial, and not grudge the expenditure of ease and health, and life itself, when called for;—such is our Lord's idea of greatness, and such is the lesson which, alike by example and precept, He has left for us all.[1]

Some men have professed to detect flaws in the teaching of our Lord. According to one view, He gave too much encouragement to the passive enduring of wrong; according to another, He did the very opposite—He was disrespectful to the rulers, and did too much to excite the disaffection of the people. According to some, He discouraged industry and all interest in worldly affairs; He taught men that it was a sin to be rich and a virtue to be poor; encouraged them to hate their father and mother, and not mind though they kindled strife even in

[1] *Glimpses of the Inner Life of our Lord.*

the bosom of their homes. It need hardly be said that such views are founded on a false view of the meaning of what Christ taught. And as for those who tell us that the day is coming when a moral code shall be in operation as much superior to that of Christ as Christ's was superior to that which went before it,—we would just say, "Let not him that girdeth on his armour boast himself like him that putteth it off." There is hardly a soul, unless it has been utterly darkened by vice, that does not discern something singularly pure and beautiful in the moral teaching of Jesus. To some, indeed, its fault is that it is too high—

> "Too bright, too good
> For human nature's daily food."

But few have failed to see the marks of its heavenly origin, and to pay to it in their hearts the homage due to pure truth. The Hindu to whom some chance had brought the Sermon on the Mount, and who, after reading it, was so impressed by its divinity, that, being unable to sleep, he got up in the night, hastened to the house of the Christian missionary, and begged for more instruction in the truth of God, represented many a soul that instinctively feels that in that sermon there is a higher element than human wisdom. "Sweetness and light" appear nowhere as in the teaching of Jesus. It has a calm, bright air, like the light of a summer morning. As we listen to Jesus, we seem borne away to some mountain of myrrh, some hill of pomegranates. As His words fall on our hearts, they calm our excited feelings as of old they stilled the winds and the waves. His lips drop as the honeycomb. We say with Peter, "Lord, to whom shall we go? Thou hast the words of eternal life."

It is this blessed teaching that the Church is called to spread over the world, in the very spirit of Christ Himself. Like the silvery rays of the sun, brightening and gladdening hill and vale after a night of storm, or like the fresh sweet beauty of spring after the gloom and hard grip of winter,— such is the teaching of Christ, let it follow what system it may.

"As dew upon the tender herb,
   Diffusing fragrance round;
As showers that usher in the spring,
   And cheer the thirsty ground:
So shall His presence bless our souls,
   And shed a joyful light;
That hallowed morn shall chase away
   The sorrows of the night."

CHAPTER VIII.

ELEMENTS OF IMPRESSION IN HIS TEACHING.
I. INTERNAL.

From the substance of our Lord's teaching we proceed to its form and manner. It may be admitted that we come down here to a lower level. The substance of truth is unchangeable; the form and manner are susceptible of a thousand variations.

But though we come to a lower level, it is not an unimportant one. Most certainly our Lord was not among those that think little of form and manner. Neither directly nor indirectly did He ever convey the notion that if only you proclaim the truth of God, it matters not how you do it. His own maxim, when He ordered the fragments to be gathered together, "that nothing be lost," demanded that care should be taken of every fragment of influence that could tell on the mind of man. While He looked mainly to the essential weight and force of the truth itself for moving the soul, and to the Holy Spirit for the vitalising power, He neglected no subsidiary means of impression, however feeble it might appear.

In this He only followed the analogy of nature and of art. The most impressive paintings do not owe all their power to the principal figures or features where the main conception of the painting lies; the background, and the filling up of the details, and the care and finish of the whole, contribute their elements of effect. The mosses and lichens of the forest indicate careful and beautiful workmanship as truly as the majestic oak, and contribute to the general impression. It is not merely the substance of our Lord's teaching that shows the hand of a master, but the forms into which He throws it, His language, His style, His figures of speech, the tone and manner of the whole. Nor is anything used by Him for stage effect; all is directed to the production of impression. His arrows are never shot to show His skill in archery, but that they may stick fast in the hearts of His enemies. His figures of speech are not designed to dazzle, but to commend His lesson and to move His audience. It is very instructive to study these features of His teaching. It may appear to some a heavy burden to have to keep so many things in view in addressing an audience. But it is not a mechanical imitation of our Lord's method that we desire to see. It is a law of our nature that what we admire we unconsciously imitate. If we carefully study our Lord's manner, looking with reverent admiration on His ways of putting truth, and of adapting it to the avenues of the heart,—the ways that lead to the springs of action in men, we shall gradually learn to follow His example, and, with God's blessing, our work will become better adapted to its great end.

In studying those elements of impression which

belong generally to the form and manner of our Lord's teaching, we are led to a twofold division, some of them being more internal, that is, connected with the state or working of His own spirit, and others, more external, connected with the structure of His discourses. This division may be adopted for convenience' sake, although in practice the two classes of qualities blend together, like colours that shade into each other, and cannot be thoroughly separated.

I. INTERNAL.

1. What we have just said is specially true of the first feature we mention—the singular *lucidity* that marks our Lord's teaching. In one sense lucidity is a structural feature, but it can be so only when there is a remarkable clearness in the speaker's mind. Generally, it is those who have most thorough knowledge of a subject, and most mastery over it, both in its principles and details, that are able to expound it most simply and clearly. A smatterer is seldom lucid. The utter absence of mist or haze about our Lord's teaching, even on the most vital topics, must strike every reader. He held truth with so firm a grasp, His view of it was so comprehensive, that He could at once seize the kernel, and hold it up, distinct and obvious, to the eye of His hearer. As He said to Nicodemus, "We speak that we do know, and testify that we have seen." For the most part His teaching is so luminous that there is hardly a possibility of misunderstanding it. The only parts where there is any obscurity are certain of the parables, and some

of the earlier discourses in the Gospel of John. But one purpose designed to be accomplished by the parables (as we shall see hereafter) was to throw a veil over the truth, so that, whilst discoverable in all its richness by the honest and diligent inquirer, it should not be apparent to careless onlookers. And in regard to the discourses in John, bearing as some of them do on the relations of the Son to the Father, the subject itself is obscure, and incapable of being made perfectly clear to the human mind. But, even in these profound regions, Jesus does not betray a trace of perplexity, or speak as if He found the subject too difficult. On the contrary, we cannot fail to admire His firmness of tread and ease of movement, even in regions where to us the light appears so dim.

Luminousness in any teacher has the double benefit of making the subject plain to the scholar, and inspiring confidence in the teacher. The luminousness of Christ's teaching inspires the fullest confidence; we feel assured that He is perfectly able to unfold to us the mysteries of the Kingdom of God.

To such a degree of lucidity as characterised the teaching of Christ we can never attain. But it is useful to pursue what we can never come up to. Paul, Peter, and John are all luminous; but they are not so luminous as Christ. If we would teach well we must learn much. If we would know our subject thoroughly, we must ponder it laboriously, and in profound dependence upon that Spirit whose function is to guide us into all the truth. Paul unfolds to us very frankly the secret of the lucidity to which he had attained : " As it is written, Things which eye saw not, and ear heard not, and which entered not into the heart of man, whatsoever things God prepared for them that love him. But unto us God revealed them through the Spirit : for the Spirit searcheth all things, yea, the deep things of God. For who among men knoweth the things of a man, save the spirit of the man, which is in him? even so the things of God none knoweth, save the Spirit of God. But we received, not the spirit of the world, but the spirit which is of God; that we might know the things that are freely given to us by God" (1 Cor. ii. 9-12, R.V.).

2. Allied to the feature we have just dwelt on is our Lord's profound *personal conviction of the reality and importance of all He taught.*

A teacher might be able to present a truth in a flood of light, but his own heart not being saturated with it, he might do so without any living sense of its value. In the case of Jesus, every solemn truth He taught had a profound hold of His own heart, and came from Him glowing with the warmth of His own convictions. Truth, in such cases, borrows from the emotions a great rousing power, making it thrill the hearts of hearers by a kind of magical spell. In His frequent use of the formula, "Verily, verily, I say unto thee," we have a proof of the intensity of our Lord's convictions. "Verily, verily, I say unto thee, Except a man be born again, he cannot see the kingdom of God." "Verily, I say unto you, Thou shalt in no wise come out thence till thou hast paid the uttermost farthing." "Verily, verily, I say unto you, He that believeth on me hath everlasting life." As Jesus uttered such truths, His voice would borrow from His heart the tones of reality, and a corresponding impression would be made on the hearts of hearers. Such utterances were parts, as it were, of His very self; they were truths of whose reality He had the deepest assurance, and which, therefore, He sought with His whole soul to press on the hearts of all.

No element of impression can be more valuable than this. "We believe, and therefore speak"— denotes the secret of the influence of soul upon soul. The doubting mind can never be influential except in the way of kindling doubt. It is impossible with "truths men half believe" to heal the "woes they wholly feel." No position can be more uncomfortable than that of one who is committed to teach, as great Divine verities, what he neither can wholly receive nor wholly reject. Obliged to put aside the great doctrines of the evangelical creed as matters about which he is not so sure as to be able to commit himself to them, he will be left with little more than the truths of natural religion, or the principles of natural morality. Even about these, perhaps, he may find some uncertainty, for doubt like a cancer is ever spreading; but should he believe that here he has solid ground beneath him, the case is not much better; for if this be all his gospel, he cannot call himself a minister of Christ's, and most certainly he cannot look for the power of the Holy Ghost to bless his words, since he cannot make up his mind whether there be any Holy Ghost. No power wielded by such a man can avail to destroy the works of the devil. What is needed by such a worker, if he really desires to be a minister of Christ's, is the teaching of the Holy Ghost; the apostles and the early Church had no want of certainty after the Spirit came down on the day of Pentecost; and all in every age, who are truly taught of God, "know the certainty of those things wherein they have been instructed."

The more that our souls are saturated with what we teach, the greater will be our power. The voice will take its tone from the heart. The truth will pass, not through dead wires, but living nerves. The hearer's heart seems to be proof against the most solemn truths spoken with indifference, or in a tone which is not in keeping with their import. But the very same truths spoken from the heart go straight to the heart. The Holy Ghost makes great use of the sincerity which He inspires. It is vain to ape the tone of genuine feeling. Divine power never accompanies the work of apes. The soul that thrills with the truths it proclaims is the favourite instrument of the Holy Ghost. It moves and melts the soul of the hearer; carrying with it the power of heaven, it does the work of God.

3. In connection with our Lord's depth of conviction, we must view His habit of *prayerfulness.* It is to be carefully observed that even He found the avocations of ministerial and missionary work distracting,—liable, unless counteracted, to impair vividness of impression, to diminish spiritual strength, and lower spiritual aspirations. It was to overcome these tendencies, to keep all fresh and bright within, that He prayed so often and so much. Solitude and renewed communion with

His Father in heaven were needed to restore and sustain the tone of His spirit; for even in the human heart of Jesus, the constant iteration of the noblest acts had something of an exhaustive effect, and it needed direct communion with the upper fountains to revive His soul.

It is when we study the Gospel according to Luke that we learn most thoroughly how full of prayer the life and ministry of our Saviour were. First, we find Him praying at His baptism, when the heaven was opened, and the Holy Ghost descended on Him like a dove (Luke iii. 21). Then, after the cure of the leper, when the multitude thronged Him, "He withdrew himself into the wilderness and prayed" (v. 16). Before the appointment of the twelve apostles He went out into a mountain to pray, and continued all night in prayer to God (vi. 12, 13). At the miracle of the loaves and fishes, He looks up to heaven, and blesses them ere He gives them to the multitude (Luke ix. 16). It is as He is alone praying that He is joined by the disciples, and that He asks them, "Whom do men say that I am?" (Luke ix. 18.) Luke tells us that His object in going up the mount of transfiguration was to pray, and that it was as He prayed that the fashion of His countenance was altered, and His raiment was white and glistering (ix. 28, 29). In sending forth the seventy disciples our Lord prefaced His charge to them by an injunction to pray the Lord of the harvest that He would send forth labourers into His harvest (Luke x. 2). Luke tells us that the Lord's Prayer was given, though not apparently for the first time, in answer to a request of one of His disciples that He would teach them to pray (xi. 1), and He records the parables that were designed to show the power of prayer,—that of the stranger coming at midnight (xi. 5), and that of the importunate widow (xviii. 3). It is from Luke that we learn that at Gethsemane our Lord bade the three brethren pray before the trial began (xxii. 40), as well as at its close (xxii. 46). Luke records also the prayer for Peter: "I have prayed for thee that thy faith fail not" (xxii. 32); and the prayer for His murderers, "Father, forgive them, they know not what they do" (xxiii. 34). From Luke, in fine, we learn that the dying word of Jesus was in prayer: "Father, into thy hands I commend my spirit." Having said thus, He gave up the ghost.

The lesson is too obvious to need to be more than stated. Whatever doubts men may throw on the efficacy of prayer, these doubts certainly get no shadow of countenance from the example of our Lord. And little can the ministry of any man be trusted where there is little or no occasion for prayer, and little or nothing to say when he goes to the throne of grace. In our case, over and above the reasons that were applicable to our Lord, there is the whole of that personal experience to be spread before God which has to do with our sins,—the guilt we incur, the defilement we contract, the disorder and confusion it breeds in our souls; the frequency with which we grieve the Spirit, and thereby interrupt the current of Divine influence; our feebleness in service, our neglect of opportunities, our carelessness about our Master's honour,

And can it be that we need less than Jesus to have our spiritual impressions and aspirations revived by fellowship with God? Do our weapons need less whetting than His? Do our spirits contract less rust from the atmosphere of the world? Do we need less than He to bring our views and aims to the standard of the Divine will, and have them rectified and elevated by the presence of God? If even His lamp needed to be constantly trimmed and supplied anew with the oil of heaven, how much more does ours, which even at best burns so dimly, and which is so liable to be extinguished by the breath of temptation, or through our carelessness in times of carnal ease!

4. A not less striking element of impression in the state of our Lord's spirit was His usually *bright, cheerful, and genial tone.* To appreciate this, we must guard against a prejudice arising from our notions of what was necessary for the great work of atonement for which He came into the world. From the fact that, as the Sin-bearer, He had to carry an awful burden; from His being called by Isaiah "the man of sorrows, and acquainted with grief;" and likewise from the fact that in some of the darkest of the Psalms, revealing His experience, there are expressions of terrible distress, many have inferred that His countenance must have been always overcast, and His tone habitually sad. But this is not what we gather from the Gospels. On the contrary, Jesus is seen there encompassed for the most part by an air of cheerfulness and gladness. Witness the opening of the Sermon on the Mount. It begins with pouring out quite a cornucopia of

beatitudes. It is not from a heart habitually sad that such silvery streams can have their flow. It is not the distressed soul that likes to think of the fowls of the air, whose wants are always provided for, though "they sow not, neither do they reap;" nor of the lilies of the field, "that toil not, neither do they spin, and yet Solomon, in all his glory, was not arrayed like one of these." Even when our Lord makes mention of "the grass of the field, which to-day is, and to-morrow is cast into the oven," it is not to press what you might suppose was the more natural lesson—the gloomy lesson of decay,—it is to draw even from that emblem a cheerful thought, a lesson of trust in Him who, as He makes provision for clothing the short-lived grass, will surely "clothe you, O ye of little faith." There is nothing more characteristic of a buoyant, joyous heart, than that spirit of trust in God which refuses to let the shadow of possible evil in the future come between it and the sunshine of the present, accepting gladly every present comfort and mercy, and believing that "sufficient unto the day is the evil thereof."

The same spirit was shown by Christ in His usual intercourse with the disciples. He did not desire them to be fasting before God in His providence should call them to fast. He would rather let them enjoy their summer day,—enjoy the bridal festivities while the Bridegroom was with them; soon enough for them would come the day when the Bridegroom should be taken away, and they would certainly have to fast in those days. Was it not a proof of the habitual gladness of Christ's tone that He went about continually doing good? A heart full of sadness would go about weeping with those that weep, lamenting life's inevitable sorrows, and bidding them bear calmly what they could not remove. But Christ goes about removing troubles, drying up tears, bringing bread to the hungry, water to the thirsty, rest to the weary, life to the dead. His words to the widow of Nain, "Weep not," to Mary Magdalene, " Why weepest thou ?" are not like the words of one who would have turned human life into a vale of tears, and made the wail of sorrow its only music. It is evident that on the very eve of His sufferings He enjoyed the glee and gladness of the children crying in the temple, " Hosanna to the Son of David," and showed by His quotation from the 8th Psalm that He deemed no praise more delightful than that which is borne aloft on the merry voices of infants. His habitual tone harmonised with that gladness which is at once ascribed to Him, and accounted for in the 45th Psalm—" Thou lovest righteousness and hatest wickedness; therefore God, thy God, hath anointed thee with the oil of gladness *above thy fellows.*"

Nor need we find any insuperable difficulty in reconciling this, the habitual spirit of Christ, with His position as the sin-bearer, and His experience from time to time of very terrible and crushing distress. Of these dreadful visitations of soul-sorrow we have a memorable instance in the experience of Gethsemane, when His soul writhed under agonies that could hardly be borne. But who does not see that Gethsemane was a great contrast to Christ's ordinary mood, showing that while doubtless His relation to man's sin and punishment could not fail to make itself felt in some degree habitually, still the more extreme experiences of that relation would come on Him in the form of sharp paroxysms that apparently were short in proportion to their intensity.

It needs to be borne in mind that both physically and spiritually man is formed for light, not darkness. Literal darkness, even for a few days, is so terrible a punishment that where it has been tried on criminals it has been like to drive them mad. Spiritual darkness and desolation of soul are as little favourable to its health and prosperity as literal darkness is to the body. It cannot be God's intention for any of His children that their minds should ever dwell in darkness, or be perpetually occupied with awful thoughts. Even under our most crushing earthly sorrows, our hearts, through the healing influence of time, usually regain a measure of serenity and cheerfulness. It is the voice of rejoicing and salvation that ought to be heard in the tabernacles of the righteous. Men say that we cannot be sincere in what we profess to believe regarding the lost state of men by nature, and their prospects of everlasting punishment, for if we really believed it, our hearts would be oppressed by a perpetual horror. But from their very constitution our hearts are not capable of dwelling constantly on the doom of sin. It is to be thought of, thought of profoundly and awfully, thought of repeatedly, but not thought of always. If it were ever before our minds, we should be immersed in unbearable darkness. "Light is sown for the righteous, and gladness for the upright in heart." While bearing in mind the doom of the lost, and not trying to stifle the anguish that thrills us when the thought becomes vivid, we are to endeavour at the same time, as our habitual tone, to cherish the bright counsel of the Apostle : " Rejoice evermore."

Thus we may come in some degree to understand how Jesus, while carrying on His shoulders the terrible burden of His people's sin, and experiencing at times such paroxysms of soul-horror, should for the most part have maintained so bright, cheerful, and happy a tone. This radiance of spirit must have had a wonderful attraction for the disciples, and served to make their intercourse a time of great delight. We do not need to accept all that Renan has written on the charming manner of the young Galilean. As an explanation of Christ's influence over the disciples it is inadequate, and Renan's way of referring to it is flippant and unbecoming. No charm of manner could account for that profound reverence for Christ, that sense of obligation to Him, and that readiness to live and to die for Him, which from the first filled the souls of thousands. But, doubtless, the presence of Christ was a sunny presence, and brought daylight and fresh air into the little company. His ordinary words were cheering words, giving joy to the sad and bringing hope to the hopeless. The incident of the storm at sea, when Jesus came into the ship and all traces of the storm vanished, was at once a fact and a symbol— a symbol of the blessed influence of His presence in times of darkness and danger. What a characteristic salutation it was with which He greeted the eleven on the evening of His resurrection : " Peace be unto you!" It was like a sunbeam passing through the gloom of death.

So, likewise, when we study the written page of Christ's life we find it wonderfully cheering to faith. Compare the Gospels with Job, or Jeremiah, or Hosea, how different is the atmosphere! In Job the whole firmament is dark, but a ray of light breaks now and again through the gloom. In the Lamentations of Jeremiah you hardly discover so much as one ray. But in the Gospels the sky is comparatively clear. It is not the prevailing lesson of the Gospels as it is in Job that man is born unto trouble as the sparks fly upward. It is not the prevailing cry of the Gospels as it is in the Lamentations, that "the joy of our heart is ceased; our dance is turned into mourning." The aspect of life set before us in the Gospels is not that of disappointment, vexation, and despair, but that of hope, success, enjoyment. The poor in spirit, the mourners, the meek, and the other classes portrayed in the beatitudes get what they crave and need. The man seeking goodly pearls finds the pearl of great price. The man who finds treasure in a field becomes the owner of the field. The woman finds her lost piece of silver. The shepherd recovers his lost sheep. The father clasps to his bosom his prodigal son.

Even when the topics are the darkest possible, our Lord's treatment of them does not want brighter elements. The twenty-fourth chapter of Matthew is a forecast of terrible events. It is a picture where the desolations of flood and fire, of deluge and thunderstorm and earthquake seem combined. It holds out but a sorry earthly prospect for the Church

—"then shall they deliver you up to be afflicted and shall kill you, and ye shall be hated of all nations for my name's sake;" "then shall be great tribulation, such as was not since the beginning of the world to this time, nor ever shall be." Nor are the fortunes of the world at large more encouraging: "Immediately after the tribulation of those days shall the sun be darkened, and the moon shall not give her light, and the stars shall fall from heaven, and the powers of the heavens shall be shaken." Yet even this picture does not want re-assuring elements: "He that shall endure to the end, the same shall be saved"—comes in both to stimulate the grace of endurance, and to show its blessed reward. And then, too, comes the grand consummation; when the storm is at its wildest, and confusion worst confounded, the sign of the Son of man is seen in the heavens. In the presence of the King, commotion ceases, as on the lake the winds and waves fell at His word. From Him that sitteth on the throne there comes forth a new-creative word: "Behold, I make all things new." And yet the doom of sin is not overlooked; for the careless servant has his portion with the hypocrites; "there shall be weeping and gnashing of teeth."

So also in the farewell discourse; it abounds with apples of gold. The sky is dark enough. Terrible mental trials and frightful physical sufferings hang over our blessed Lord. The disciples are to be parted from Him who has been their light and joy. They are to be plunged into all the troubles and terrors of a conflict with the world and the devil. Yet amid all this darkness, cheerfulness prevails.

"Let not your heart be troubled" is the key-note of the whole. It is full of reassuring and comforting words. It is the presence of these two features, calmness and consolation, but especially the predominance of the last, that constitutes the great charm of this discourse. It is this that has made it for the mourning Christian a fountain of comfort in all generations. Strange that in our darkest hours, when we most crave brightness, we turn to words uttered by Jesus in the very hour and apparent triumph of darkness! How wonderful must have been the quality of the heart that could be radiant and cheerful amid the thickening elements of such a storm! How profound the sympathy that, with all its own unspeakable load to bear, could pour out words so fitted to cheer the miserable in every age!

All this may surely show us how earnestly a radiant cheerful spirit should be cultivated by all Christ's servants. We may think that if men see us habitually sad and woebegone on account of their sins, the sight will bring them to themselves—they will be touched by the thought of the misery they are causing us. But experience does not confirm this view. In the home of the drunkard, it is not the wife utterly crushed and broken-hearted, who drags herself through her work in heartless prostration, that is likely to touch her husband's conscience; but rather the noble woman who keeps a buoyant heart amid all her discouragements, and while "much in sorrow, oft in woe," tries as far as possible to conceal the tokens of it from him who is the cause of it all. He is more likely to be brought to himself by hopefulness and self-command than by despair. So in the Christian ministry, while our appeals must sometimes be bathed in tears, it is not sadness but gladness that should be our habitual tone. The tears, from their very rarity, may have a remarkable effect. Paul could remind the Ephesian elders that for two years he had not ceased to warn them day and night with tears; yet none of his epistles is more sunny, more full of thankfulness and of bright views of the riches of God's grace and love than the epistle to that very church. A countenance habitually depressed and a funereal tone ill become the ministry of reconciliation. The gospel message is glad tidings of great joy.

5. We have yet to speak of one of the most powerful of the internal elements of impression in our Lord's teaching—*the harmony of His life with His lessons.* His life and example lent force to His precepts even in regard to the highest and most difficult of the attainments that He ever urged. If He spoke of the blessedness of the poor in spirit, the meek, the peacemakers, the pure in heart, He Himself beautifully exemplified all. If He urged trust in the heavenly Father, the absence of all care, of all dread of want while you are doing your Father's will,—His life was a perfect picture of this spirit. If He taught men not to fear them that killed the body, He himself was utterly regardless of all that man could do to Him. If He exhorted them to set their hearts not on earthly but heavenly treasure, the world and all its riches were literally nothing to Him. Thus His life was as clear and consistent a sermon as His words. He had no fear of any *tu*

quoque when He hurled His charges against the scribes and pharisees, of binding heavy burdens and laying them on men's shoulders, while they themselves would not touch them with one of their fingers. If men should say that His standard was too high, His own life might be appealed to, to refute the charge. From infancy to the cross it showed no flaw, and all through, it might have been described in the words spoken to the Baptist: "It becometh us to fulfil all righteousness."[1]

Alas, it is hard to calculate the amount of harm that is done through the want of harmony between our preaching and our lives! And it is not of

---

[1] In dwelling on this topic in his *Practical Theology*, Van Oosterzee is not content with noting the harmony between our Lord's teaching and His life. He notes a sevenfold harmony which, somewhat fancifully, he compares to the seven prismatic colours, blending in a perfect ray of light. 1. The first is the harmony of His teaching with His *person;* He speaks like the only begotten of the Father, full of authority, full of grace and truth. 2. His teaching is in harmony with *the Scriptures*—not with traditions, like the teaching of the Scribes; not with the mere letter of Scripture (although it agrees with that too, as, for example, His prophecy of the resurrection roots itself in Scripture facts and language), but emphatically with the soul and spirit of Scripture. 3. With the *deepest wants of His hearers.* "Lord, to whom shall we go? Thou hast the words of eternal life." 4. With *the demands of the moment.* His words are not abstract words, but words expressly adapted for the time, therefore for all time. They bear the stamp of real life. 5. His word is in harmony *with itself.* Amid apparent diversity, His word is pervaded by a higher unity. He develops it more at one time than another, but it is always the same truth unto salvation. 6. *With His walk.* His sublimest precepts are at once exemplified and enforced by His faultless example; His life is one continued preaching; His preaching is not doctrine merely, but life. 7. In harmony with *the Father*, whose face He often seeks in prayer, and before whom He could testify at the end that He had revealed and glorified the Father's name upon earth."—(*Practical Theology*, pp. 72-74.)

ministers only that this is to be said. Inconsistency between practice and profession is like dry rot in the Church, and neutralises fearfully any influence for good. Abroad, at home, in colonies, in India, China, Japan, we hear the monotonous but painful tale of men and women calling themselves by the name of Christ, but not walking worthy of the vocation wherewith they are called. It is the ready excuse that young persons offer for trifling with the voice of conscience, that they are but doing as others do. It is the palliation of their declension that backsliders are always giving us, they were in contact with men or women bearing Christ's name, but certainly not following His precepts. But if this be a source of much evil in any, it is a source of superlative evil in Christian ministers. And it is an evil for which there can be little excuse. It does not spring from the want of rare or unattainable gifts. It springs from a carelessness in common things for which there is little palliation. Watchfulness and prayerfulness will bring about a thorough harmony between our preaching and our lives. Nor can any influence be better or higher. Sometimes a whole country-side is influenced by the consistent life and blameless spirit of a hard-working, affectionate, self-denying minister, whose life has exhibited no visible stain, and whose heart has never been known to refuse any service of love to young or old, rich or poor. Such men seem to combine the saintly repose of a life of retirement and contemplation with the unwearied beneficence of a life of activity. In contact with their Master, alike in the closet and in the field of duty, they have caught His spirit in both, and made it manifest in all the aspects of their life. They remind us of the legend of the godly monk, who one evening was meditating on his Lord, when lo! He appeared at his side. It was an hour when the monk's duty called him elsewhere. Fain would he have lingered to enjoy his Lord's company; but the claim of duty seemed to come before everything else. Returning from his work, he found his Lord still in his cell, and was greeted with the words—"If thou hadst stayed, I had gone; because thou didst go, I have stayed." Delight in Christ's company makes our lives consistent and our labours fruitful. "And of Benjamin he said, The beloved of the Lord shall dwell in safety by him; and the Lord shall cover him all the day long, and he shall dwell between his shoulders" (Deut. xxxiii. 12).

CHAPTER IX.

ELEMENTS OF IMPRESSION IN HIS TEACHING.
II. STRUCTURAL.

THE elements of impression in a public teacher that depend on the state of his own spirit operate unconsciously,—they result from the spontaneous activity of his soul, working in accordance with its strongest impulses. But there is another class of influences, in the application of which there is more scope for deliberation and selection. These influences belong to the structure of his addresses, and are connected with the kind of arguments he employs; the use he makes of any common ground there may be between him and his audience; the means he makes use of to arrest, to interest, to illustrate, to apply; and generally, his way of making the truths which he proclaims effectual for the great ends for which they are proclaimed. The present chapter is devoted to an exposition of some elements of this kind in the public teaching of our Lord.

1. And first in this class we note His *appeals to the Old Testament Scriptures.*

Perhaps we are inclined to wonder that He did not make more use of Scripture than He did. In the earlier part of His ministry it was more for purposes of defence than of direct instruction that He appealed to the Bible. In the wilderness He used it to repel the temptations of the devil; in battling with His enemies He often used it to silence them, as when He appealed to the example of David to justify His views of the Sabbath, or to the words spoken to Moses at the burning bush, to show that there was a resurrection of the dead. But in His earlier ministry we have little account in the Gospels of work done by Him in the way of formally expounding the Scriptures. One memorable exception there is,—His exposition of Isaiah lxi. 1 in the Synagogue of Nazareth. The result of that exposition, however, did not show a people prepared for such instruction, and did not encourage the continuance of the practice.

But from the beginning our Lord made plain in many ways His reverence for the Scriptures as the record of God's will and the fountain-head of all saving truth. His indignation was great at the public instructors of the people for making the Word of God of none effect by their traditions. It was vain to suppose that even one rising from the dead could have a greater effect on men than the Scriptures: "If they hear not Moses and the prophets, neither will they be persuaded though one rose from the dead." If the people showed great concern about outward acts of worship, joined to great aversion of heart to God, it was just as Isaiah had foretold. In the days when disaster was to overtake Jerusalem, the signal for leaving the place would be the fulfilment of a prophecy by Daniel, respecting "the abomination of desolation." Scripture incidents were frequently employed to embellish and point His discourses. The men of Nineveh repenting at the preaching of Jonah; Jonah himself being three days and three nights in the belly of the fish; the doom of Sodom and Gomorrah; the fathers eating manna in the desert; the devil a murderer from the beginning,—are samples of His ready and effective use of Scripture incidents. But that He regarded the Bible as a great mine of Messianic truth which at that time even He had not opened up fully in His discourses, is plain from His words —"Search the Scriptures, for in them ye think ye have eternal life, and it is they that testify of me."

It was at the very end of His ministry, and indeed after His resurrection, that He began in earnest to open up the mine. The first glimpse of its treasures was given on the way to Emmaus, when " beginning at Moses and all the prophets, he expounded to them in all the Scriptures the things concerning himself." Afterwards, when the disciples were assembled, He opened their understandings that they might understand the Scriptures. And when the Comforter came, in fulfilment of the promise, it was to guide them into all the truth. So that, before they were called to go forth into all the world as witnesses to Him, their minds were abundantly stored with truth drawn from the great record of revelation,—the Scriptures given by inspiration of God.

No ministry follows the model of Christ's which does not make both authoritative and ample use of the Word of God. Authoritative, we say, because we do not come up to our Lord's example if we quote the Scriptures merely as a book of interesting incidents or striking examples, or as a book of high tone and profound moral and spiritual insight. "If they hear not Moses and the prophets, neither will they be persuaded though one rose from the dead." Such words ascribe to the Bible a force quite unique, an authority peculiar and unexampled. And as our use of Scripture should be authoritative, so it should be ample. Its incidents are very varied. Its characters are very marked. Its range of teaching is very large. Its experiences of human life embrace all varieties—from the lowest depths of sorrow and despair to the loftiest heights of joy and delight. Its revelation of God presents Him in a great variety of capacities: Father, Judge, Redeemer, Teacher, Guide, and Sanctifier. The forms in which truth is presented in the Bible are very numerous: history, biography, proverb, song, prophecy, parable, didactic treatise, familiar letter, apocalyptic vision. There is no excuse for our not making our discourses full of Scripture. And it is not necessary to be always demonstrating its authority. The impression will not be less powerful if there underlie our teaching a profound reverence for the Word of God, as being given by His inspiration, and as profitable for doctrine, for reproof, for correction, and instruction in righteousness. All experience shows that in the Word of God thus used there is a great element of power. An unseen force makes of it a hammer to break the rock in pieces, a fire to burn up the works of the flesh, a sword to divide between the joints and marrow, a lamp to discover the ways of peace, a granary stored with the finest of the wheat, a rock that drops with honey, a cloud that distils refreshing dew. Of the Bible as of the sword of Goliath it may be said that there is none like it; preaching is powerful in proportion as it is biblical; the ablest essays which disregard its authority are little better than water spilt on the ground.

2. Hardly less common was another method of our Lord—His *appeals to ordinary human experience,* as justifying views which He advanced and duties which He urged. This may be called the homely element of Christ's teaching. It gives it a peculiarly practical character. It brings His instructions home to the business and bosoms of men. " Neither do men light a candle and put it under a bushel, but on a candlestick, and it giveth light unto all that are in the house." " No man can serve two masters: for either he will hate the one, and love the other; or else he will hold to the one, and despise the other." " Which of you, intending to build a tower, sitteth not down first and counteth the cost, whether he have sufficient to finish it? . . . Or what king, going to make war against another king, sitteth not down first and consulteth whether he be able with ten thousand to meet him that cometh against him with twenty thousand ?"

What our Lord would press through such appeals is, that if in common life men act on such principles, surely they ought to acknowledge them in matters of infinitely higher moment. We do not need to enlarge on the charm which this practice gave to our Lord's discourses, the intense sense of reality which it imparted to His teaching. And it is very remarkable that though in ordinary hands this line of remark is apt to become undignified, it never becomes undignified in the hands of our Lord. Homely allusions, designed to enforce the most solemn principles and obligations, are apt to appear incongruous, and to disturb our serious feelings. It is wonderful how our Lord could bring into contact things most solemn and things very common, yet not offend our sense of congruity. He could picture a householder with an empty cupboard surprised by a midnight visitor, stealing away to a friend's house, thundering at his door, and begging the loan of three loaves, while the friend, angry at the disturbance, growls from bed a surly answer—really a picture full of humour, probably the most humorous sketch in all His ministry,—and yet in His hands most fitly following up that beautiful lesson in prayer when He taught men to say, "Our Father, which art in heaven."

This power of turning to His purposes the most homely incidents of common life not only lightened His method of teaching, but enabled Him to clinch very effectively His arguments and appeals. No man can quarrel with his own ways, repudiate his own practices, traverse his own judgments. The practice shows how clever and ready-witted our Lord was, always able to find weapons close at hand for His purpose, able to turn them quickly and smartly to account, hitting the nail upon the head, and establishing His point with convincing power. But let us observe that it needs common sense to appeal to common sense. Eccentric minds dealing with the common affairs of life are apt to become incongruous and ludicrous. You must have good sense, and its twin sister, good taste, to keep clear of absurdity, and utter only words of truth and soberness.

There are preachers that despise this homely element, and think it vulgar. But it must be a false canon that repudiates the practice of our Lord. It is a canon that, with its prosy abstractions and dry lines of thought, would often be more honoured in the breach than the observance. What a relief to an audience when, by a sort of chance, such a preacher wanders into the homely region, and relieves his dulness by some allusion to familiar life! We may be sure that we are making a great sacrifice of impression when we confine ourselves to stiff, dignified abstractions. And we may be equally sure that if we clinch a lesson by showing its harmony with some well-known maxim of common-sense, some well-known law of human life, we touch a chord which will not fail to vibrate in many souls.

3. But our Lord makes a far larger use of the spontaneous principles of our nature. *Appeals to our intuitions*, intellectual and moral, underlie a great part of His teaching. He does not argue much; by a more direct process He secures our assent. In proof of this remark let us take the first, or rather the whole series of beatitudes, in the Sermon on the Mount. "Blessed are the poor in spirit: for theirs is the kingdom of heaven." How is it made to appear that the kingdom of heaven belongs to the poor in spirit? A great teacher must make very sure of his first position. But there is not an attempt at proof. Nor does it seem to be meant that the truth is to be received simply on authority.

In the very form of laying down the proposition there is an appeal to an intuitional something in the soul that responds to the statement. The truth is made to shine by its own light, and thus commends itself to acceptance. "Blessed are they that hunger and thirst after righteousness: for they shall be filled;" "Blessed are the peacemakers: for they shall be called the children of God;" "Blessed are the pure in heart: for they shall see God;"—these are not so much new revelations as they are clear and explicit exhibitions of truth with which we seem to have had a dim, shadowy acquaintance before. The candid mind readily admits the fitness and beauty of the connection between the graces denoted and the rewards annexed. It seems so suitable, so beautiful, that such rewards should be given. The readiness and universality with which this is acknowledged shows our Lord's skill in availing Himself of the intuitions of the human soul. By a stroke of heavenly genius He goes straight to the chords that respond to His words, and sets these vibrating in every breast. At Killarney it is only as the result of much experiment and careful observation that the guide knows the precise spots where the echoes he is to waken lie slumbering among the mountains. But Jesus appears all at once to have gained perfect knowledge of all the echoes of the human heart, and complete control over them. No man disputes the beatitudes. They awaken echoes in the very depths of our nature.

Or let us take a sample of His appeals to what are more strictly our *moral* intuitions. Let us attend to his commentaries on the sixth and seventh commandments. After giving the views of the men of old time He substitutes His own: "I say unto you, That whosoever is angry with his brother without a cause shall be in danger of the judgment; and whosoever shall say to his brother, Raca, shall be in danger of the council; but whosoever shall say, Thou fool, shall be in danger of hell-fire." . . . "Whosoever looketh on a woman to lust after her, hath committed adultery with her already in his heart." These are no doubt in a sense revelations of the Great Lawgiver, authoritative decrees of a great king. But do they not waken echoes in our moral nature? The principle that the heart is the seat and fountain of sin is one to which we cannot but respond. Our Lord does little more than apply an acknowledged principle. And startled though we are to find branded as great sins what may appear to be only silent and apparently harmless movements of our hearts, a moment's reflection shows us that the judgment of our Lord is true. The thought of wickedness is sin.

It is not to be supposed, however, that all truths which Christ came to proclaim found an echo in men's inner nature. The announcement of His approaching death was met by Peter and the apostles with a strong protest: "Be it far from thee, Lord; this shall not be to thee." Nicodemus did not at first accept the doctrine of the new birth, nor the woman of Samaria that of the living water. And there were many things that Jesus would have told them but for His consciousness that they would awaken no echo—they would encounter too many obstacles among the prejudices and traditions that still prevailed. "I have many things to say unto you, but ye cannot receive them now." It was more especially in the sphere of "heavenly things" that this reticence had to be practised. "If I have told you earthly things and ye believe not, how shall ye believe if I tell you heavenly things?" In other words, there was little or nothing in their intuitions for such truths to appeal to. Most probably they would have only awakened prejudices in opposition.

It is important to mark this fact. It shows that Christ came to reveal as well as to appeal. He came to make known truths previously unknown, and not merely to rouse our slumbering consciousness, or give vividness to our dim conceptions. He did not raise our consciousness to the rank of an original or supreme authority, He used it only as a help. He did not make it a standard, but only a witness. He did not employ it on all occasions, but only when it was capable of bearing witness. What we affirm is, that wherever there was anything in the intuitions of men's minds to appeal to, our Lord did not fail to recognise the fact. He did not like to lay the whole stress on the principle of obedience to authority. Where any help was to be got from men's own ways of asking, or ways of thinking and feeling, He eagerly availed Himself of that aid. Nothing was to be lost. Any echoes that could be evoked from the conscience, any sense there might be of moral fitness, any perception of what was becoming on the part of the great God were carefully brought into action in the service of the kingdom; while at the same time it was made plain that the fountain of authority was infinitely higher, and that truth came to men with the unchallengeable sanction, "Thus saith the Lord."

4. A fourth element of impression in the structure of our Lord's discourses is found in the *variety of level* which He occupied in His expositions of truth and duty, ranging from the level of ordinary human life to the sublimest regions to which the mind of man can rise. Corresponding to this variety of level is the variety of tone in which the several subjects are handled, ranging again from that of ordinary conversation to the impassioned tones of the most sublime eloquence. In Augustine's well-known work *De Doctrinâ Christianâ*, Book IV., where the practical work of the ministry is considered, three methods of speaking are enumerated, viz. the *submissa dictio*, the *temperata dictio*, and the *grande dicendi genus*. In our Lord's method of teaching we find all the three.

Of our Lord's way of enforcing the more homely aspects of truth, enough has already been said: we shall now turn our attention more to His method of dealing with subjects of the higher kind—topics that directly touch the most vital and solemn of all our interests. This class of topics is one from which many preachers recoil. Young preachers in particular are supposed to be shy of dealing with subjects that are fitted to rouse the soul to its depths, as if they felt that greater experience and maturity of powers were needed to do justice to themes of such sublimity.

It was not so with our Lord. There is no subject

He handles more frequently than the solemn retributions of the day of judgment. He follows the soul as it passes from this world into the presence of the Judge, whether to be plunged into hell, or carried by the angels to Abraham's bosom. He is not afraid to set forth both the severity and the goodness of God,—His severity to the unprofitable servant who tied up his talent in a napkin, and buried it in the ground; or to the guest at the wedding feast who came to the entertainment without having on the wedding garment. The goodness of God is in like manner unfolded, as in the parable of the Prodigal Son, where the tenderness of the Divine compassion is so beautifully shown; or in the parable of the Debtor, whose debt of ten thousand talents was not too great for the clemency of his lord. It is usually in His delineations of coming retribution, and in contrasting the awards of the righteous and the wicked, that our Lord rises to the sublimest level, and His words glow with the profoundest emotion. The contrast at the end of the Sermon on the Mount between the house built on the rock and the house built on the sand, goes, at least for the moment, to every heart. And there is seldom a reader over whom a tremor of awe does not pass when all nations are assembled before the Son of man, now come in His glory, and the holy angels with Him; when He divides them from each other, as a shepherd divides the sheep from the goats; and, after setting forth in detail what has been done by the one, and left undone by the other, declares their doom in words awful in their very simplicity: "These shall go away into everlasting punishment, but the righteous into life eternal."

Not less striking or less admirable is the calmness with which our Lord contemplates the progress of His kingdom in the world, the violence with which it is assailed, and the tremendous conflicts through which it has to fight its way. Of final discomfiture or failure He never shows the shadow of a fear; He is never forsaken by a sublime confidence in the future, which seems to spread itself before Him in a vision of triumph, in which all His faithful servants will share in the rewards and glories that shall be pre-eminently His own. In His closing address He partly draws aside the curtain that conceals the future, tells of the many mansions in His Father's house, and of His going to prepare a place for them, and returning to take them to be with Himself. Nor is it merely with sublime hopes for the future that He cheers His servants. To their faith He offers not less glorious privileges for the present. He speaks of the heavens opened, and the angels of God ascending and descending on the Son of man. He reveals a wonderful communion between faithful hearts and the God of heaven: "If a man love me, he will keep my words, and my Father will love him, and we will come unto him, and make our abode with him." He lays bare the secret of a kind of omnipotence in prayer that was within their reach: "If ye abide in me, and my words abide in you, ye shall ask what ye will, and it shall be done unto you."

Thus wonderfully does Christ mingle the element of sublimity with His preaching. And yet in rising to these heights He is neither excited nor ecstatic, but maintains the calm self-possession appropriate to one familiar with the highest themes. To keep pace with Him in such regions, to rise with Him to such heights, is to us manifestly impossible. And yet even here, though with caution, the successful minister must not shrink from following His example. To handle these sublime truths is part of the duty committed to us. And, moreover, the human soul has a craving for the sublime. It does not like to be pinned down to the low level of common things. The eye is not satisfied with the grey tints and sombre flats of a level country; it craves, at least occasionally, a brighter and richer view—the glories of an autumnal sunset, or the shining peaks of snowy mountains, or the bright blue of the sky, or of the sea. Religious teaching, level and monotonous, may have every quality of solid excellence, but in the human heart there is a craving for something more. It is true that there is no class of truths where men of vulgar taste and ambitious rhetoric are so apt to make the subject ridiculous and to disgust their hearers. There is no region where magniloquence and tawdry metaphor are so much out of place as the region of death, judgment, and eternity. But those who lavish their vulgar drapery on such themes have not studied in the school of Christ. Nor does the fact that in connection with such subjects disastrous mistakes have sometimes been committed, affect our position that the Christian preacher is not to turn away from them. Not that he is to make of them his every-day topics, for then the danger will be to strip them of their thrilling power; rather ought they to be regarded as the great festival topics appropriate to times of special exercise and high endeavour, when we leave the noise and dust of the world far behind us, and on the wings of faith and love soar away to the gates of heaven.

5. A fifth, and very remarkable structural peculiarity of our Lord's teaching, is His abundant use of *illustration*. This, however, introduces us to so wide a subject that we shall reserve it for special consideration in our next chapter.

6. We therefore note here, in conclusion, various *felicities of style* that are conspicuous in our Lord's method.

(*a.*) Prominent among these is the remarkable *finish* which marks all His discourses. There is absolutely no instance of redundancy, or carelessness, or uncouthness of speech. All is expressed with admirable correctness and precision. It is not easy for us to understand the process by which our Lord attained this result. We have no knowledge what opportunities He may have had of practising speaking during the thirty years of His silent preparation. But there is abundant proof of a very admirable intellectual and spiritual discipline, leading to the utmost precision both of thought and expression on the subjects that occupied His mind. The eagerness with which, at the age of twelve, He conversed with the doctors in the temple, would lead us to believe that He would gladly avail Himself of every opportunity of conversation that might present itself to Him. His nature was evidently social; He liked company; He had no turn for the hermit's life. But, whatever were His opportunities of speaking, it seems beyond doubt that He cultivated habits of very careful and orderly thinking, and such thinking naturally clothes itself in corresponding language. If men should infer, from the simple structure of our Lord's discourses, that matters of style are of little or no importance, they would draw the very inference most opposite to the truth. The best pains that can be bestowed on the style of religious discourses is that which makes them plain, simple, and precisely adapted to the object in view. Illiterate speakers who talk at random may sometimes, by sheer genius, hit the nail on the head; but, in the great majority of cases, their want of consecutiveness, their repetitions, their flabbiness and uncouthness, make a fearful mess of the topic they handle. Men that are but half-educated, with a vulgar taste, fall into similar errors. The labour that strips one's spoken style of superfluity, makes all simple and orderly, and brings out one's meaning with the admirable clearness and conciseness that marked every utterance of our Lord, is far from being wasted labour. We see the influence of our Lord's style on the apostles—at least on such of them as have left speeches or writings behind them. All is clear and orderly, and at the same time most penetrating and impressive.

(*b.*) In our Lord's style we may further notice great *facility of expansion*. Expansion is the quality that helps, as Whately puts it, in the digestion of a discourse,—dilutes it sufficiently to let it be taken up and appropriated by an ordinary mind. Many familiar instances will readily occur: "If thine eye offend thee—if thy hand offend thee." " If ye salute your brethren only—if ye love them that love you." " Lord, thou deliveredst unto me five talents: behold, I have gained besides them five talents more. Lord, thou deliveredst unto me two talents : behold, I have gained two other talents besides them." " Then shall two be in the field; the one shall be taken, and the other left. Two women shall be grinding at the mill; the one shall be taken, and the other left." "I am the living bread which came down from heaven. If any man eat of this bread, he shall live for ever : and the bread which I will give is my flesh, which I will give for the life of the world. Verily, verily, I say unto you, Except ye eat the flesh of the Son of man, and drink his blood, ye have no life in you. Whoso eateth my flesh, and drinketh my blood, hath eternal life; and I will raise him up at the last day. For my flesh is meat indeed, and my blood is drink indeed."

(*c.*) Even more remarkable, however, than His power of expansion is His faculty of *concentration*. To go straight to the heart of a subject, and bring out its pith and marrow in a single happy expression, is a mark of profound genius. A whole world of spiritual truth seems to be given in essence in the word to Nicodemus : " Ye must be born again." Hardly less is packed up in the word spoken to the woman of Samaria : " God is a Spirit, and they that worship him must worship him in spirit and in truth." How many foolish ideas were scattered, and what a gloriously suggestive truth brought into the light in the words—" They that are whole need not a physician, but they that are sick "! A vast amount of practical theology is contained in that antithesis—" The Sabbath was made for man, and not man for the Sabbath." Other examples are the following:—"A man's life consisteth not in the abundance of the things which he possesseth;" "The spirit is willing, but the flesh is weak;" "Where the carcase is, there shall the eagles be gathered together." Evidently our Lord was fond of proverbs that sum up a great amount of practical wisdom in very few words: "A prophet is not without honour save in his own country;" "Physician, heal thyself;" "Herein is that saying true, One soweth, and another reapeth."

But probably the most striking of all the forms of concentrated speech used by our Lord was in prayer, and especially the Lord's Prayer. On the very surface, a prayer of but six or seven lines in length, containing the leading matters suitable to be asked of God in all ages, in all countries, and by all ranks and conditions of sinful men, must be a wonderful production. But the more it is pondered the greater does the marvel become. The more profound the knowledge that Christian men acquire of human want on the one hand and Divine grace on the other, the more rich, suggestive, and indeed wholly inexhaustible are these petitions found to be. A proof of this is, that from the earliest times many of the best minds in the Christian Church have been expounding that prayer, and yet the subject is not exhausted. Hardly ever has a competent writer addressed himself to it without making some addition to what it has been shown to contain. Nothing is to be more deprecated than the common practice of rattling over the petitions in public without affording a moment's time to think on the wonderful depth of their contents. Each several clause carries us out on a new excursion to the infinite:— so vast is the variety of particulars and the range of possible fulfilment which rise before the thoughtful and exercised heart.

We have exhausted our space but not our subject. As the thoughtful reader studies the discourses of Christ, feature after feature of excellence and power will present themselves to his mind, and a profounder conviction will form itself of the truth of the criticism—" Never man spake as this man."

CHAPTER X.

ELEMENTS OF IMPRESSION IN HIS TEACHING.
III. ILLUSTRATION.

THERE is no feature of our Lord's method of teaching that is more universally appreciated than His habit of illustrating. It is an obvious fact that from first to last His discourses swarm with illustrations. One of the most characteristic and prominent class of His discourses, His parables, may be said to be illustrations, pure and simple. This class of illustrations is so important that we shall reserve it for separate consideration. But apart from the parables, His ordinary discourses and conversations sparkle with illustrations as the sky by night sparkles with stars.

One thing is already very obvious—our Lord had no sympathy with those who object to illustration on principle. It is regarded by some as an inferior mode of instruction. It is alleged that because some men are not capable of giving, and others are not capable of receiving, truth by means of the primary organ, the logical faculty, an inferior and less trustworthy organ, the imagination, is resorted to as a medium of instruction. Not only is the imagination inferior to the logical faculty as an organ of giving and receiving truth, but it is much more liable to deceive. Men are liable to be led to wrong conclusions by false or irrelevant analogies.

It is plain, we say, that our Lord did not sympathise with this objection. If He had been dealing with none but skilled and trained logicians, He might have seen it right to adhere to the strict methods of logic, as a mathematician, teaching geometry, adheres to the strict method of Euclid. But our Lord was dealing with popular audiences. His hearers generally were not trained logicians, but men whose ways of receiving truth were moulded by the practice of ordinary life. To such men illustration is one of the most common and most useful mirrors of truth. Hence our Lord made the most plentiful use of it, guarding at the same time against all possible abuse.

In all discourses, and especially long discourses (our Lord's were never long), few things are so repulsive as dryness, and discourses which are destitute of illustration are sure to be dry, and unsuitable to the popular mind. Now, the faculty of illustration, like the faculty of observation, is one that requires to be diligently exercised, and that is susceptible of almost indefinite improvement through exercise. Hardly any one is destitute of the germ of the faculty of illustration, for the perception of analogies and contrasts is one of the most ordinary attributes of the human mind. But a large proportion of preachers allow it to be neglected, and comparatively few are impressed (as Dr. Guthrie was) with its importance so as to make the cultivation of it one of the chief objects of their care. In teaching the young we instinctively fall back on illustration, and it is generally those who have been compelled to illustrate truth in the family, the Sunday-school, or the Bible-class, that become most successful in the use of it. We feel instinctively, as we handle the young mind, that a long spell of abstract statement wearies and repels it; it must have a story, an anecdote, or a figure. It is well to remember that men are but children of a larger growth, and that by most of them bare exposition or dry discussion is as little relished as by children. In discoursing to ordinary flocks, preachers have just as much need to think how they may brighten and illustrate their remarks as in dealing with children. If they fail they must pay the penalty, and that will commonly be found in a weary, uninterested audience, and the preacher's labour spent in vain.

In considering our Lord's method we may first note the sources from which He drew His illustrations; second, their peculiar form; and third, the purpose for which they were used. The parables, however, will not be included in the present inquiry.

(1.) *Sources.*—If we collect and classify our Lord's illustrations we shall find that with hardly an exception they all spring from these two—external nature and human life. This implies a co-relation of three things—*Christian truth* (the thing that has to be illustrated), *human life,* and *external nature* (the sources from which the illustrations came). No one can deem it surprising that Christian truth should stand related to the operations of nature. Both have the same Author, and both are revelations of the same Being. It was by the Son that God made the world, and it was by the Son that He revealed Himself in the Gospel. It is no wonder that He who revealed the Father in the gospel should have found numberless analogies to that revelation in the world of nature, which was but a revelation of the self-same God. It may excite some surprise, however, that in the sphere of human life He should have found so many resemblances to the truth of God. Has not the machinery of human life been thrown too much out of gear by sin to be adapted to such a purpose? Not so, in the judgment of our Lord. "If ye that are evil know how to give good gifts to your children, how much more shall your Father which is in heaven give good things to them that ask him?" It would seem from this that there is still a sphere in human life that furnishes analogies to the ways of God. The entire sphere is not so co-related, but a part of it is, and it is in that part which has been least shattered by the forces of evil that our Lord found His illustrations of the order and operations of the kingdom of heaven.

The analogy that connects the *world of nature* with the revealed truth of God is one of profoundest interest, and it affords a delightful field for the faculties of congenial minds. The analogy is seldom obvious; it commonly lies below the surface. To bring it to light requires a certain insight or penetrating power, "the vision and faculty divine" of the poet. Of modern poets none has shown more of this gift than Wordsworth, in so far as the sights and sounds of nature bear on the truths of *natural religion*. Keble makes nature speak in a more evangelical strain; the morning sun is the fit symbol of Him who makes all things new, but when the sun sets at night he only contrasts with the

> Sun of my soul, thou Saviour dear,
> It is not night, if Thou be near.

The angels' song is

> Like circles widening round
> Upon a clear blue river,
> Orb after orb, the wondrous sound
> Is echoed on for ever:
> "Glory to God on high, on earth be peace,
> And love towards men of love—salvation and release."

Some of our Scotch preachers, like James Hamilton, William Arnot, and Hugh Macmillan, have shown the same poetical insight, with a large power of application. The charm of their writings lies in their way of bringing out the analogies of nature and grace; and the genius of the writers lies in the felicitous way in which they hit off the analogies, and show the relation of the one topic to the other.

(2.) *Form of our Lord's illustrations.* It is to be observed, that there are two ways of dealing with analogies between the processes of nature and the ways of God. The one is realistic, the other idealistic. The one is prose, the other poetry. The one didactic—chiefly for use; the other æsthetic—more for ornament.

Of all instances of the prosaic method of treating analogy, Butler's work is the most remarkable. The object of the book, as explained in the title-page, is to trace the analogy of religion, natural and revealed, to the course of nature. The subject is capable of poetical treatment, but very wisely Butler has adopted the other mode. It may be hard on the reader—as Tholuck said of the book, one tires of walking on dry sand,—but it is fortunate for the subject. Where the object of a writer is to establish and elucidate truth, the more prosaic his treatment of analogy the better. If the object be to embellish what is known and admitted, the poetical mode of treating resemblances may safely come in. For it is in the more idealistic or free poetical use of analogy that the danger lies of dazzling the vision and misleading the judgment. The prosaic use of analogy is not so subject to this risk.

Now it is chiefly to the more prosaic method that our Lord's analogies belong. "Ye are the salt of the earth. Ye are the light of the world. I am the vine, ye are the branches. If these things be done in the green tree, what shall be done in the dry?" Our Lord's object was to establish truth. With such a purpose, it would not have been suitable for Him to intrust Himself, as His ordinary habit, to the wings of poetry. And if the four Gospels had abounded in poetic flights and visions, their historical character might have been more easily attacked, and we should have wanted the strong argument for their absolute truth which their calm matter-of-fact aspect so clearly supplies.

Thus it is that certain of our Lord's illustrations seem tame in comparison with some in the Old Testament of similar tenor. Compare two emblems of the Divine solicitude for men: "As an eagle stirreth up her nest, fluttereth over her young, spreadeth abroad her wings, taketh them, beareth them on her wings, so the Lord alone did lead him, and there was no strange god with him." "How often would I have gathered thy children together, as a hen gathereth her chickens under her wings, but ye would not!" In the imagery of the psalms and prophets the idealistic spirit often soars to heights sublime. In the Apocalypse you have it in its most brilliant and gorgeous form. Compared with the splendour on either side, our Lord's imagery is somewhat bare and tame. Not that it altogether wants touches of poetry. There is beauty as well as force in the imagery of the lilies: " Consider the lilies of the field; they toil not, neither do they spin; and yet I say unto you, that even Solomon in all his glory was not arrayed like one of these." The parable of the Prodigal Son in its very simplicity is a beautiful poem; so is the parable of the Lost Sheep; and the tragic elements in the Rich Man and Lazarus could hardly be surpassed. In certain delineations of the future our Lord allowed His fancy an ampler sweep: "Then shall the King say unto them on his right hand, Come, ye blessed of my Father, inherit the kingdom prepared for you from the foundation of the world: for I was an hungered, and ye gave me meat: I was thirsty, and ye gave me drink: I was a stranger, and ye took me in: naked, and ye clothed me: sick and in prison, and ye came unto me." "In my Father's house are many mansions: if it were not so, I would have told you. I go to prepare a place for you." "He shall send his angels with a great sound of a trumpet, and they shall gather together his elect from the four winds, from one end of heaven to the other."

But if in handling illustrations drawn from the field of nature our Lord seldom soars into the higher regions of poetry, but keeps to the more prosaic method, this feature is still more apparent in emblems drawn from human life : " Neither do men light a candle, and put it under a bushel, but on a candlestick . . ." "No man putteth a piece of new cloth unto an old garment . . ." "If the blind lead the blind, both shall fall into the ditch . . ." "No man having put his hand to the plough, and looking back, is fit for the kingdom of God."

In such instances our Lord just appeals to the common-sense of men, but by using an illustration He exemplifies that rule of vivid discourse by which you express the general by the particular. He does not in an abstract way bid us beware of bestowing on coarse rough men arguments beyond their capacity, or gifts beyond their taste, but He says, " Give not that which is holy unto dogs, neither cast your pearls before swine." He does not reprove the Pharisees for passing over offences of lesser magnitude, and being very particular about smaller sins, but He exclaims, " Ye blind guides, which strain out a gnat, and swallow a camel." He does not say drily that consciousness of our emptiness, the sense of dependence, docility, and guilelessness, are marks of His followers, but He says, " Whosoever shall not receive the kingdom of heaven like a little child, shall in no wise enter therein." He does not say that heaven is capable of accommodating a large and varied family, but, " In my Father's house are many mansions." He does not say that He will be careful of their interests when He goes thither; but, " I go to prepare a place for you "—just as the two disciples had gone before to prepare the place in which they were. And yet there are preachers who think they are following in Christ's steps when they translate His bright, graphic emblems into abstract propositions and weary prose!

We cannot but remark how our Lord's illustrations fulfilled the rule that they ought to be drawn from familiar objects. Transparency is the true quality of all that is designed to illustrate, and for this end the analogy must be one that is familiar to the hearer. And there is this further advantage in such illustration, that the preacher is in less danger of spending undue pains on the dress of the figure. In those who have to deal with the awful realities of sin and grace, death, judgment, and eternity, the elaborate dressing out of illustration is highly unbecoming. The wisest course is to follow in the footsteps of our Lord: to aim simply at instructing and impressing the audience; to seek to be homely without being vulgar, and plain without being commonplace.

(3.) *Purpose of our Lord's illustrations.* Coming now to consider more minutely the reasons for which our Lord made so much use of illustration, we remark that the purpose to be served was twofold,—to elucidate truth and to apply it. Illustration in His hands deals with truth in its relation to the intellect, and in its relation to the will. In its relation to the intellect, the purpose of illustration is to make truth clear; in its relation to the will, it is to make truth practically effective. Sometimes an illustration will serve both purposes,—nay, it will even do more: it will state a truth, elucidate it, and enforce it all together. When our Lord says, "Ye are the light of the world. A city that is set on an hill cannot be hid. Neither do men light a candle, and put it under a bushel, but on a candlestick; and it giveth light to all that are in the house. Let your light so shine before men, that they may see your good works, and glorify your Father who is in heaven"—He at once states, explains, and enforces the Christian duty of so living as to influence others.

It is only what we should expect that many of our Lord's illustrations should bear on those truths, whether doctrinal or practical, which were most conspicuous in His teaching. (*a.*) Prominent among His doctrinal truths is *the fatherly character of God.* This is beautifully brought out, as we have seen, in the parable of the Prodigal Son, and in the homely question, "What man is there among you, whom if his son ask bread will he give him a stone? if he ask a fish will he give him a serpent?" Other illustrations bring out the *judicial* character of God, brought in the gospel into harmony with the paternal. (*b.*) *The inwardness of true religion.* Not that which entereth in defileth a man, but that which cometh out. The cup and the platter may be clean outwardly, but horribly foul inside. Alms and prayers are to be offered in secret, not to be seen of men. (*c.*) *The practical fruitfulness of true religion* is shown by the figure of the house built on the sand and that built on the rock; the parable of the Sower; or the question, Do men gather grapes of thorns, or figs of thistles? (*d.*) *Our spiritual dependence on Christ.* The fourth Gospel being that in which this theme is most enlarged on, the illustrations of it are found chiefly there. Christ is the bread of life and the water of life, and we must come to Him to obtain these. He is the true vine, and we must abide in Him in order to be fruitful. He is the door of the sheepfold, and if we would be lawful inmates of it, we must enter by Him. He is the way, and the truth, and the life, and if we would come to the Father, we must come by Him. He is the resurrection and the life, and if we would live for ever, we must believe in Him: "He that believeth on me, though he were dead, yet shall he live." (*e.*) Prominent among the *practical* truths illustrated by Christ is the great duty of *trust*. "Consider the fowls of the air;" "Consider the lilies of the field;" "Consider the grass, which to-day is, and to-morrow is cast into the oven," and draw from all the lesson of trust. (*f.*) The duty of *prayer* is enforced by analogies among men, especially by the parables of the Friend at Midnight and the Importunate Widow. (*g.*) The duty of *service*, as really the highest condition in Christ's kingdom, is enforced by the symbolical act of washing the disciples' feet, and by the parable of the Sheep and the Goats. Other features of the kingdom of heaven, as we shall see in our next chapter, are illustrated by other parables.

Thus did our Lord leave behind Him pictorial witnesses, as it were, for all of the greatest truths which He came to teach. What pictures are to a book of history, our Lord's illustrations are to the Gospels. The things that are seen become revealers of things unseen and eternal. The sluggish mind is stimulated by the active eye and the active ear; and the sluggish conscience is roused from its slumbers when it is seen how the pains and care bestowed on the life that now is rebuke the apathy so often manifested about the concerns of the life to come.

CHAPTER XI.

PARABOLIC DISCOURSES.

THE parables stand out in the teaching of Christ as the pyramids in the scenery of Egypt, or the Alps and glaciers in that of Switzerland. They are not only prominent and remarkable phenomena, but they are found nowhere else. There are no pyramids but the Egyptian; no snow-clad peaks (at least within easy reach) but the Swiss; and virtually no parables but our Lord's. The parable was emphatically Christ's instrument. We have a few samples of it in the Old Testament, like Jotham's parable of the trees electing a king, or Isaiah's parable of the vineyard, or Ezekiel's of the eagles and the twig of cedar. But in the hands of Christ the parable culminates, and we may say, terminates. For strange to say, none of the apostles, not even those of Jewish birth, seem to have attempted this form of teaching. When the beloved disciple in the Apocalypse brought in the imagination as a handmaid to truth, it was in a totally different form. St. Paul's allegory of Mount Sinai in Arabia, and the Jerusalem which is above, is not in the form of the parable. The early Christian fathers did not revive it. The "Shepherd" of Hermas embodies the spirit of it, but not the form. In more recent times, Christian literature and art have been enriched by allegorical books and pictures, by stories for children, and by religious romances, all in the spirit of the parable, but none of them identical with it. There could hardly be a more striking testimony to our Lord's originality. To put a sermon into a dozen of lines, or a drama into half a page; to bring out the highest lessons as vividly as in the most elaborate composition; to leave them rankling in the conscience, and grappling with the will, thus modifying one's whole view of life and duty, is a feat of spiritual dexterity beyond human powers. The parable is like the bow of Ulysses,—ordinary hands cannot wield it. It remains alike a monument of Christ's originality and a trophy of His power.

It is needless for us, therefore, to discuss the parable as if it were possible for the modern preacher to revive it. All that we can reasonably hope to do is to transfuse its spirit into our lessons, and especially our lessons for the young and the ignorant. We ought never to dream of abandoning the imagination as a brilliant auxiliary in the service of Christianity. But we must use it in such forms as we may hope, with God's help, to be able to turn to practical account in present times.

Among other ways of classifying the parables, two may be suggested as having a bearing on the homiletical and pastoral aspect of the subject: first, they may be classified according to the *audiences* to which they were addressed; or, second, according to the *purpose* for which they were designed.

With regard to the audiences to which the parables were addressed, we may note four:—(1.) The ὄχλος, the mixed multitude that used to throng and follow Christ. (2.) The priests and rulers at Jerusalem. (3.) The μαθηταί, or disciples generally. (4.) The twelve, the special μαθηταί, or confidential followers of our Lord. Some parables were spoken to individuals, or smaller groups. The four classes, now enumerated, may be reduced to two: 1st, the outer world, comprehending the multitude and the rulers; 2d, the circle of disciples, who were more or less in sympathy with Christ, and ready to receive instruction from His lips.

In narrating the parables the Evangelists usually indicate the kind of audience to which they were spoken, and stress is laid on differences in this respect. In regard to the group of parables of which "the Sower" is first, our Lord gave a very important reason why He addressed such discourses *to the multitude*. And in regard to one parable, that of the servants waiting for the coming of their Lord, Peter asked, "Lord, speakest thou this parable to us, or to all?" evidently implying that this was an important element for ascertaining its drift and fixing its interpretation.

The reason which our Lord gave for speaking in parables *to the multitude* was a solemn and startling one. In their case, His purpose was not simply to reveal truth, but partly to veil it. In his journeys He was followed by a promiscuous multitude, whom He desired to sift like Gideon's army, in order that He might deal the more effectually with those that should be left. There were many delicate points connected with the establishment of His kingdom, on which He desired to make known His views in some form, but in the circumstances it would not have been safe to fling out these views carelessly for the information of the whole world. Setting up a new economy which was to embrace the world, He had to guard against needlessly exciting the jealousy or the suspicion of the existing rulers, whether civil or ecclesiastical. Now, the form of the parable was such that while careless and unspiritual hearers saw nothing important in it, it was fitted to excite the interest of those who had spiritual sympathies, and to urge them to inquire earnestly into its deeper meaning. Suppose that our Lord had broadly and all at once proclaimed to the world the truth contained in the words in the parable of "the Sower,"—"the field is the world," words indicating the extent of the spiritual conquest at which He aimed,—it is hard to say what might not have followed. But careless hearers thought little or nothing on the matter; it was only the sympathetic few, the disciples, whose interest was awakened, who came to Christ desiring further explanation, and to whom He announced the world-wide dimensions of His kingdom, and the way in which it was to grow. As for the multitude, their attitude seemed to reveal the careless state of their minds, and their indifference to spiritual treasure;—it showed that they were not among those of whom it is said, "To him that hath shall be given," but on the contrary among those whose eyes were judicially blinded, and from whom there should be taken away even that which they had.

It may be thought that if this was the purpose of some of the parables, they cannot be regarded as having had for their object the elucidation of truth. But in point of fact they did elucidate truth to those who studied them, and whose eye pierced the veil. It was only to the careless that they conveyed nothing; to the earnest heart they taught, and still teach, much valuable truth pertaining to the kingdom of God.

The other mode of classifying the parables is that which has regard to the *purpose* for which they were intended.

I know not how many divisions of them might be suggested on this line, according to the varied view that might be taken of their purpose. The classification which we adopt here is simple, and confessedly general. We have already had occasion to notice our Lord's habit of viewing men both in their individual and in their social capacity. That habit appears in the parables. Certain of these deal with "the kingdom of heaven,"—deal with the followers of Christ in their united or social capacity. And certain of them deal with men individually: they are designed to bring some part of Divine truth to bear directly on the individual soul or conscience.

I.

The parables that deal with the kingdom—the social body—are mainly expository. Most of them are found in Matthew. For that Evangelist the idea of the kingdom seems to have had a peculiar attraction.

To nearly every parable which He records the formula is prefixed—"The kingdom of heaven is like." Even where the parable is more applicable to the individual than to the social body, it commonly has this prefix. But the predominating bearing of the parables recorded by Matthew is on the Church, the one body with many members.

Regarding the kingdom of Christ, these parables give much information which could not have been communicated in a direct form, except by means of lengthened disquisitions and explanations. No single body that had ever existed in the world was a thorough counterpart of the Church of Christ, or fitted to convey a thoroughly correct impression of it. The Jewish Church was too much identified with the nation; its ordinances were too carnal, and its structure too rigid, to give a fair conception of what Christ's society was designed to be. It seemed to our Lord most fitting to convey this idea of His Church in a series of glimpses, and by means of natural symbols. In this way we have in the parables a prophetic vision of some of the most essential features of the Church.

(1.) Thus, in regard to its *origin*. It was not to be set up by force, or by any human authority, whether civil or ecclesiastical. It was to be a vital growth, like that of seed cast by the sower into the ground. The whole life of His Church was to have its root in the Word. It was to spring from conviction of the truth working in the hearts of men, and making them fruit-bearing. But this process would not proceed uniformly without let or hindrance. The result would be very different in each case according to the circumstances in which the Word was received. Great care would be required on the part of the husbandmen to remove obstacles, otherwise the process would be arrested, and even destroyed.

But the process of sowing would be obstructed from another source. Efforts would be made to mix tares with the wheat. In other words, counterfeits would be mingled with the genuine elements of the Church, in order to corrupt it, and assimilate it to the world. Nor would it be possible for the skill of the husbandmen wholly to frustrate this attempt. Men would not see a perfectly pure Church on earth, until, at the great harvest, the Master would come and separate the tares from the wheat.

(2.) Next, as to the *growth* of the kingdom. It would be partly visible and partly invisible. The visible growth would resemble that of the mustard plant, growing from the smallest of seeds to a tree in which birds made their nests. The invisible growth, the silent influence of the Church, its power to transform society, to mould institutions, to purify the moral atmosphere, to elevate the tone of life, would resemble the leaven, making its way gradually and silently through the lump, until the whole was leavened.

(3.) Another point relates to what may be called elements of value in the kingdom. Enlightened men would come to estimate the kingdom very highly. To them it would become like treasure in a field, like a pearl of great price, worth losing everything else in order to possess it. Great men would express their value for it thus—" Yea, doubtless, I count all things but loss for the excellency of the knowledge of Christ Jesus my Lord, for whom

I have suffered the loss of all things, and do count them but dung, that I may gain Christ and be found in him."

(4.) Still another point is the *service* of the kingdom. It is evident that in our Lord's view this was a very important point. There was great danger of the servants forgetting that they were but servants. The absence of the Lord might tempt them to make their own interests their end. In a great variety of parables our Lord strives to rectify this tendency. They must remember their Lord. It is He that has called them into the vineyard, and bargained for their service. It is He that has given them their talents, and bid them occupy until He come. His coming again is the great consummation of the history of His Church. Some of them will then be found to have been desperately unfaithful, their hands being stained with the blood of the servants whom He has sent to gather the fruits, and even of His own Son. Want of vigilance, forgetfulness that He is coming again, will be the sin of others, who will be surprised in a state of carelessness and disorder when He appears. Some who are not forgetful of His coming will be caught asleep when the cry of the Bridegroom is heard. Some, who have had extraordinary experience of His forbearance and forgiveness, will be found tyrannising over their fellow-servants, unmindful of the mercy that has been shown to themselves. In the case of some, whose lives have been full of mercy and good fruits, it will be seen that all unconsciously they have been serving Christ, because they have been kind to His brethren. In the case of others, the reverse will appear; having neglected all their opportunities of feeding the hungry and clothing the naked; having lived in selfish ease and cold indifference to the claims of the needy, they will be arraigned for neglect and disloyalty toward the Lord Himself, and will have the doom of the negligent and heartless servant. It is interesting to observe that it was towards the close of His ministry that these views of service, responsibility, and retribution, were expounded most fully and urged most emphatically.

The bearing of such parables on the constitution and life of the Church, or general body of Christ's followers, is apparent; but it is not to be supposed that they have no lessons for the individual. Many of them come home very closely to the individual conscience, and none more so than the large and important class which we have grouped last, as bearing on the *service* of the kingdom. And indeed it must be remarked, that while it is convenient to view the followers of Christ in their twofold capacity—as individuals, and as members of a community, —the two aspects often run into each other, and cannot be wholly detached by any hard line.

II.

We find at the same time another class of parables that have less to do with the kingdom and more with the individual. And as it is Matthew who has given the fullest account of the Church-parables, so it is Luke, and in a less degree John, to whom we are indebted chiefly for reports of the other class. And as the leading aspects of the Church are illustrated by the parables of

Matthew, so in those of Luke and John we find many of the most vital points connected with the individual soul. Among these are—

(1.) *God's feeling toward the sinner.* The most fatal obstacle to the return of the sinner to God arises from wrong ideas of God's feeling toward him. Usually when we are offended, and our anger is roused, it is a bitter anger that is excited, ready to load the offender with hatred and malediction. By ascribing a similar bitterness of feeling to God, we widen the gulf between Him and us, and make a mutual approach impossible. It is of vital importance to know that the anger of God, directed against our sin, has no bitterness in it, but is accompanied with warm love and longing toward our persons. This is illustrated by the parable of the Prodigal Son so beautifully and powerfully that it would seem as if nothing could ever be added. It is often counted the very prince or pearl of parables, giving a revelation of God's heart that must leave all without excuse who are not convinced by it that "God is love."

(2.) *The convicted sinner's feeling toward God* is set forth in a parable hardly less complete,—that of the Pharisee and the Publican. And the principle of contrast is brought in to heighten the effect. The Pharisee's prayer is a wonderful revelation of the self-righteous heart. Things are not far wrong. Anything that was wrong has been easily put right, and the man's life is so good that he can only thank God for its excellence. But the man knows nothing of sin. The publican has been convicted, and has felt himself undone. He can only throw himself on God's mercy: " God be merciful to me, a sinner!"

(3.) *God a forgiving God.* The parable of the Two Debtors shows that His forgiving grace is boundless. Ten thousand talents was a prodigious sum for any man to forgive. But it was only the symbol of God's forgivingness. " Where sin abounded, grace did much more abound."

(4.) *Christ the way to the Father, and the propitiation for sin,* are shown in the parable of the Good Shepherd. He is " the door " of the sheepfold, and " the good Shepherd giveth his life for the sheep."

(5.) *Christ the source of all spiritual life and strength.* This is taught in the parable of the Vine and the Branches. " As the branch cannot bear fruit of itself, except it abide in the vine; no more can ye, except ye abide in me." " If a man abide not in me, he is cast forth as a branch, and withereth; and men take them, and cast them into the fire, and they are burned."

(6.) *This life vitally connected with that which is to come.* Nothing more impressive in this point of view can be conceived than the parable of the Rich Man and Lazarus. It is one of the parables to which men listen with breathless interest. Less striking, but bearing on the same point, are the parables of the Unjust Steward, and the Pounds.

(7.) *Prayer not only an incumbent duty, but a blessed privilege.* This is shown in the parable of the Importunate Widow, and also in the illustration of the father who will not give his son a stone when he asks bread.

(8.) *The Christian duty of neighbourliness* is brought

out with consummate art in the parable of the Good Samaritan. The heart in which God dwells is tender and sympathetic; it "rejoices with them that do rejoice, and it weeps with them that weep."

Thus we see that, unsystematic though the arrangement be, many of the leading truths of Christianity are embodied in the parables. And the similitudes are all drawn from familiar objects. Whether they be furnished by the operations of nature, or by the ways of men, they are level to every capacity, because familiar to every mind. By being linked to objects of familiar interest and frequent occurrence, the truths which they teach are often suggested to the mind.

It is plain that Christ's mind, so quick in perceiving analogies, and so ready in throwing them into suitable form, might have produced parables by the hundred, if He had been so disposed. The question, therefore, naturally presents itself,—On what principle did He select the parables which have been given us? What end had He in view in giving these? Other questions will follow this: When and where did our Lord prepare His parables? And what is the lesson, the permanent homiletical lesson, for preachers and other Christian instructors of the present day, to be deduced from the great use He made of this form of address?

First, as to our Lord's principle of selection. From what has been already said it will be seen that there were certain great truths, bearing on His kingdom on the one hand, and on the welfare of souls on the other, which He deemed it right to clothe in this form of speech. Looking round the whole spiritual horizon, as it were, considering what men needed, and what He desired them to become, our Lord fixed in His mind on certain truths as those that were most adapted to His purpose, and determined to find for these truths, among the things familiar to men, analogies that would help to impress them. We see in this a striking proof of the grasp and penetration of His mind. To form an estimate of the condition and tendencies of man, and of the truths that were fitted to meet that condition, such that what He threw out would form for all time the best food for the hungry, the best guide for the perplexed, and the best mould for Christian character and means of spiritual influence, was a wonderful effort of creative foresight and power. When the earth was launched on its orbit, with the precise mass, velocity, and distance from the sun that were adapted to keep it moving with undeviating uniformity for myriads of years; when the animal and vegetable substances were so balanced as to supply each other's wants from age to age; when man and other animals were formed with organisations to be reproduced generation after generation in undiminished vigour and activity—in all such operations there was a wonderful effort of creative forethought and wisdom. But even this grand reach of thought and plan is eclipsed by that of Christ, selecting the truths that would be needed to mould men's minds and hearts through all coming ages, and the very forms of illustration by which these truths might be launched most advantageously on their momentous career.

This consideration suggests the answer to the

next question—When and where did our Lord prepare His parables? As He brought them out, they have all the look of finished products, of analogies that had long before been apprehended by His mind, and verified by much observation and thought. It is not for us to penetrate the region in which Jesus as a man came into closest communion with the Father, deriving from Him all that was requisite for His several functions of Prophet, Priest, and King. But thus much we may well believe: that in the days of profound thought at Nazareth our Lord's human mind would be occupied with the great truths pertaining to His Church, and likewise to the souls of His people, which His public ministry was to proclaim, and with the parables or other illustrations under which these truths were to be set forth. It is easy to conceive that He may have settled, long before, the parable that would be best suited to illustrate some particular truth, so that, when the occasion came, the parable would be ready. Just as we must believe that long before the last Supper He must have determined to institute a rite of commemoration, and must have settled the precise terms in which He would hand it down to the Church of all future ages, so we can hardly help thinking that the same preparation must have been made in reference to all the great truths which He was to set rolling through the ages in their chariots of illustration. We speak with reserve of matters on which we have received no direct communication. But if our view be right, does it not throw a new light on that feeling of serene content with which our Lord could say at last, "I have finished the work which thou gavest me to do;" and, "I have given them the words which thou gavest me"? Of all the great truths which He had received from the Father, to be communicated before His death, there remained not one which He had not now made known, and which He had not clothed in an appropriate garb. He had preached righteousness in the great congregation; He had not refrained His speech; He had not concealed God's loving-kindness nor His truth from the great congregation. In that, as in all other departments of His work, His task had been completed, and His soul was at rest.

But what a different feeling was this of Christ's from that which other men have in the retrospect of their work! Who among us, as he draws nigh to the close, it may be, of a long life, but has to mingle innumerable regrets and confessions of inefficiency with his acknowledgments of God's mercy for having enabled him to do a little? Who ever comes up even to his own ideal of useful service? We have to confess that we are unprofitable servants; we have to bring the very best of our services to be sprinkled with the blood of Christ; and it is only the sense of His infinite grace and merit that keeps us from sinking in despair. There is something even pathetic in many a good man's verdict on his own efforts—

"And yet to mean so well and fail so foul."

But with Jesus it was quite otherwise. The retrospect of His life discovered no truth omitted, no message neglected, no form of illustration, no vehicle of truth, inadequate or imperfect. Who shall duly think of this and not confess, "Truly this man was the Son of God"?

Our last question respects the lesson to be derived by us for our ministry from our Lord's love of the parable. We have already said that it is not in its very form that we shall do best to copy it. But there is something for us to learn beyond the general truth that illustration ought to form a chief attribute of all our instructions. We are surely taught *to be prepared* with suitable illustrations—suitable both to ourselves and to others—of the chief truths which we are called to proclaim. We know what is meant by "the leading doctrines of the faith." The duty arises from Christ's example to have some well-considered illustration in our treasury by which to explain and commend each of these doctrines. How should we illustrate justification by faith? How should we bring home to the intellect and to the heart the doctrine of substitution? How should we distinguish between sanctification and justification? How should we illustrate the need of purity? How should we show the value and efficacy of prayer? We say again, It is our duty to cultivate the faculty that discovers analogies; and, with this view, we ought often to bring together the truths of Revelation on the one hand, and the processes of nature and the ways of men on the other. In some minds, however, this may be a very difficult thing. In the case of such does it not become them to go to their Master and ask from Him vehicles for conveying the truths He has already given? Must not the prayer be pleasing to Christ that springs from the desire to make our teaching in its very form the counterpart of His,—to make it rich with such illustrations as those which sparkled in His discourses? We have known cases in which this power was asked in prayer, and with remarkable results. "Take heed," our Lord once said in another connection, "that ye despise not the least of these little ones." So let us take heed that we despise not the least of those helps by which truth is rendered effective. If our Lord took such pains to clothe truth in the dress of figure, can any of His servants be justified in casting it carelessly aside?

CHAPTER XII.

PUBLIC DISCOURSES—THE SERMON ON THE MOUNT.

IN one obvious respect the Sermon on the Mount lies beyond the reach of imitation, and even the attempt to imitate—in its thoroughly Oriental character. At the first blush it is seen to be constructed in a way that differs fundamentally from the sermon of the West. It wants the continuity and flow which we always look for in a religious discourse, and is made up of proverbial and antithetic statements, each of which is more like the germ of a separate discourse than a part of one continuous address. It is more like a wonderful mosaic, like the essence of many discourses pieced together, than a single sermon, with the three things which it is said every sermon ought to have,—a beginning, a middle, and an end. The ability to frame and deliver such a discourse implies no small share of that composure of spirit and calmness of manner which sit more readily on the Oriental than on the Western public speaker. It presents in a remarkable degree two features of Oriental discourse which might almost be considered incompatible—*terseness* and *luxuriance*. Nothing could exceed the terseness with which its truths are stated: "Blessed are the poor in spirit: for theirs is the kingdom of heaven." " Ye are the light of the world. A city set on an hill cannot be hid." " Where your treasure is, there will your heart be also." Yet the exuberance of the Oriental fancy weaves round these terse sayings an almost endless festoonery of metaphor and symbol.

It is interesting to inquire into the final cause of this. Why was the world's teacher so thoroughly Oriental, and why were His most elaborate lessons cast in so Oriental a form? One answer to this question is obvious:—Truth presented in the Oriental form takes the firmest hold alike of the memory and the imagination. Its compact terseness makes it handy for the memory, while its luxuriant illustration adapts it to the imagination. This form, moreover, is suitable to the purposes of a revelation which, in its very aspect, must be authoritative, and which, for practical purposes, must be frequently quoted and made use of in small portions. The terse proverbial form carries authority in its very structure; it challenges belief, it forbids all question or denial. Following the emphatic " Verily, I say unto you," the short utterances of our Lord lodge themselves at once in the conscience and the heart. The Western style of preaching seldom admits of short quotations —extracts contained in a single line. Were one called to carry in one's head a sermon by Chalmers, or Liddon, or Spurgeon, and to quote and apply it, bit by bit, on a thousand occasions of ordinary life, the task would be found impossible. Except Matthew Henry, hardly any preacher or commentator has appeared who could condense his thoughts into pithy clauses of half-a-dozen words, easily quoted and easily remembered. In whatever way the Sermon on the Mount may have been first delivered, nothing could be better adapted for transferring practical truth to the memory, the conscience, and the heart.

It is quite remarkable, indeed, how many expressions in the sermon have become "household words," indigenous, as it were, in our very language and literature. The candle under a bushel, the mote and the beam, wolves in sheep's clothing, casting pearls before swine, the single eye, serving two masters, the right hand not knowing what the left hand doeth, sufficient unto the day is the evil thereof, are not merely household words, but the ideas represented by them have become practically unchallengeable; they are moral axioms, admitted alike by friend and foe.

And thus we see another advantage of the Oriental method. Peculiar though it be, it presents great facilities of combination; it may be transfused very readily into other forms of thought and expression. A Western mind can take the gems from Eastern discourses, and set them without loss of lustre in the more flowing addresses of the West. He may give them as quotations, or he may melt them down and mingle their substance with the train of his own reflections. Thus, let the West advance as it may to new developments in every department of knowledge, there always remains a sense of obligation to the East—a feeling that from it have come to us the seeds and elements of our best possessions.

One other remark ere we pass from this aspect

of the subject. Our Lord is more Oriental than any New Testament writer. The apostles are less Oriental than Christ, and the early Christian writers are less Oriental than the apostles. St. Paul is the connecting link between the two styles. The truths that came first in the detached Eastern form are reproduced by him with more of the logical continuity and flow of Western speech. Perhaps this makes the contrast between our Lord's teaching and St. Paul's appear greater than it really is. In any comparison of the two, we must bear in mind the difference between truth taught by analogy, parable and proverb, the favourite methods of our Lord, and truth presented in accordance with the dialectic process which came so naturally to the apostle.

Have we not in these facts a striking incidental proof of the authenticity of our Lord's history and teaching, as delineated in the Gospels? He belonged to that age, and so did the writers of the Gospels. It is ridiculous to think of writers of the second century developing a teacher whose style of thought and mode of expression were so widely different from their own.

Viewing the Sermon on the Mount homiletically, we remark of it that it is in the strictest sense an address *to* an audience, not a mere essay or treatise delivered *before* them. From first to last the idea of the audience is present to the speaker. Though He begins by speaking *about* people, using the third person ("Blessed are the poor in spirit: for *theirs* is the kingdom of heaven"), we see that very early in His address He changes the *they* into *you;* indeed, at an early point He repeats a statement, apparently

for the very purpose of making this transition:
"Blessed are *they* that are persecuted for righteousness' sake—blessed are *ye*, when men shall revile *you*, and persecute *you*." The second person, once attained, is for the most part kept up all through, and, indeed, there are many times when even the plural *ye* is not close enough, and when it is exchanged for the more personal *thou*: "If thou bring thy gift to the altar, and there rememberest that thy brother hath ought against thee; leave there thy gift before the altar, and go thy way; first be reconciled to thy brother, and then come and offer thy gift." This is an instructive fact for preachers, indicating in the first place that true preaching is a soul-to-soul intercourse—is the transaction of important business between the preacher and the individual members of his audience; and further, that in every instance of thoroughly successful preaching a process goes on of getting nearer to the hearts of the hearers, corresponding to the movement of an earnest man in conversation who comes physically closer and closer to those to whom he appeals: holding them as it were by the eye—the closest grip of all.

> "He holds him with his shining hand,
> 'There was a ship,' quoth he:
> 'Hold off! unhand me, greybeard loon!'
> Eftsoons his hand dropt he.
> He held him with his glittering eye,
> The wedding guest stood still,
> And listens like a three-year child,
> *The mariner hath his will.*"

The Sermon on the Mount has not only no text, but not even any announcement of a subject. In the circumstances, we are probably to regard it as an exposition of principles connected with the kingdom of heaven—of rules, aims, and characteristics demanding the attention of all who desired admission into the heavenly fellowship. Five main topics divide the discourse, but they are nowhere announced:—1. The character and privileges of the kingdom (Matt. v. 1-16). 2. Its rule or discipline, which is substantially the old moral law, but more spiritually and searchingly applied (chap. v. 17-48). 3. The service of the kingdom, consisting not of outward forms ostentatiously observed, but of inward worship and a thoroughly truthful and filial spirit towards the Great Head of the kingdom (chap. vi.). 4. The social spirit of the kingdom—its spirit of brotherhood; inasmuch as all are the children of one Father, they ought to avoid the spirit of censoriousness, not casting out motes from their brother's eye, but observing the golden rule, "Whatsoever ye would that men should do unto you, do ye also unto them" (chap. vii. 1-5). And 5. The fruit of the kingdom, suggesting a most vital and discriminating test, to be applied at last to all professing members, of which the effect will be to separate the real from the fictitious, to bring forward the one for reward and the other for condemnation (chap. vii. 6 to end). Stated more briefly we have—1. The character; 2. The rule; 3. The service; 4. The spirit; and 5. The fruit of the kingdom.

But our present purpose does not require us to go into these divisions. Our object is to bring out the chief homiletical features of the discourse; and for that purpose it will be best to advert,—first, to some of its peculiarities of *structure;* and, second, to some of its peculiarities of *substance.*

I. STRUCTURE.

1. Here first we notice its remarkable *symmetry.* This great feature of Oriental discourse is more thoroughly and elaborately worked out in the Sermon on the Mount than in any other of our Lord's longer discourses. As has been shown by Professor Forbes in his *Symmetrical Structure of Scripture,* it exemplifies that method of parallelism or symmetry which we find in the poetical and other books of the Old Testament, such as the Psalms, the Proverbs, and the Prophecies. The Beatitudes furnish the earliest specimen. We do not inquire whether their number be properly seven, the perfect number, as some contend; the eighth beatitude so-called being in their view not a real one, because it is not, like the rest, associated with a spiritual grace. But the symmetry of the other beatitudes strikes every eye; the several verses all beginning alike, and all of them, in their second clauses, giving a reason for the affirmation of the first. But there are many other instances of parallelism :—

Ye are the salt of the earth : Ye are the light of the world.
If thy right eye offend thee, pluck it out, and cast it from thee, etc.
If thy right hand offend thee, cut it off, and cast it from thee, etc.
If ye love them that love you, what reward have ye?
　　　　Do not even the publicans the same?
If ye salute your brethren only, what do ye more than others?
　　　　Do not even the publicans so?

Behold the fowls of the air: for they sow not, neither do they reap, nor gather into barns; yet your heavenly Father feedeth them.

Consider the lilies of the field, how they grow; they toil not, neither do they spin: and yet I say unto you, That even Solomon, in all his glory, was not arrayed like one of these.

Ask, and it shall be given you; For every one that asketh, receiveth;
Seek, and ye shall find; And he that seeketh, findeth;
Knock, and it shall be opened unto you. And to him that knocketh, it shall be opened.

We observe the same structure in our Lord's treatment of topics that are handled at some length in the sermon. Thus, in the fifth chapter, the sixth, seventh, and eighth commandments are treated symmetrically: the old idea of their import being uniformly prefixed by, "Ye have heard that it hath been said by them of old time;" and the new by, "But I say unto you." So also, in expounding the service of the kingdom: the three things—almsgiving, fasting, and prayer—are treated symmetrically; first the current abuses of these are indicated; then the manner in which our Lord desired that they should be severally observed.

The circumstance of so remarkable attention being paid to symmetry in this discourse is instructive to preachers of all time. For though it be true that *such* symmetry was peculiarly Oriental, yet it was the means to an end which is not Oriental merely, but universal. It was a remarkable help towards arresting and impressing the hearers. It shows what care our Lord must have taken with the structure of His more elaborate discourses. Though they have no appearance of art or elaboration, they are distinguished by properties which we cannot attain without much painstaking care. The perfection of art is to conceal itself. *Ars est celare artem.* If it was through the exercise of His human faculties that our Lord constructed His discourses, we cannot think of such exquisite symmetry and finish of style but as the result of a purpose not only to find words for His thoughts, but to find the very fittest words that language supplied. The Sermon on the Mount is a perpetual rebuke to flabby, wordy, uncouth, clumsy discourse. The Lord's Prayer is a perpetual rebuke to loose, rambling, unsymmetrical, unrhythmical devotions. If the example of our Lord is to furnish a rule, carelessness of style, on the part of the messengers of the Cross, is at once discreditable and a source of inefficiency.[1]

[1] No words have been more misapplied than those in 1 Cor. ii. 1, 4—"And I, brethren, when I came to you, came not with excellency of speech, or of wisdom, declaring unto you the testimony of God. . . . And my speech and my preaching was not with enticing words of man's wisdom, but in demonstration of the Spirit and of power." From these words it has often been inferred that a rude, uncultured way of putting the Gospel message is not only no drawback, but an actual help to efficiency. But surely St. Paul could never have meant to lay down a rule which should contradict his own practice. For although at times, when he is rushing on impetuously towards the close of an argument, his language is unfinished and elliptical, yet on most occasions it is singularly select and beautiful. Many passages in his writings are models of eloquent, expressive, most beautiful composition. It is evident to every fair reader that what is stigmatised as "excellency of speech, or of wisdom," and "enticing words of man's wisdom," is, something opposed to, and subversive of, Divine wisdom. Beyond doubt, what is deprecated is the way in vogue among the philosophers of developing all truth from the human reason, as opposed to the humble reception of truth as God's revelation. Like other writers of Scripture, Paul spoke as he was moved by the Holy Ghost; but from

In noticing the symmetrical character of the sermon, we ought to pay special regard to the element of *contrast* which pervades it. Contrast is a remarkable mode of giving to statements a definite outline and an emphatic form. It is usually managed by the pronoun *but* :—

> I am not come to destroy—*but* to fulfil.
> Lay not up for yourselves treasures on earth : . . .
>> *But* lay up for yourselves treasures in heaven. . . .
> If thine eye be single, thy whole body shall be full of light.
>> *But* if thine eye be evil, thy whole body shall be full of darkness.
> Wide is the gate, and broad is the way, that leadeth to destruction, and many there be that go in thereat:
>> Because strait is the gate, and narrow is the way, that leadeth to life, and few there be that find it.

2. Another very obvious feature in the structure of the sermon is the abundant use of illustration. Hungering and thirsting after righteousness—the salt of the earth—the salt that has lost its savour—a city set on an hill—treasures where thieves do not break through nor steal—serving two masters—the lilies of the field and the fowls of the air—Solomon in all his glory—the mote and the beam—pearls before swine—the strait gate and the narrow way—wolves in sheep's clothing—grapes of thorns and figs of thistles—the house on the rock and the house on the sand. One hardly realises till one makes the collection how figures stud this sermon like stars in the Milky Way. It is remarkable too, that they do not create any impression of superficiality, nor

Genesis to Revelation it is apparent that the style consecrated by the Holy Ghost is not rough, uncouth, and unsymmetrical but clear, elegant, eloquent, and always impressive.

do they, like some of the sermons of Jeremy Taylor for instance, weary us by their excessive abundance. The reason is, that there is so much profound truth under them. They illustrate without overlaying. Compactness and richness are equally remarkable in the sermon; it is like those structures in nature, which, though hardly visible to the naked eye, turn out, under the microscope, to be little worlds, exhibiting wonderful contrivance, great simplicity, and an exquisite beauty and finish in every part.

3. A third feature in the structure of the sermon is its appeal to the various faculties of the soul. It is not all addressed to the reason, or to the conscience, or to any single faculty of the mind; it appeals to all. It appeals to *instinct, e.g.* to our instinctive love of life and comfort: "It is better for thee that one of thy members should perish, and not that thy whole body should be cast into hell." The reasoning faculty is called in: "If ye that are evil know how to give good gifts to your children, *how much more* shall your Father which is in heaven give good things unto them that ask him?" Conscience is summoned to judge: "Why beholdest thou the mote in thy brother's eye, but considerest not the beam that is in thine own eye?" Our *fears* are addressed: "Agree with thine adversary quickly, whilst thou art in the way with him; lest at any time the adversary deliver thee to the judge, and the judge deliver thee to the officer, and thou be cast into prison." Hope is not allowed to slumber: "Blessed are they that mourn: for they shall be comforted." Of appeals to the imagination we need say nothing; for every figure is an appeal to the imagi-

nation; and the exercise of the imagination, which the sermon encourages so abundantly, is not only instructive, but also delightful.

II. SUBSTANCE.

Passing now to notice the substance of the sermon, we may first advert to what has been a stumbling-block to some—the fact that it contains no such distinct announcement of the way of salvation as does the conversation with Nicodemus, or even with the woman of Samaria. Some go so far as to say that the sermon does not belong to the new covenant, but to the old—to the period before, not the period after, the death of Christ. A single word to vindicate its scope and character may not be out of place.

Let us observe, then, that it is addressed to *disciples*. "Seeing the multitudes, he went up into a mountain," as if for the purpose of sifting His audience; "and when he was set, *his disciples*"—those who were so earnest that the mountain could not separate them—"came unto him." To this more select and instructed audience our Lord unfolded the character of His kingdom, showed the work to which their energies were to be given, and the change on the face of the world which they were to aim at producing. The sermon was the pattern that had to be worked out, the ideal that had to be realised, the theory of life that had to be turned into practice. It was an ideal for the community as much as direction for the individual. It was a prophecy as well as an exhortation—a forecast of the results of the work with which the name of Jesus was to be identified. If it was only an ideal then, it is in part a reality now. Living Christianity has always been in vital contact with the Sermon on the Mount. It is a picture of the moral millennium toward which the Church is ever stretching its hands. It is the pattern of the New Jerusalem; here are all the materials for the foundations of precious stones, the gates of pearl, and the streets of transparent gold. To realise this ideal is to hear the proclamation, " Behold, the tabernacle of God is with men, and he will dwell with them, and they shall be his people, and God himself shall be with them, and be their God."

No doubt there are many sneers still directed at the Sermon on the Mount. The scoffing criticism is perhaps still on some lips, that it showed great ignorance of human nature. Now there was nothing that Jesus knew better than human nature. And it is remarkable, that though to human nature as it is, this vision was a mere Utopia, He propounded it in all seriousness and in all good faith. What manner of man was this that could not only set forth to His disciples what ought to be, but foretell what in a measure would be? What a wonderful control He must have felt that He possessed over all moral forces when He could commit Himself, as a practical teacher, to such a model, and feel sure that it would be realised more or less over all the civilised world! What faith He must have had in His ability to set the successive generations of good men for hundreds of years in motion after the realisation of His ideal!

Further, let us observe, that it was necessary for Christ, while beginning His work, to show clearly the relation of the new economy to the old. He must show that the new was not to be a subversion but a development of the old, and that the law, while still retaining all its authority, was in the first instance to show to man his imperfections, and lead him to seek for another righteousness; and thereafter, under the influence of a new spirit, to be the rule of his life, the indication to him of the will of his Lord.

But though the Sermon on the Mount does not set forth fully the doctrine of redemption, that doctrine underlies it, and may easily be found in it. It is true the sermon rather shows to man his duty on the one hand, and his sin, want, and need on the other, than indicates in detail the sources of gracious blessing as provided in the gospel. Very plainly it is the doctrine of this sermon that man is a sinner. He needs a righteousness, a righteousness which must exceed the common standard, must exceed the righteousness of the Scribes and Pharisees. As a sinner he must appeal to God for *justifying* righteousness—for forgiveness; he must pray, " Forgive us our debts." As a sinner, too, he must appeal to God for *sanctifying* righteousness; he must pray, "Deliver us from evil." The sermon is full of considerations showing the awful position of man before God. It brings him face to face with God, makes him enter the closet and shut the door, and feel that none but God is there. It shows him the searching character of God's law, finding sin in every angry thought, in every irregular sensual feeling. It holds up to him the highest possible standard—the very perfection of God: " Be ye therefore perfect, even as your

Father which is in heaven is perfect." It summons him to specific duties of acknowledged difficulty, requires him to forgive and love his enemies, to place unwavering reliance on God, and to be perfectly sincere in all his service. It indicates the rigour of the law, once a sinner comes within its grasp: "Thou shalt by no means come out thence till thou hast paid the uttermost farthing." It presses the necessity of a choice: "Enter ye in at the strait gate." It requires of us the moral courage that chooses a different road from that of the many, and it warns us, repeatedly and solemnly, of the danger of our being cast into hell.

Rightly apprehended, what is the effect of all this but to bring the sinner into the depths, to stop his mouth, to make him cry for mercy to pardon and grace to help? Though there is a certain severity about the sermon, it is not the untempered severity that drives to despair. It is spoken with authority, but not the authority of a stern, unsympathising rabbi. There is not a little sunshine in it, not a little that is fitted to encourage. Pre-eminent in this respect is the opening word of the sermon: "Blessed are *the poor in spirit:* for theirs is the kingdom of heaven." It is not by accident that this stands first. It is the key-note of the whole. The object is to foster the sense of poverty, and then reveal and impart to faith the infinite stores of the kingdom of heaven. All are available for the poor in spirit. Let them enter into the kingdom as little children, and they will find ample provision for all their needs.

In other ways, too, our Lord encouraged the poor

in spirit. If, on the one hand, He showed them God as a strict lawgiver and judge, on the other He showed Him as a considerate Father. There is a delightful blending in the sermon of the judicial and paternal elements of God's character. From whatever is good in fallen humanity it rises to a corresponding but far higher goodness in God: "If ye that are evil know how to give good things to your children, how much more shall your Father which is in heaven give good things unto them that ask him?" And it draws the heart up to God. It has an attractive, elevating tendency. "Our Father, which art in heaven," it says, making us lift up our soul, like the Psalmist (Ps. xxv. 1), to Him. It encourages the spirit of trust—that spirit that is the perennial fountain of peace and joy, and that takes away the sharpness of anxieties, the bitterness of trials, and the gloom of sufferings. Thus, in its whole drift and tendency, it is an evangelical sermon. It does not say all that might be said. But what it does say is fitted to bring the earnest soul into the attitude of desiring and seeking for more; and then, that law of the kingdom comes into operation: "To him that hath shall be given, and he shall have abundantly."

And no sermon ever ended with a more searching or striking peroration. The discourse, which begins with a sevenfold blessing, ends with the crash of doom. For warning men to take heed how they hear, nothing can be better adapted than the last figure—that of the house, built perhaps with much care, but on a false foundation, swept away by a resistless torrent, and crushed in utter ruin. Nothing could more clearly foreshadow the moral history of the world in relation to Christ's kingdom. Well does that Preacher know that the stone which He is now unloosening from the mountains is to roll on to the end of time—that the truths He is now proclaiming are to have everlasting results. The account to be given by men of that sermon represents the whole reckoning of the day of doom; the crash of the house mingles with the crash of falling worlds; and the desolation of the inhabitant merges in that of lost souls. Little do they apprehend the nature of this sermon who imagine that when Jesus delivered it He was a mere reformer of Judaism, an improver of the legal dispensation. The Son of man knew His work from the beginning; He knew what kingdom had been delivered to Him of the Father; and in the knowledge of this, and nothing less than this, "he spoke as one having authority, and not as the scribes."

CHAPTER XIII.

THE COLLEGE OF THE TWELVE.

If there were nothing else to prove the supernatural origin of Christianity the history of the twelve apostles might furnish an unanswerable proof. No twelve men ever made such an impression on the world. We need not measure their influence by such memorials as the magnificent temples that to this day bear their names—such as Saint Peter's at Rome,—wonderful though these are, and tokens of a marvellous influence. What we are to consider in these men is their unexampled spiritual power, the power by which they were enabled to transform the lives and characters of their fellows, to teach the ignorant, to reclaim the erring; to make men noble, pure, and generous; to restore the image of God; in a word, to bring down, in large measure, the spirit of heaven to earth.

We have to take into account that when they joined Christ they were unlearned and ignorant, with no antecedents of promise, full of prejudices, subject to infirmities, even childish infirmities, utterly unlikely to become great and powerful men. Some were fishermen, and one was a publican. Fishermen are generally an isolated class, living much among themselves, prone to superstition, obstinate in their traditions, believing in lucky and unlucky days and omens, with no book-learning, and little of the smartness that comes of intercourse with the world. Publicans, collectors of taxes, are not an attractive race, not even at home, and much less in such countries as Syria was then. We have to remember also the shortness of the time during which Jesus and His apostles were together—not more, in all likelihood, than three years. It is an unprecedented wonder that such men should in that little time have been trained for such marvellous work. That Jesus, who was apparently but a working man like themselves, should have so wonderfully transfused into them His own spirit, His mighty plans for the world, His noble aspirations, the love that many waters could not quench, the zeal that no persecution could smother, the courage that defied them that kill the body, the faith that removed mountains, the purity of character that mocked calumny, as well as the teaching power that spread over the world the mysteries of His kingdom, is a wonder for which among mere natural causes we shall search in vain for any that has even the semblance of sufficiency. Whatever changing phases the battle between faith and unbelief may assume, whatever weapons, new or old, it may be found necessary to employ in defence of the faith, the world can never cease to be profoundly impressed by the unparalleled fact, that the greatest and most enduring revolution ever known was conducted by publicans and fishermen of Galilee.

The means which our Lord had of influencing

these men were very few and simple. No wealth, no books, no social or ecclesiastical connections, no philosophy, no science, not a single literary or philosophical acquaintance had He to help Him in the process. "Speech and fellowship," as has been said, were His only apparent means of influence. By speech He enlightened them, by fellowship He attached them. In speech He was always clear, racy, striking, and wonderfully decided. His mind was made up on every question; His views were certain, self-evidencing, self-commending. His remarks were not cursory observations as of a clever man taking a glance at a subject: they were the fruits of a knowledge that seemed to embrace all facts, and of a wisdom that seemed to comprehend all their relations.

It is a very foolish idea that in the course of His three years' ministry our Lord changed His plan. That He began on one tack, saw that it was not satisfactory, and changed to another; began as a reformer of morals, and changed to a preacher of salvation; began as John the Baptist had done, and ended by claiming to be the Messiah, is a weak as well as a baseless position. If ever teacher began public life with clear vision and mature views, Jesus was that teacher. If ever public man worked right on upon the same line of things, Jesus was that man.

If His speech was thus unexampled, so was His fellowship. What a charm there must have been in His simplicity and transparency of character, His kindly sympathy, His ever-thoughtful love, His goodness and His gentleness! How many little anecdotes of personal kindness and loving consideration must every one of the little band have had to remember! It is remarkable that, save in the temporary panic of the crucifixion, none of them but Judas ever left Him, or seemed to think of doing it. Paul, with all his nobility, failed to keep Mark with him during even one campaign, Barnabas left him at another, and in his Second Epistle to Timothy he speaks of Luke as his only remaining companion. But Jesus kept even Judas almost to the last. The very thought of leaving Him was repulsive. " Lord, to whom shall we go? Thou hast the words of eternal life."

The idea of the college of the twelve was in the main original. It had a certain resemblance to the methods of the Greek and Roman philosophers, and probably it was not without precedent of some sort in olden time in the schools of the prophets, and in days more recent in the schools of the Hebrew Rabbins. What was especially characteristic of the relation of Jesus to His disciples was, that they were to itinerate with Him, to live and eat, to walk and work along with Him, sharing many of His trials and some of His joys—becoming, as far as possible, identified with Him. It was the best way of multiplying Himself that the circumstances of His earthly life admitted of. No one of us is in a position to follow His example literally. But in spirit some approach may be made to it. A young minister, for example, may try to multiply himself by means of the young men of his flock. Some have a rare gift of finding out the most susceptible of these—getting them about them in classes and meetings, and perhaps sometimes in walks and at meals—explaining to them their plans, infusing into them their enthusiasm, enlisting their sympathies, and drawing out their talents. At first it might be thought that the elders of a congregation would be the most likely persons to become to the minister what the twelve were to Jesus. But in the case of a young minister, the elders are generally men in middle or advanced life, and they want the elasticity of character and suppleness of manner that can be easily turned to new modes of service. Often valuable for mature and steady Christian character, they are not seldom deficient in practical service.

But the apostles, profoundly venerable though their after lives and labours have made them, were not the old men of the painters when Jesus called them. Some of them seemingly were but lads, working with their fathers in fishing occupations; even after the resurrection of Jesus, the title they got from the stranger on the sea-beach was "children" —παιδία, lads;—their disputes were often childish, as to which would be greatest, and their friendly contests—one apostle outrunning another on the way to the sepulchre—showed how young they were in mind. So that the relation of a minister to the godly young men of his flock is not an inappropriate analogy. Dr. Chalmers in Glasgow, gathering young men around him, pouring his own views and spirit into them, rousing them to aid in his territorial schemes, and thus training the youths who in after years became the *élite* of the Christian laity of the west, comes as near as may be on a mere common level to the example of Christ and His twelve.

Let us mark of the twelve, that they seem to have belonged to the more serious families—to what may be called the religious aristocracy of the district. Some of them were related to each other, and some had been under the instructions of John the Baptist. One group were natives of Bethsaida; another appear to have belonged to Capernaum. These families seem to have been exceptions to the mass, for the people generally were hardened in wickedness. Though there was less of the foulness of sensual pollution in the cities of the northern lake than there had been in those of the southern in the days of Abraham, there was not less of the depth and inveteracy of sin. If the mighty works that were done by Jesus in them had been done in Sodom and Gomorrah they would have remained until that day.

We have adverted to the deep impression made on the world at large by the fact that most of the apostles were fishermen. The impression has usually been that which arises from the palpable distance and disproportion between the original calling of the men and the work to which they were appointed. It is more rarely that men have apprehended the symbolical meaning of the craft, and its appropriateness as a training for the more spiritual work. The symbolical callings of the Bible which are applied to the office of the ministry have all their significancy; but in certain respects that of the fisherman is the most suggestive. The shepherd or pastor; the watchman on the walls of Zion, set to warn men of danger; the soldier fighting the good fight; the husbandman with his hard plodding and patient waiting for God to give the increase; the vinedresser, pruning, watering, grafting; the builder, choosing his strong foundation and building carefully on it; the physician, faithful, vigilant, and tender; the nurse affectionately cherishing her children; the father in Christ entreating them with tears, and rejoicing, like the father of the prodigal, in their conversion—are all instructive emblems, but none conveys the precise idea symbolized by the craft of those whom Jesus called to be fishers of men.

First, it is an aggressive craft, differing from the Old Testament emblem of the shepherd, whose occupation is mainly conservative. The shepherd has to tend an existing flock; the fisherman has to find and secure his fish. Then, there is in the symbol of men-fishers the idea that those whom they are set to catch are unwilling to be taken, and as fain to escape from them as fish from the fisherman, although their purpose is not to destroy but to bless. Further, there is the notion of certain qualities needed for a successful fisherman—diligence, skill, patience, courage, and faith. Diligence, for the fisherman must look well to his nets and his ship. Skill, for he must adapt himself well to the habits of the fish. Courage, for he must expose himself to stormy elements. Patience, for many of his efforts will end in disappointment, the net will often come up empty; and faith, for success depends on conditions over some of which he has often no control. Now, these are the very qualities most needed for the ministry.

Moreover, the business of fishermen implies a certain separation from the world, which also has its counterpart in the life of the godly and devoted minister. On the sea the fisherman is away from the haunts of other men. As night is often the season for his work, he pulls away from the lights of the city, or the modest taper in his cottage window, and thinks of other men enjoying their fireside comforts or their calm repose, while for him there is only the bitter embrace of the cold north wind. But this very isolation throws fishermen more on each other's company, and generates a deeper sense of brotherhood. When religious awakenings occur of the rapidly spreading kind, it is observed that they move very fast among fishermen, and that sometimes they are confined to them alone. This fact is an illustration of the closeness of the sympathy that binds them together, and the readiness with which they communicate what they have to each other. So we may say of the servants of Christ that they are thrown peculiarly on one another, and ought to be bound together by peculiar ties of sympathy and regard. In a certain sense the true minister must feel that he is not of the world; he must be ready to give up its joys and pleasures; ready at his Master's call to go where there is little or nothing to soothe and cheer—where there is much to repel and vex. He must be prepared for storms, and even for the appearance of his Master asleep on the pillow, as if not caring that His servants should perish. Such experiences, however, must serve as occasions for rallying faith and re-establishing trust; for taking hold anew of the assurance, which is the strong tower and refuge of the faithful in every hour of need: "Lo, I am with you alway, even to the end of the world."

A very important statement in reference to the choice of the twelve apostles is made in these words of Luke: "It came to pass in those days that he went out into a mountain to pray, and continued all night in prayer to God. And when it was day, he called unto him his disciples: and of them, he chose twelve, whom also he named apostles." It is in many ways an instructive scene. If He was constrained to spend a whole night in prayer before choosing His apostles, should not we feel called to great deliberation and earnestness of prayer before giving ourselves to His service? And once we are ministers, ought not our choice (so far as it is our choice) of coadjutors to be very solemn and prayerful too? Do we not go about the selection of Sabbath-school teachers, the recommending of persons to be elders or deacons, and the like, in a spirit far from devout? But surely the disciple is not above his master, nor the servant above his lord. We may believe that Jesus had His mind full of the far-reaching influence which His apostles would have, and the need, therefore, of great care that the best men should be selected, and that they should have much of the blessing of God. If we wish to know something of His prayer, we may find it, in substance, in the 17th chapter of John. That they might be sanctified by the truth—that they might be kept from the evil in the world—that God would keep them through His own name; and especially that they all might be one. And if the petition was added, "Neither pray I for these alone, but for them also that shall believe on me through their word, that they all may be one"—may we not feel that the intercessions of that night were not limited to the twelve, but embraced all their successors? Is there no possible link, then, between that mountain-top and every company of candidates—not indeed for the apostolic, but for the ministerial office? May we not think of ourselves as having had an interest in these prayers? And if, even remotely, the heart of Jesus was drawn out that night for all future workers in His vineyard, is this not fitted to have a powerful influence on us, and fire us with the ambition to serve Him as He was served by the first batch of disciples?

It appears that Christ made choice of the twelve out of a much larger number of disciples who even already had become attached to Him. Doubtless He chose them, not because they were all alike, but because, while alike in some things, they were in many things different. A modern writer has attempted to find in each apostle the representative of some special type of Christian character or mode of service. There may be more ingenuity than solidity in some of the qualities specified; but here in substance they are:—

Peter, the Rock, represents the principle of confession—of bold and fearless avowal of discipleship—of disregard of the power and influence of this world.

Andrew—the manly breaker up of the way, who went and found his brother Simon, and brought him to Jesus—represents the evangelistic principle—the leaven-like spirit of the Gospel—the diffusive character of Christianity.

- James, one of the Sons of Thunder, who was not permitted to give to Christ the active service of his life, but was the first to shed his blood for Him, represents the principle of martyrdom.
- John, the Beloved Disciple, more a man of contemplation than of action, a seer of visions when in the Spirit, represents the principle of calm contemplation, mysticism, ideal depth.
- Philip, who like Andrew went to communicate the good tidings to others, and invited Nathanael to "come and see," to test by experience the good that could come out of Nazareth, represents the principle of experimental knowledge—the inward evidence of the truth.
- Nathanael, the Israelite indeed in whom was no guile (supposed to be the same as Bartholomew), represents the type of transparent simplicity and childlikeness of character, and entire consecration to God.
- Thomas, so prone to doubt, represents the spirit of scepticism (in the original sense), of criticism and free inquiry, but in union with true devoutness and attachment of soul.
- Matthew, in whose Gospel the Old Testament is so much made use of, and who brings so much testimony from the older sources to bear on Christ, the principle of ecclesiastical learning and antiquarian research—the spirit that brings the past to bear on the present and the future.
- James, the son of Alphæus, who led the Council of Jerusalem to the decision that united both parties—the principle of ecclesiastical government and union.

Judas, or Thaddeus, if he be the writer of the Epistle, may represent the principle of pastoral fidelity, discipline—extrusion from the Church of unworthy members.

Simon Zelotes, on the supposition that his surname denoted a personal quality—pastoral activity, readiness for work—for enterprise—for peril and trouble.

Judas Iscariot—the secular administration of the Church.

The over-ingenuity of this table in some points may be admitted without giving up the fact that the College of the Twelve were a body of men who were not copies but complements of one another. It was a miniature likeness of the Church—a picture in small compass of that fulness and variety of gifts and graces which is ever the characteristic of a living Church. We learn that there is intended to be a certain manifoldness of character in the ministers of Christ's Church. Those brethren who recognise but one type of Christian character, or of Christian service, and if not opposed are very suspicious of all who do not conform to that type, are not walking in Christ's steps. It is not desirable that all our ministers should be alike. It is not desirable that every one should be of the type of Paul, any more than of the type of Peter, or the type of James or of John. It is desirable, nay necessary, that all should have the Spirit of Christ; but Jesus Christ Himself has laid it down, and it should ever be recognised, that His servants have gifts differing one from another.

It will always be a mysterious circumstance why

Judas Iscariot was placed among the apostles. Even conjecture can hardly throw light on this strange fact. Why there should have been a son of perdition in the chosen band baffles our conception. It can hardly be doubted that Jesus Christ selected Judas knowing his real character. Why He did so we really cannot tell, unless it was for the purpose of a warning to us all. Through all the unbroken eighteen centuries Judas Iscariot has stood as it were in the pillory, in the full gaze of all mankind, a terrible spectre of greed and treachery, to show us how near one may come to the Only-begotten Son and yet be a devil, how familiarly one may handle sacred things and yet be in the gall of bitterness and in the bond of iniquity, how close one may come to the gate of heaven and after all be a child of hell.

It is to be remarked as striking that the whole of the twelve were chosen by our Lord near the beginning of His ministry. He did not begin with a small number, to be afterwards enlarged; He completed the college at once. This shows us how mature His own mind was as to His work, and as to the men best fitted to aid in it. This plan had the advantage, too of securing a united testimony and an intelligent co-operation all through. It gave the apostles the benefit of that charm which arises from early association in an enterprise, an enterprise which begins with small beginnings and goes on, through many dangers and conflicts, to a glorious issue. We think in this connection of the association of Luther and Melanchthon; we think of Cranmer, Latimer, and Ridley; we think of the Pilgrim Fathers; we think of others who have nursed together an infant cause and lived to see its maturity and its triumphs; we think of the effects of adversity in making them cling the more to one another, to their cause, and to their Lord. Had the twelve been but straggling adherents, attached one now, another then, they would not have had that interest in the cause and that steadfastness to each other which helped to give such strength to their testimony, such efficiency to their labours, and such glory to their lives.

The elaborate charge which our Lord addressed to His twelve disciples when He sent them to the lost sheep of the house of Israel (Matt. x.), furnishes a beautiful illustration of the true spirit of Christian service. From first to last it takes for granted the spirit of thorough consecration and unswerving trust. To men of worldly temper, who have no faith in spiritual forces, and to whom the idea of a supernatural fellowship with God is but a devout imagination, nothing could appear more Quixotic than the enterprise itself, and the weapons furnished for conducting it.

The first word is most significant—" He gave them power." Power in Christian work springs not from brilliant talents, nor careful culture, nor eminent scholarship, nor social position, nor the influence of the great, but from Christ alone. However useful such things may be as instruments, they have not an atom of spiritual power. The men of might in the Christian Church are the men who have much of the spirit of Christ. Furnished with power from Him, they may look down on those whose patronage is often counted such a benefit to their cause. For in truth, men of worldly rank and means are far more in need of a Church full of Christ's spirit than such a Church can be of them.

The message which He gave them to proclaim was, that the kingdom of heaven was at hand. It was a simple message, but based on one of our Lord's most favourite ideas—the coming together in the gospel of heaven and earth, the coming of heaven to earth, the transfusion into earth of the spirit of heaven. Such a message may well stimulate every preacher; for how should it raise his spirits and quicken his energies to remember that the enterprise in which he bears a part contemplates nothing less than the bringing this sin-stricken earth into contact with the spirit of heaven.

To illustrate the gracious purpose and tendency of their ministry, their message was to be accompanied by numberless works of beneficence. They were to heal the sick and raise the dead, to cleanse the lepers and cast out devils, and as they had freely received so they were freely to give. The gospel is not the threat of a creditor, nor the summons of a taskmaster; it is glad tidings of great joy. It bears gifts for the body, though its main inheritance is for the soul; it has the promise of the life that now is, as well as of that which is to come. Though supernatural power has ceased, this connection may still be maintained. If we cannot heal the sick by a word, we may do much for them through the medical missionary and the Christian nurse; if we cannot raise the dead, we may prolong the days of the living; if we cannot cleanse the leper, we may cleanse the cesspools of moral and physical corruption; if we cannot cast out devils, we may assail forms of vice which turn men and women into demons. Our preaching should be in close connection with all that tends to lighten the burdens and brighten the life of humanity. Where there is a grim and hard indifference to every human interest even the gospel message fails to win.

In the charge of our Lord to His apostles, the most conspicuous topic of all is the opposition they would have to encounter. For that opposition, and for all the effects of it, He strives to nerve them, especially by infusing the spirit of serene trust— of a holy regard for Him, and a holy regardlessness of all that might be against them. If they found themselves like sheep in the midst of wolves, they were to remember that it was He who had placed them there. And the heart of the Father was the same to them as that of Jesus. "Are not two sparrows sold for a farthing, and not one of them shall fall to the ground without your Father? But the very hairs of your head are all numbered. Fear not, therefore; ye are of more value than many sparrows." The spirit of trust is one of those attainments that are difficult because they are so simple. It seems so reasonable that we should trust God; it is often so hard to do it. Yet no spirit is so strong as trust, or so rich in blessing. Childlike in itself, it breeds heroes, and it is equally sublime in the highest officers and in the humblest servants of the kingdom.

And out of trust comes the spirit of patient endurance. It was a long time of trial they would have, but victory was sure in the end. "Ye shall be hated of all men for my name's sake; but he that endureth to the end, the same shall be saved."

Meanwhile, they must be courageous and resolute. It is a fearless confession of Christ that becomes His servants. This is the characteristic feature of the whole charge, and if we claim to be successors of the apostles we must respond to this call. If Christ has any right to be our Master He may well claim our supreme homage and confidence. "He that loveth father or mother more than me is not worthy of me; and he that loveth son or daughter more than me is not worthy of me. And he that taketh not his cross and followeth after me is not worthy of me. He that findeth his life shall lose it, and he that loseth his life for my sake shall find it."

The charge to the twelve recalls the song of Deborah, with the scorn she poured on the lazy tribes, and her blessing on the brave. " Why abodest thou among the sheepfolds, to hear the bleatings of the flocks ? Gilead abode beyond Jordan: and why did Dan remain in ships ? Asher continued on the sea-shore, and abode in his breaches. Zebulun and Naphtali were a people that jeoparded their lives unto the death in the high places of the field."

It was with this high military spirit that our Lord sought to inspire the twelve. With all His humility He spoke out frankly about Himself, and summoned them to a bearing worthy the followers of such a leader. The "higher criticism" may affirm that in the synoptic Gospels Jesus makes no such lofty claims for His person as are made in the fourth. But a profounder criticism will detect in the 10th chapter of Matthew's Gospel a claim and a challenge which cannot be surpassed. The person of Christ gives such power, dignity, and glory to His cause as to make a timid and sneaking tone disgraceful on the part of His officers. When the world comes to an end, and the awards of eternity are apportioned, the very smallest service done in His name will derive from its connection with Him a value and a glory unknown in any other field. It is the most certain of all future events that He shall reign from sea to sea, and from the river to the ends of the earth. A cause which brings the kingdom of heaven to earth; which scatters salvation and all other blessings wheresoever its banner comes; whose leader bears on His vesture and on His thigh the name "King of kings and Lord of lords;" and whose heroes and martyrs are to shine in heaven like the stars of the firmament, demands a manly and intrepid bearing on the part of every one who holds a commission from its Lord.

In the light of this ringing charge to the twelve, is not the ordinary tone and attitude of Christ's ministers somewhat too tame? Does it not want something of that spirit of firmness and fearlessness which is more characteristic perhaps of the piety of our soldiers and sailors when they come out on the Lord's side? We dare not overlook the military ring of this charge. All preaching, all mission work, all revival work, becomes telling when it has this warlike ring. This is the characteristic feature of all the Christian histories, biographies, speeches, and appeals which move men's hearts, and induce them, when the Master calls for labourers, to answer, "Here am I, send me."

CHAPTER XIV.

DEALINGS WITH THE TWELVE.

WHILE our Lord during His life did occasionally send out His apostles on special errands and with special instructions, His ordinary method of training them, as we have seen, was clinical rather than systematic. For the most part, He took them with Him, as He pursued His own course from city to city, and from hamlet to hamlet, and taught them how to do their work by showing them how He did His. They heard His discourses, they followed His discussions, they learned His views of sin and grace, of man and God, of the law and the gospel, of death and life; they saw His methods of angling, so to speak, His methods of dealing with various sorts of men; they heard His prayers, saw His miracles, and felt the magnetism of His presence, and the charm of His tenderness, grace, and humility.

But besides having His example to learn from, they were themselves the objects of a more direct training. In fact, the pastoral training of the twelve was one of the great objects of our Lord's public life. In many points of view, this fact is worthy of attention. It has an important bearing, for example, on the structure of the Gospels.

Sceptics have asked such questions as, How could the apostle John know what passed between Jesus and Nicodemus, when the interview was a secret one? How could he report the conversation with the woman at the well, when there were none but Jesus and the woman present? And they have concluded that these conversations, like Livy's speeches, must have been imaginary. But the explanation is obvious,—the disciples would be told all by Jesus. And Jesus had this special reason for telling them, that at the time he was training them how to deal with such very cases. Just as a doctor, going round the wards of a hospital with his students, would give them a history of any important case *up to the time of its being brought into the hospital;* so Jesus would most naturally inform His apostles what took place between Him and Nicodemus, or between Him and the woman at the well, in order that they might rightly understand the cases, and know how to act when similar cases should arise. In any due and comprehensive view of the purport of the four Gospels, it is never to be forgotten that, in addition to the other objects which He prosecuted, Jesus all the while was training the twelve.

And His success in this work was remarkable. No instruments seemed less adapted to their work than they were when our Lord first called them; certainly none were better fitted for it when He left them to continue what He had begun.

I. One very important branch of this training was designed to quicken the *spiritual apprehension* of the twelve: to make them quick in apprehending the truth of God, as that truth was contained in His word and illustrated by His providence, more particularly with reference to the objects for which He had come into the world.

Three stages are easily to be remarked in this course of training. The first and longest is that which occupies the chief part of the public ministry. The second, that which immediately precedes the last scenes, when we are repeatedly told, Jesus began to announce to the disciples that He was to be condemned and crucified; the third, that which immediately follows the resurrection, when He threw such light on the Scriptures, and especially on the Messianic elements contained in them. A fourth period might be stated,—that which was inaugurated by the mission of the Comforter after the resurrection. At first they could hardly be said even to see men as trees walking; at last, under the guidance of the Spirit, they were able to give clear and convincing explanations of saving truth. Yet even the most enlightened of apostles had to own that here we see through a glass darkly—indicating that the progression is not yet ended, and that by far the most remarkable advance in knowledge is yet to come.

In the earlier stages of our Lord's intercourse with the twelve, and in particular, during His Galilean ministry, He followed the lines which the prophets laid down, by seeking to enlighten them more fully in the spirituality and holiness of God, the superiority of the moral to the ceremonial element of obedience, and the supremacy of the spiritual element in all acceptable worship, and in all holy living. He laid down such positions in a more emphatic way than the prophets had done, bringing the spirituality of the kingdom of God into stronger and brighter relief. It was only after the spirituality of God, of His law, and of His worship was well established in their minds, that the apostles were prepared to be instructed in what was more peculiarly characteristic of the new dispensation, and especially in the coming humiliation and death of their Master, and the purpose which was thus to be served. Had this strange aspect of their Lord's career been announced to them bluntly at the beginning, it would probably have utterly stupefied and confounded them. Their spirituality of view, their faith, their belief in the predominance of the spiritual over the sensible, would not have been strong enough to bear it. As it was, the announcement of what was at hand was almost too much for them. Peter opposed it with all his usual vehemence. But Jesus put Peter firmly down, and the purpose of the coming death came to be understood and appreciated. But their prejudices were not wholly removed until the third stage of their progress—that which took place under Christ's teaching, when He opened their eyes after the resurrection. So much was found in the law and the prophets and the psalms, showing that Christ must suffer, that the stumbling-block of the cross was then entirely removed. The more we think of this result in the case of the twelve, the more marvellous does Christ's influence on them appear. The history of the world presents no case in which prejudices were so completely removed,

Q

and views, new to the recipients, but old in their sources, so successfully implanted, and endowed with such living power. And all this achieved without anything like rebellion, or schism, or separation, so that after the resurrection, with the exception of Judas, who fell away on other grounds, Christ's views of the kingdom, as well as of the old economy, held complete possession of them all.

II. In a more directly spiritual line of influence we see how our Lord trained the apostles to steady, unwavering trust in Him, as the great Head of the kingdom, and as the fountain of all the grace, strength, and blessing which it dispensed.

It was in order that they might make a right use of the stores that were treasured in Him that He was so earnest in desiring that they should have true views of His person. Very different from the egotistical vanity that delights in the incense of admiration was the spirit in which He asked, "Whom do men say that I, the Son of man, am?" And as far removed from the complacent self-importance of a vain man acknowledging a compliment was his congratulation when Peter said, "Thou art the Christ, the Son of the living God," —" Blessed art thou, Simon Bar-jona, for flesh and blood hath not revealed it unto thee, but my Father which is in heaven." That in Him dwelleth all the fulness of the Godhead bodily—that we are complete in Him who is the Head of all principality and power—that out of His fulness all we receive, and grace for grace—were truths of the most vital importance, in which it behoved the apostles to be thoroughly indoctrinated. To this end many of the miracles were directed, in so far as their effect on the apostles was concerned. The raising of Lazarus, for example, was not meant merely to attest his power, far less was it a mere act of kindness to a bereaved and beloved family, but emphatically it was designed to show to the disciples the vastness of Christ's resources, not merely in the world of the living, but even in the realms of the dead.

So also the miracle of walking on the sea, and the miracle of hushing the winds and the waves. Before such stupendous exhibitions of power, all the tricks of magic, all the mysteries of legerdemain were as nothing and vanity. But our Lord's desire through them was not to be admired or wondered at, but trusted. Needless though it was in Peter to ask leave to come to Him on the waters, still it was an act of trust, and as such the request was granted. But Peter's trust was feeble and flickering, and the cry of terror soon came from his sinking heart. But even that cry of terror brought a new manifestation of gracious power, and a new proof how worthy He was of implicit trust. When our Lord asked, "Will ye also go away?" the most gratifying feature of Peter's answer was its expression of trust—" Lord, to whom shall we go ? thou hast the words of eternal life." When the disciples came to Him with the request, "Lord, increase our faith," He took the opportunity to enlarge their horizon in that direction to the very furthest bound—" If ye had faith as a grain of mustard seed, ye might say unto this sycamine tree, Be thou plucked up by the root, and be thou planted in the sea; and it should obey you."

In His farewell address, one of the points which He most elaborately and strongly urged was the necessity of abiding in Him, a point illustrated very expressively by the similitude of the vine and the branches. And the whole tone and tenor of that address goes to commend the spirit of trust. No doubt it seemed at first that all had been said in vain. Where was their faith when "all the disciples forsook him and fled"? But an army may give way in a moment of panic, and yet in a little while be rallied for noble service. And though the faith of the apostles gave way for the moment, the subsequent rally was very glorious. The long training and many prayers of the Master were not lost after all.

In this connection we naturally single out the cases of two of the apostles with whom our Lord had very special dealings in reference to their faith in Him—Peter and Thomas. Referring to Peter's confidence in his own strength, but real weakness, Jesus said, "I have prayed for thee, that thy faith fail not." Some might have thought it more appropriate to pray that his courage might not fail, since courage was the attribute that would be specially tried. But in our Lord's view faith was more important than courage. That Peter should have a profound impression that Jesus Christ was the Head of the kingdom of heaven, and the only fountain of salvation and blessing, and that he should be brought into the habit of clinging to

Christ, and drawing from Him by faith accordingly, was more for the apostle's own good, and for his usefulness in the Church than that he should have an enlarged supply of courage, whether physical or moral. And when the crisis came after the ascension, it was Peter's faith that carried the Church through—a faith summed up in his memorable utterance: " Neither is there salvation in any other: for there is none other name given under heaven among men whereby we must be saved."

The Christian Church has always been profoundly touched by the manner of Peter's restoration to office after his great fall. It took place at the Sea of Galilee, after a second miracle of a multitudinous draught of fish, similar to that when Jesus had said to him, " Henceforth thou shalt catch men." There was no need to inquire now whether Peter had faith. He could not but have faith. But it was desirable to inquire whether he had something more, something that springs from faith, but is more than faith—whether he had that personal love to Christ that would give the true tone and flavour to his work in the Church. We observe, however, that though faith was not the object of inquiry, the grace sought for was still one of which Jesus Himself was the immediate object. It was really an inquiry as to whether in Peter's heart Christ held the place of supreme regard, and whether Peter was prepared, not only to look to Him for all His supplies of grace, but to go forward to his duty in the Church simply as His servant and deputy. If there had lurked in Peter's mind a vestige of any independent ambition—if he had not been prepared in simple reliance on Christ, and out of love to Him, to accept the charge to which he was called, he would not have had the foremost place in laying the foundation of the Christian Church.

In the case of Thomas, unbelief had got the hold which it sometimes obtains of a very honest but scrupulous heart which is really longing to believe, but which fancies that it must have evidence not merely sufficient but demonstrative. Like Jacob, when told that his son Joseph was alive and governor of Egypt, he could not at first take in such blessed intelligence. How Jesus overcame the unbelief of Thomas is one of the most beautiful incidents of the post-resurrection history. But all these incidents and observations go to establish the infinite importance, in order to ministerial efficiency, of a right view of the Saviour's person, and a lively condition of the graces that grasp Him, and lean on Him, and draw from Him. The object of all the training which the disciples underwent in relation to Christ's person may be gathered from two sayings—one, Christ's own, the other, His apostle's: "Without me, ye can do nothing;" "through Christ strengthening me, I can do all things."

III. In His training of the twelve, we find our Lord very careful to wean them from certain carnal views and habits natural enough to the human heart, but utterly opposed to efficiency in the service of the gospel.

The most serious of these carnal views, and that

which was most frequently cropping up, was love of pre-eminence—desire for greatness in the kingdom of Christ. Now it is a dispute among themselves which of them shall be greatest; now it is a request of the mother of James and John that they may sit on His right hand and His left when He comes in His glory; now it is a question, put in apparent honesty, Who is the greatest in the kingdom of heaven? That such a spirit should have prevailed, and that such questions should have been put, must have been deeply trying to our Lord. That after the example He had set of profoundest self-renunciation; after the way He had met the Tempter, when he offered Him all the kingdoms of the world and the glory of them; after all His endeavours, by life and lesson alike, to teach humility and self-denial; after all His efforts to inspire them with higher aims and nobler purposes of life, they should still be squabbling about pre-eminence and worldly honour, was an experience fitted to try the most patient heart, and to disappoint the least sanguine teacher.

There were two forms which this temper assumed —first, a general craving for distinction and pre-eminence before men as the result of their connection with Christ; and second, a particular craving for pre-eminence one over another within the sacred enclosure of His Church. Both of these tendencies our Lord discouraged to the utmost. In regard to the first, the craving for worldly honour and distinction, He showed it to be utterly unworthy of the children of heaven. It was entirely opposed to the order of His kingdom. The greatest there was the servant of all. Honour there did not come from what one got, but from what one gave. Humility, self-repression, devotion to the welfare of others, were the great sources of distinction in His kingdom. The Son of man had not come to be ministered unto but to minister, and to give His life a ransom for many. The servant was not above his Master, nor the disciple above his Lord. The high and haughty temper of the world could find no place in the kingdom of heaven. Whosoever would enter that kingdom must become a little child; guilelessness, simplicity, transparency, humility, were the true marks and tokens of its members.

In regard to the spirit of James and John, and others who desired pre-eminence over their brethren, our Lord was equally decided. The government of His kingdom was to be not lordly but brotherly. One Lord they had, but only one. One Master alone was entitled to prescribe their course. Their consultations and church assemblies were to be carried on with a clear recognition of His supreme authority, and with the single object of finding out His will. Calm brotherly consultation and prayer were the means for ascertaining that will. Meetings of this kind would not want Divine authority and control: "Lo, I am with you alway, even to the end of the world."

How needful are these counsels of our Lord in every age! How prone is the love of pre-eminence to show itself; how impatient are many of the dull level of equality, and eager for places of artificial elevation above their brethren! How continually and earnestly watchful faithful ministers, especially those conscious of the higher gifts, would need to be against this tendency! What constant supplies they would need from Christ Himself to keep down self at every corner of their path, and make them abound in the charity that seeketh not her own!

It is to be observed, however, that in a sense our Lord did recognise inequalities among His servants. Three of His apostles, Peter, James, and John, were honoured with an especial share of His confidence and affection. Two of them, John and Peter, had special tokens of superior consideration, the one in being the disciple whom Jesus loved, the other in being recognised as the leader of the band. For Jesus did to this extent acknowledge the pre-eminence of Peter. "Simon, Simon, Satan hath desired to have you ($ὑμᾶς$, *plural*, the whole band), that he may sift you ($ὑμᾶς$) as wheat: but I have prayed for thee (*singular*), that thy faith fail not: and when thou art converted, strengthen thy brethren." Undoubtedly the Lord singled out the natural leader of the band for special prayer and a special charge in the hour of deadly trial. If the leader could be kept from falling away the rest would be saved. But the pre-eminence which our Lord thus acknowledged was simply the pre-eminence of natural gifts and spiritual grace. It is the kind of pre-eminence that shows itself by capacity for difficult and it may be unpopular service; by readiness to labour, by skill and tact and success in overcoming difficulties, and building up the cause of Christ. But it is one thing to acknowledge such pre-eminence, and allow it its natural sphere of successful exercise; and it is another thing to create offices of pre-eminence without Christ's warrant, and accumulate power, honour, and rank upon those who fill them. All this is foreign to the spirit of Christ's instructions. It springs from the carnal policy which He was so eager to discourage. One ambition only is worthy of Christ's disciples—to follow in the footsteps of the Master, who came not to be ministered unto but to minister, and to give His life a ransom for many. As time rolls on, and the clouds of fashion and prejudice are scattered, the names that shine brightest in the Christian firmament are the names of those who have surrendered all worldly distinctions and comforts, and consecrated themselves most thoroughly to the service of Christ and of humanity. Names like that of Livingstone in Africa, Burns in China, and Patteson in the South Sea Islands, are for ever acquiring a new lustre in all Christian eyes —are shining out with a ray that more and more resembles that of the "bright and morning star." How miserable, in the light of such lives, is the spirit that schemes, and longs, and labours for worldly distinction in the Church of Christ! "O my soul, come not thou into their secret; unto their assembly, mine honour, be not thou united!"

IV. One other general feature we notice in our Lord's method of training the twelve,—His desire to enlarge their views, to deliver them from all that was mean and petty, and make them in these respects worthy children of their Father who was in heaven.

Small enough, in all conscience, the views and

spirit of the apostles sometimes were. Even James and John, two of the *élite*, were narrow enough in their proposal that they should command fire to come down from heaven and consume the village of the Samaritans that would not receive Him. " But he turned and rebuked them, and said, Ye know not what manner of spirit ye are of. For the Son of man is not come to destroy men's lives, but to save them." Was ever a fuller meaning packed into words so few, or was ever a nobler direction given to hearts that had been trailing in low and unwholesome levels? How unworthy it would have been of the Son of man to show irritation at a personal affront, and forget His noble mission in the ignoble desire to destroy those who had annoyed Him! Doubtless He might have found precedents in abundance in the doings of kings and conquerors without number, in whose eyes the greatest of all offences has been to thwart their projects and refuse them homage. How much higher the ambition of Christ, how much higher the ambition to which He would urge His servants, to be ready to pass by personal slights and offences in the absorbing desire to save immortal souls; to brush aside in this spirit the petty affronts of which little men are ready to make so much, as a great surgeon would disregard the stinging reproaches of an excited patient, on whose person he was performing an operation mercifully designed to relieve his suffering and to save his life!

So, also, when John reported to Jesus that they had seen one casting out devils in His name, and they forbade him because he followed not with them

—"Jesus said unto him, Forbid him not, for he that is not against us is for us." His mind soars high beyond the littleness of sectarianism, beyond the interests of the denomination, even beyond the interests of orderly and authorised procedure. In a world groaning under the tyranny of Satan, He rejoices to hear of any one who is working to set captives free. The thought of their good fills His soul; other interests are petty and unworthy in comparison of this grand result, the eternal salvation of men.

But all through His public life, and all through His intercourse with the twelve, Jesus showed a largeness of heart which was alike grand in itself and elevating in its influence. Peter comes to Him to ask a question and to suggest an answer: "Lord, how oft shall my brother trespass against me and I forgive him? Until seven times?" Evidently Peter has some complacency in this very generous proposal. But how utterly is it eclipsed by the soaring reply of the Master: "I say not unto thee, Until seven times, but until seventy-times seven"! And this sublime quality of the Divine forgiveness is illustrated by the debtor whose lord forgave him the debt of ten thousand talents, as well as by the father of the prodigal son, who forgives him heart and soul, and loads him with tokens of his unchangeable affection. A lawyer asks Him, Who is my neighbour? He gets his answer in the parable of the good Samaritan,—in a tale of bountiful beneficence which left no want unsatisfied, and no suffering unsolaced. If we inquire into the quality of His miracles, we find in the feeding of the multitude and in the miraculous draught of fishes—miracles that were each repeated—evidence of the same largeness of heart, a heart that liked to be beneficent on a princely scale. When we see Him among the sick, there goes virtue out of Him that heals them all. When He surveys the toils and sufferings of humanity, the offers to which He is prompted are offers of unlimited richness: " Come unto me, all ye that labour, and are heavy laden, and I will give you rest." " He that drinketh of this water shall thirst again; but he that drinketh of the water that I shall give him shall never thirst; but the water that I shall give him shall be in him a well of water springing up unto life everlasting." When John the Baptist sends his messengers to make that strange inquiry of Jesus, " Art thou he that should come, or look we for another?" it is pleasing to Jesus to be able to give His answer in words that denote the amplitude of the blessings which He dispenses: " The blind receive their sight, and the lame walk, the lepers are cleansed, and the deaf hear, the dead are raised up, and the poor have the gospel preached to them." When He sends forth the twelve to prepare His way, they are to scatter a whole cornucopia of blessings: " Heal the sick, cleanse the lepers, raise the dead, cast out devils; freely ye have received, freely give." The woman that was a sinner is forgiven all; the thief on the cross is promised that he would be that day with Christ in paradise; Peter is reinstated without a word of reproach; Thomas is taken on his own terms, and restored like a wandering star to his orbit. Finally, when the apostles get their last commission, it is in these sublime words:

"Go ye into all the world, and preach the gospel to every creature."

This grandeur of view and largeness of beneficent aim on the part of Jesus Christ is a very remarkable feature. On the part of one sprung from the lower class of the people, accustomed to the hard lines and scrimp supplies of poverty, who to all appearance had no resources of His own with which to devise liberal things, this imperial generosity, this world-wide beneficence, denoted one higher than the children of men. Would that the same feature were ever reflected by His Church, both in its collective capacity and in its individual membership! Let us at least try to cherish the thought that narrowness of view and poverty of aim and expectation are not in keeping with the bearing of Him who, having bought His Church with His blood, seeks to endow her with all His possessions, and to bless her with all spiritual blessings. Let us rise above the pettiness of mere denominational interests, as if the great thing were to keep all we can for ourselves and our brethren, or to benefit one section of the Church, no matter what happens to the rest. Would that, among other gifts, our ascended Lord would give us that spirit of princely spiritual munificence which spreads its blessings over the whole world,—that nobility of soul which is never weary of forbearing and forgiving,—that catholicity of heart which looks not every one on its own things, but every man also on the things of others; that loyalty to our Lord and Saviour which will never be satisfied until there is heard the voice of many angels round about the throne, and the living creatures and the elders, the number of them ten thousand times ten thousand, and thousands of thousands, saying with a loud voice, " Worthy is the Lamb that was slain to receive power, and riches, and wisdom, and strength, and honour, and glory, and blessing!"

CHAPTER XV.

DEALINGS WITH DIFFERENT CLASSES.

I.—THOSE OUTSIDE THE KINGDOM.

THE point which we now reach in the survey of our Lord's ministry is one of great practical importance. For the great object of the Christian ministry is to deal with all classes of men, in order to bring men into the kingdom of God, and to transform their character once they are there. Our labour is vain if we fail to turn men from darkness to light, and from the power of Satan unto God, and to carry them on from stage to stage in the life of faith and holiness. How did our blessed Master go about this work? Did He use the same method with all sorts and conditions of men? If not, how and on what principles did He vary His method? These questions will afford us materials for very interesting and profitable practical study.

The first and most memorable thing to be noted in connection with our Lord's pastoral dealings with different classes is His habit of ranking His hearers in two great divisions, between whom there was a most vital difference. Many instances of this will occur to every one familiar with the Gospels. It is quite natural that Matthew, who of all the Evangelists had the keenest eye for contrasts, should record the greatest number of them. It is remarkable, too, that before noting this feature in our Lord's ministry, he should have noted it in John the Baptist's, or rather, should have recorded John's forecast of the searching nature of the ministry of Jesus: " Whose fan is in his hand, and he will throughly purge his floor, and gather the wheat into his garner; but the chaff he will burn up with unquenchable fire."

Accordingly, in the Sermon on the Mount, the two classes are represented by the two *gates*, the two *ways*, and the two *endings*—life and destruction. The same division is made in the summing up of the discourse, where the hearers are either like the wise builders that built on the rock, or the foolish that built on the sand. So of the Ten Virgins, five are wise and five are foolish; and the difference is anything but trivial; the wise are admitted into the palace, the foolish are irretrievably shut out. The parable of the Talents recognises, though less formally, the same division: some improve their talents and are rewarded, others wickedly and slothfully neglect them and are punished. So, likewise, in the parable of the Sower; part of the seed, through various causes, is lost, part of it bears fruit in varying degrees.

But of all forms in which Christ taught this truth, the most solemn and impressive is the parable of the Sheep and the Goats. The great assembly here divided into two is not limited to those that heard Christ personally, but embraces " all nations." It is not easy to determine the precise application of this parable. But the division of the whole into two parts is as complete as when a shepherd divides his sheep from the goats. The criterion of judgment is remarkable—the presence or the absence of practical sympathy towards the brethren of Christ in their times of distress. The final issue is described in terms of simple but awful distinctness: "These shall go away into everlasting punishment, but the righteous into life eternal."

It cannot be disputed, that as our Lord looked over the people that listened to His discourses, there was ever before His mind this notion of the twofold division and the final twofold destiny. It was a most solemn and impressive thought, and doubtless it had a great influence in quickening His ardour and intensifying His appeals. Yet, naturally, it is a thought far from pleasant, either to the people or to the preacher. That there should be only two paths from this world to eternity, and that the one should issue in life and the other in destruction, is a truth anything but welcome to the human mind. Human nature, in such a case, makes a desperate effort to find a *tertium quid*. Many who have no reason to believe that they have entered in at the strait gate, cannot bring themselves to think that they are walking on the road to destruction. They would fain find a third path, not quite so narrow as the one, and not quite so broad as the other, and leading up, not to absolute life or absolute destruction, but to something between. It is this desperate reluctance of men to accept our Lord's alternative that makes purgatory so attractive in the Church of Rome. The idea that our state for ever and ever is to be finally determined by our conduct in this short life and in this feeble condition of being, is very unpopular, and men are ready to grasp a straw in the hope of extending the probation. Liberal theology sets aside this outstanding feature of our Lord's teaching, makes all characters to shade off, by minute touches, into one another, and finds accommodation for all, sooner or later, in the house of many mansions. But what right have we to set aside in this manner the great lesson of our Master? If we make so much as a pretence to fidelity, must we not teach precisely as He taught, especially in a matter of such vital importance?

Yet nothing could be more miserable than to follow Him here in the letter, as some do, without following Him in the spirit. Men that have heaven and hell for ever on their lips are not always men whose hearts tremble at the awfulness of the difference. Preachers who realise profoundly that every member of their audience is travelling to the one place or to the other, will not be glib and easy in their references to them; the effect of their profound conviction will come out more in the intense reality and earnestness both of their preaching and their prayers, and in the directness and fervour of their appeals to their hearers at once to accept the offers made so graciously to them in the Gospel.

Proceeding, then, on this great division of the two classes of hearers, let us go on to point out the differences in our Lord's method of dealing with the various kinds of men and women that lay on either side the line.

I. THOSE OUTSIDE THE KINGDOM.

In His dealings with this class, the most important difference was, His treatment of openly lost sinners on the one hand, and of respectable but self-righteous, and therefore non-justified persons on the other.

I. His treatment of the openly lost was one of the most striking features of His whole ministry. It brought on Him the scorn of those who were incapable of understanding a noble deed. He was nicknamed "the friend of publicans and sinners." It was uttered against Him as a reproach—"This man receiveth sinners." It was even believed by one that was friendly to Him, Simon the leper, that had He been a prophet He would have disdained the homage of the woman that was a sinner. Such persons could not appreciate the spirit that longs to save the lost, nor see that a nature so pure as Christ's stood in no more danger of defilement from personal contact with the guiltiest of the race, than the sunbeam that falls on the dunghill.

The cases in which Jesus showed kindly consideration for persons steeped in guilt were,—some real, and one imaginary. Of the former was the case of the woman of Samaria; that of the woman taken in adultery; that of the woman that was a sinner; and that of the thief on the cross. The imaginary case was that of the Prodigal Son. It is to be observed of these cases, that the persons concerned were not all roaming and rioting in the pleasures of sin; most of them had been brought to bay either by the law of the country, or the circumstances of their position; so that, in a sense, they were subdued. In all of them our Lord seems to have apprehended a similar state of feeling; a hopelessness of regaining their lost character and earthly position, far less the favour of God, *through any power inherent in themselves or in those who were around them;* as far as any resources of their own were concerned, they were consciously lost. If anything was to be made of such persons it must be by leading them *to look away from themselves,* and giving them an impressive sight of God's blessed provision for saving the lost. Sometimes our Lord formally unfolded the provision of grace; but more frequently he conveyed the sense of it in a less formal way. To the woman of Samaria, He said, "*If thou knewest the gift of God,* and who it is that saith to thee, Give me to drink, thou wouldest have asked of him, and he would have given thee living water." Here was a direct proclamation of God's saving grace; but usually it was made known less directly. The truth is, the whole of Christ's earthly career, and especially His miracles of healing, were exhibitions of the grace of God. If you ask, Why did not our Lord *preach* grace more? Why did He not deliver more addresses corresponding to the evangelistic addresses of to-day? the answer is, —He *lived* grace. His whole life was a sermon of grace. The tenderness of His spirit, the readiness of His sympathy, the cordiality of His manner, the frankness and freeness of His cures, the fervour of His invitations, the heavenliness of His life, were all exhibitions of Divine love, and were thus the means of rekindling hope where its lamp had long been extinguished, and where nothing remained but the blackness of despair. The very sight of Christ, the interest which He took in the fallen, the very looks He cast on them, appear in some instances to have kindled a new sense of heavenly goodness, and a new faith in the possibility of restoration to pardon and to purity, when the dire experience of lust raging within, and the cold frown of the respectable world without, had quenched all faith in either.

Some of these lost sinners seem first to have been drawn to Christ by a spirit of vague, wistful wonder, with something of the feeling of the woman who said, " If I may but touch the hem of his garment, I shall be made whole." What made the woman that was a sinner wash Christ's feet with her tears, and wipe them with the hairs of her head? She had not been forgiven at the time; but having seen and heard Christ, having perhaps heard some of His parables of grace, she appears to have felt the beating of a long-lost hope in her bosom—felt that so gracious a Being was able and probably willing to raise even her up from the horrible pit and the miry clay, to fulfil to her the promise in Hosea, giving her the valley of Achor for a door of hope, and making her—poor *blasée* creature though she was— to sing as in the days of her youth. When such as she entered into communication with Christ, belief in heavenly grace had already begun to dawn, but vaguely and dimly; what they needed was, confirmation of their flickering trust, a solid foundation for hope and peace. It was this He gave to the woman that was a sinner—" Be of good cheer, thy sins be forgiven thee:" and to the thief on the cross —" Verily I say unto thee, To-day shalt thou be with me in paradise." The glimpse of grace which they had got when yet afar off, and which they had cherished so lovingly, was changed into a nearer and most satisfying view. Their cry from the depths was answered by the assurance of plenteous redemption; and with the pulse of a new life beating in their veins, and the hope of glory brightening their future, they lifted up their heads, and went on their way rejoicing.

The pastoral lesson that comes from this for dealing with the lowest samples of humanity, when subdued and brought to bay by the evil tenor of their lives, is obvious. In the like circumstances, a similar experience, a similar despair of getting out of the mire of sin has often been felt. Probably there was a reason why so many of these cases, recorded in the Gospels, were cases of abandoned women. For when a woman loses herself in sensual vice, or other gross criminality, the ruin is more thorough, and the hope of recovery is much less than in the case of men. The devil can make shorter work with the weaker sex. Christian ladies who, in visiting prisons and penitentiaries, have become intimately acquainted with criminal women, have often remarked in them a peculiarly hard, reckless, hopeless state of mind. To awaken in them any longing for a better life, or any belief in its reality, or in the possibility of attaining it, has often been most difficult. But it has been strongly felt that the first step towards restoration must be to inspire them with faith in the reality and possibility of recovery, and of a better life. And it has been very interesting to observe cases in which the very beauty and purity of the visitor's own spirit, her unwearied love and patience in seeking the poor prisoner's good, was the first step towards that prisoner's reformation. It broke up the hard crust of scepticism; it broke down the hard rebellious spirit that refused to believe in the existence of goodness; it dissipated the gloomy suspicion that had persisted in ascribing even the labour of love to some unknown form of self-seeking. And this dawn of faith in the reality of human sympathy proved a blessed stepping-stone to faith in the goodness and sympathy of the Divine Redeemer, for the goodness of the lady-visitor was but a drop derived from the great ocean, a reflected ray of the great Sun of Righteousness. It was easier after this to lead the thoughts to the fountain for sin and uncleanness, opened for the house of David and the inhabitants of Jerusalem. The life of Jesus came to have a reality unknown before, and the doctrine of redemption through His blood began to be viewed with the eagerness of a personal interest. Wherever our aim is to inspire faith in the reality of the Divine goodness nothing is more important than that our own spirit and our own bearing should form steps towards the great conclusion. And wherever men and women seem hopelessly sunk in sin, the first step towards their recovery is when they see that in no sense is it from within, but wholly from without, from the goodness and grace of God revealed in Christ, that their deliverance must come.

II. Very different was our Lord's treatment of the self-righteous. While to the consciously lost and hopeless He brought near the grace of a forgiving God,—to the consciously righteous He applied the test of a holy law. But we must discriminate between two classes embraced in the term self-righteous, for it included hypocrites, living in sin, but observant of all the ceremonies of religion; as well as a class of sincere, respectable men, who thought that, on the whole, they fulfilled all that was required by the law.

In reference to the former, the perverted Pharisees, whose notion of righteousness was limited to ceremonial observances, and who outraged the law in its weightier obligations, the attitude of our Lord was that of stern rebuke and indignant denunciation. We often feel surprised at the tremendous severity of the tone in which He inveighed against them. We must remember His remarkable insight into the human heart—a circumstance which makes His example applicable to us in but a limited degree. Still, the impression remains on our minds that there must be cases in which even for us the proper mode of dealing with sin is that of stern and crushing rebuke. There are cases in medicine where the true treatment is to administer a shock; and there are similar cases in spiritual disease. It is evident that religious hypocrisy was surpassingly odious to Christ. For men to imagine that God could find satisfaction in a round of ceremonies while judgment, mercy, and truth were trampled on, was a fearful insult to the God of holiness. Such a spirit implied a terrible moral levity—the levity that could degrade the holiest things of God, and trample them under the feet of men. In such a state of mind our Lord could discover no ground for that faith whose very nature it is to look up to the High and Holy One, to whom it owes all reverence and submission. To speak of the love and grace of God to such would only have been to cast pearls before swine; the only way to do them real good was to shell them, as it were, out of their position, to hurl woe upon woe against them, if perchance they might be terrified into belief in a righteous Judge, and seeing their condition begin to ask, What must we do to be saved?

It was in this way that our Lord taught His ministers most emphatically that though they were to be ministers of grace and reconciliation, yet the reproof of sin would ever be a most essential though a very difficult part of their office. "Every part of the duty of a minister," says a distinguished writer, "is more easy than to maintain in vigour the spirit he needs as the reprover of sin, and the guardian of virtue."[1] Our Lord left men in no doubt what He thought of sin. The denunciations of it which He uttered were really what cost Him His life. And when Peter followed Him on the day of Pentecost and other days, he was equally explicit. He arraigned his hearers as murderers of the Prince of Life. He made no mystery of what they deserved. And then, when their anxious faces and cries of distraction showed that his words had told—that they were subdued and brought to bay, he brought out for them, as it were, that grace of God which is so rich and free to every penitent, and he promised them all the blessings of redemption through the blood of the very man whom they had crucified and slain.

[1] *Saturday Night*, by Isaac Taylor, p. 183.

The other class of self-righteous persons with whom our Lord dealt were respectable men, without hypocrisy, but who had a higher opinion of themselves than they ought to have had. The young ruler, who believed that from his youth he had kept all the commandments, was one of these. So also were some to whom the first part of the Sermon on the Mount was addressed—persons who did not know that "unless their righteousness exceeded that of the scribes and Pharisees, they could in no wise enter into the kingdom of God." In dealing with such persons, Christ's method was to show the searching nature of the Divine law, and for this end He showed them that the law imposed a test which human nature could not endure. He showed that the word of God was quick and powerful, sharper than a two-edged sword, dividing even between the joints and marrow, and that it was a discerner of the hearts of men. A lascivious look is adultery, a savage feeling is murder. This is the way to deal with respectable formalism. The spirituality of God's nature, and the corresponding spirituality of His law, show how hopeless it is to expect salvation by works. He that sets our iniquities before Him, our secret sins in the light of His countenance; He that desires truth in the inward parts, who is of purer eyes than to behold iniquity, and who cannot look upon sin, has a far higher standard of judgment than most suppose. The law by its very nature is law; it knows no relaxation and no indulgence; if once its condemnation falls upon you, "thou shalt in no wise come out thence till thou hast paid the uttermost farthing."

III. A third class of persons outside the kingdom with whom our Lord had often to deal were cavillers,—persons who sneered in their hearts at His doctrine, and tried to trip Him up before the people. It was one of the most memorable features of His ministry, that He was always so ready for this class, and that He so uniformly succeeded in turning their position, and in making their very cavils the occasion of utter defeat. This shows the thoroughness of His composure, and the marvellous discipline of His mind and command of His faculties. It may likewise be regarded as an indication of God's readiness to give special and peculiar help to those who in the course of their duty are exposed to such cavils. Missionaries to the heathen, and labourers at home who come in contact with freethinkers, may find invaluable hints in our Lord's method of dealing with this class. Among His various ways of meeting them, we may note the following:—

1. Appeals to the paramount authority of *Scripture*,—the cavillers in this case being persons who admitted that authority. Sometimes His appeal to Scripture was in the direct form, as when He said to the Sadducees, who wished to throw ridicule on the resurrection, "Ye do err, *not knowing the Scriptures* nor the power of God." Sometimes it was to a Scriptural example: "Have ye never read what David did, how he entered the temple, and did eat the shewbread, which it is not lawful for any but the priests to eat?"
2. Referring the thing objected to to *an admitted principle*, which He sometimes brought for-

ward as a proverb, or at least as an admitted maxim of common sense. How could He cast out devils by Beelzebub, when common-sense might show them that no kingdom divided against itself could stand? His eating with publicans and sinners need not create surprise, since every one knew that "they that are whole need not a physician, but they that are sick." If His disciples did not adopt all the ways of life characteristic of the old economy, it was because no one of common-sense put new wine in old bottles, or a new patch on an old garment.
3. The *argumentum ad hominem:* "Which of you having an ox or an ass fallen into a pit on the sabbath day, doth he not straightway pull him out?"
4. *Making His hearers judges* in a supposed similar case, and thus getting them to condemn themselves. The parable of the Two Debtors is an example: it was put to Simon, who had been cavilling in his heart at Christ's treatment of the woman that was a sinner, whether the debtor that had been forgiven much, or the one who had been forgiven little, had most love; and when Simon gave his answer, the vindication of the woman, and of Jesus' treatment of her, was complete.
5. *Allegorical:* the principle being the same as in the last case, but no formal appeal for an answer being made to the objectors. In such allegories as the Prodigal Son and the Good Samaritan the point objected to is placed in

a peculiarly bright and convincing light, and the position of Christ vindicated so triumphantly, that the objectors seem annihilated—they are not to be found.

6. *Dramatic*, as when He set a child in the midst of the company, to show who should be greatest in the kingdom of God.

Perhaps the most instructive thing in our Lord's method of dealing with cavillers was His frequent practice of using their cavils as pegs on which to hang some of His most beautiful discourses. The parable of the Good Samaritan, for example, owed its birth to the question of a lawyer, " Who is my neighbour ? "—the object of the lawyer having been to tempt Him. Another act of derision, on the part of the Pharisees, gave rise to the parable of the Rich Man and Lazarus; and, to give but one other instance, that beautiful word to the young—the very charter of their standing in the kingdom of God—" Suffer little children to come unto me," was occasioned by the attempt of the disciples to hinder the parents from bringing their children to Him. This practice of our Lord's, of making man's captiousness a mint to coin heavenly treasure—of turning man's exhibitions of malice and evil into occasions for bringing forth the riches of Divine grace—of making heavenly wisdom spring from the soil of folly—was a very remarkable one, and might of itself have justified the saying, " Never man spake as this man." In nature nothing is more remarkable than the manner in which beauty springs from the womb of corruption; the rotten leaves of past years feed the plants and enlarge the produce of the future;

the very dunghill becomes the nursery of the choicest flowers, the most fragrant smells, and the most delicious fruits. The origin of evil has always been, and will continue to be, an inscrutable mystery; but that which throws most light on it is, the way in which the sin of man is made to illustrate the grace of God. The same thing is true of the use which our Lord made of the annoyances which He encountered so often in His work. The way in which these spurts of malice became occasions for the manifestation of surpassing wisdom and grace was typical of the grand culminating fact of Calvary, where the greatest crime that miscreants ever committed became the occasion of the most glorious act of love that God or man ever conceived.

IV. A fourth class of persons outside the kingdom with whom our Lord had dealings were those who remained unbelieving and impenitent, notwithstanding all that He said and did among them. Here, too, as in the case of the ungodly self-righteous, our Lord's language was very severe: " Woe unto thee, Chorazin! woe unto thee, Bethsaida! for if the mighty works, which were done in you, had been done in Tyre and Sidon, they would have repented long ago in sackcloth and ashes. But I say unto you, It shall be more tolerable for Tyre and Sidon at the day of judgment, than for you. And thou, Capernaum, which art exalted unto heaven, shalt be brought down to hell; for if the mighty works, which have been done in thee, had been done in Sodom, it would have remained until this day. But I say unto you, That it shall be more tolerable for the land of Sodom in the day of judgment than for thee." And again: "The men of Nineveh shall rise in judgment with this generation, and shall condemn it; because they repented at the preaching of Jonas; and, behold, a greater than Jonas is here. The queen of the south shall rise up in the judgment with this generation, and shall condemn it: for she came from the uttermost parts of the earth to hear the wisdom of Solomon; and, behold, a greater than Solomon is here."

The tone of rebuke in these passages is so similar to that of the words directed, as we have seen, against ungodly hypocrisy, as to lead us to conclude that, in the judgment of Christ, to trample on God's law and to reject God's Son are offences of equal magnitude. This is a conclusion that the world will not readily accept. To tread on the moral law, it is allowed, indicates a very disorderly nature, and to continue to do so against all remonstrance and call to repentance and reformation exposes one to just retribution. But declining to acknowledge the claims of Christ, and declining to receive salvation at His hands, are acts which many place in a very different category. What we are to think of Christ is matter of opinion, and it were hard to treat those who are not impressed by His claims as if they were thieves or liars. Against this it is enough to place the solemn judgment of Christ that Tyre and Sidon, and Sodom itself, were less guilty than Chorazin, Bethsaida, and Capernaum. The great sin of the latter cities was rejection of Christ; the older cities were full of scandalous sins, some of them sins of sensuality, outwardly the most stinking and offensive of all. But if the moral law is a reflection of the Divine attributes, and on that account worthy of our highest reverence, so also is the person of Jesus Christ. Rejection of Christ involves the same antagonism to God as the violation of His law: especially when Christ is rejected in such circumstances as those in which the Galilean cities rejected Him,—amid a blaze of miracles that might have convinced the most incredulous. To refuse to own Him thus, when He comes bringing salvation, argues an inveteracy of opposition betokening the carnal mind which is enmity against God.

One purpose of this tone of sharp rebuke in the case of unimpressed hearers, as in the case of godless formalists, was doubtless to startle them, and give them a last chance, as it were, of escaping the consequences of their guilt. There is nothing in our Lord's tone to indicate that sense of wounded vanity on His part which you often find in the rebukes of men ambitious of a popularity which they have not attained. In His severest reprimands we may note an undertone of compassion, the feeling that burst forth so as to overpower Him when He foretold the doom of Jerusalem,— Jerusalem that stoned the prophets and killed them that were sent to her. In most cases the tone is that of the righteous judge. If men sin wilfully after they "have received the knowledge of the truth, there remaineth no more sacrifice for sins, but a certain fearful looking for of judgment and fiery indignation, which shall devour the adversaries." It is an awful proof of the viciousness of sin that through the revelation of a Father's love and a Saviour's grace it is capable of being aggravated to greater degrees of criminality, and of leading on to a more fearful doom. Surely we may gather from this that no ministry can be faithful which does not solemnly reprove and warn all who refuse the Lord Jesus Christ. We must not be afraid to tell them what Christ declared, that the men of Nineveh will rise up in the judgment against them to condemn them. Our warnings, delivered in the right spirit, may be the means of startling them into repentance; anyhow, we shall dispel the delusion that the death of Christ justifies indifference to the real nature of sin, or that there is any way but that of personal acceptance of Him, and continual communion with Him, by which we may flee from the wrath to come.

CHAPTER XVI.

DEALINGS WITH DIFFERENT CLASSES.

II.—THOSE ON THE BORDERS OF THE KINGDOM.

It is no wonder that the supernatural powers of Jesus, His popularity as a teacher, the boldness of His tone, and the originality of His thoughts drew great multitudes after Him. In these multitudes were persons of all possible degrees of spiritual earnestness, between a mere vague curiosity at the one extreme, and an intense desire for salvation at the other. Many might be described as just hovering about the gate of the kingdom, not always conscious of their motives, but accessible to Christ's influence, and receiving from Him the treatment which He deemed most suitable for their case. In this chapter we are to consider some of these cases. How did our Lord deal with those who had some desire to follow Him, but whose minds were not made up; or how did He deal with those who had a genuine desire to be members of His kingdom, but needed guidance and encouragement to fix their choice?

I. The first remark suggested by these questions is, that our Lord, in various ways, signified His dislike to a mixed multitude of followers,—a mere conglomerate of so-called disciples, not bound together any more than they were bound to Him by any spiritual tie. He had none of that weak complacency in mere numbers, which in these days of statistics and social rivalry among churches are often exalted far above their true worth. When people came to Him through inferior motives, He did not repel them absolutely, as we shall see. He sought to raise them to a higher point of view; but He did not encourage such motives, and He was by no means satisfied when they rose no higher. It seems to have been because the mere fame of His miracles brought this unsatisfactory kind of people too much about Him that after performing a cure He so often added the injunction: "See thou tell no man." Sometimes, when the proportion of this kind of people was too large, He would take steps to thin their ranks, either by going up into a mountain, or by crossing over to the other side of the lake. When He did see multitudes under some kind of genuine anxiety, He was moved with compassion towards them; yet He evidently felt that it was not the best employment of His strength to work among a mass. By drawing a few men and women together, who, being filled with His spirit, should be living disciples, He would in the end convey a far better impression of the kingdom, and draw men more effectually towards it, than by having a great crowd of nominal followers, most of them with a name to live, but really dead. "Fear not, little flock," He said, "for it is your Father's good pleasure to give you the kingdom." Their being a little flock was rather a help than a hindrance to their subduing the world. Every true missionary to the heathen shares this feeling. A little church of living believers is a far more efficient evangelising agency than a big church with a mass of worldly-minded adherents. The policy pursued by certain missionaries of the Church of Rome among the heathen, to draw to their banner, by whatever means, a mass of nominal proselytes, is the very opposite of the course deliberately adopted by our Lord. The notion of what is called "a national church," in the sense of Hooker or of Coleridge,—a church co-extensive with the nation, and embracing all and sundry in its ample pale, although there may be no spiritual cohesion among them—is likewise opposed to His idea. "Herein is my Father glorified," He said, "that ye bear much fruit: *so shall ye be my disciples.*" "Why call ye me Lord, Lord," He once asked with indignation, "and do not the things which I say?" "If a man abide not in me, he is cast forth as a branch, and is withered; and men gather them and cast them into the fire, and they are burned."

II. This serves to explain a second fact—the use by our Lord of very searching tests in accepting disciples, and the faithful announcement to them beforehand of the earthly loss and suffering that were almost certain to follow their connection with Him. He did not wish men to become His disciples without counting the cost, and the cost, as He Himself reckoned it, was far from light. The scribe that was willing to follow Him whithersoever He went was reminded that the foxes had holes, and the birds of the air had nests, but the Son of man had not where to lay His head. To many it seems somewhat hard in Jesus to refuse the request of the two disciples to be allowed to follow Him, when the one of them only wished to bury his father, and the other to bid farewell to those in the house. More general but hardly less stringent was the test for all: "If any man will come after me, let him deny himself and take up his cross daily and follow me." And again: "If any man come to me, and hate not his father, and mother, and wife, and children, and brethren, and sisters, yea, and his own life also, he cannot be my disciple." In the 6th chapter of John our Lord pursued a course of remark, of the effect of which it is said: "From that time many of his disciples went back, and walked no more with him." Obviously His purpose was to impress the truth that true discipleship was a much profounder thing than many of the people supposed. The line which He followed makes it clear that He would not have approved the practice sometimes followed at revival meetings—to ask all to stand up who have in their hearts decided for Christ. Our Lord would rather have put them through a course of probation, before either asking or accepting such a declaration. No one can suppose that He would have subjected to needless discouragement any one whose interest was excited towards Him even by insufficient considerations; nevertheless it is certain that our Lord deemed it right not to accept too readily the profession of discipleship. It was in the same line that His thoughts were moving in the parable of the Sower. The seed that fell on stony ground and the seed that fell among thorns had the same promising look at first as the seed that fell in good soil; nevertheless He taught that the early promise would not be realised. And both He and His apostles foretold clearly that the Church, especially in its earlier ages, would be exposed to ordeals of great severity, and so of great sifting power. The whole book of the Apocalypse evinces the vastly important part which, in the providence of God, persecution was to play in determining the reality of men's professions of conversion. And all goes to establish that our Lord felt profoundly the significance and vital importance of true discipleship. From this we infer that to admit persons lightly and easily to the responsibilities of discipleship as some do now, is contrary to the mind of Christ; and that the profession of young disciples ought to be asked and accepted only as the result of much solemnity, deliberation, and earnest prayer. All this, however, is perfectly in accordance with the absolute freeness of the Gospel offer, and the great longing desire of Jesus that all men should come to Him at once and receive His blessing. His object was to lead men to cherish from the first a due sense of the infinite worth of His salvation, so that, like Paul, if rivals to Him should present themselves, they might "count all things but loss for him—might count them but dung to win Christ, and be found in him."

III. The preceding particulars are more negative than positive. More directly, we now remark that it was our Lord's practice to endeavour to raise to a higher level all that came to Him with comparatively earthly aims—making use of the benefit or blessing which they did prize to suggest the idea of what was higher, and to excite their hearts towards it.

1. The first case of this kind we mention is connected with the miracle of the Loaves and Fishes. The miracle had been wrought on the east side of the lake, and Jesus had returned by boat to Capernaum, when next day, many of those who had seen the miracle, finding Jesus, seemed desirous of having more of His company, with the hope, probably, that their bodily wants would be again supplied. Our Lord appears to have had good grounds for charging these people with a very carnal purpose—with seeking Him because they did eat of the loaves, and were filled. Realising how wretched a motive this was, while He whom they followed was able to bestow on them such infinitely higher blessings, He said: "Labour not for the meat which perisheth, but for that meat which endureth unto everlasting life, which the Son of man shall give unto you." On the basis of what they had done He sought to inspire them with a far loftier desire. If they had counted it worth while to follow Him for the sake of a mouthful, the good of which would last but for an hour, how much more worth their while was it to come to Him for that bread of life, of which whosoever ate should never hunger again? This, of course, gave rise to a conversation and inquiry as to whether Jesus really was in possession of this bread from heaven. On that point He made the most explicit assertion of His power. What He said did not fall into good soil in the case of many; they

were offended on account of the magnitude, the sublimity of the claim which He presented. But it may be that in the case of some the course which He urged struck home to the conscience. Certainly there is no more fruitful means of rousing the conscience, in the case of men who believe in eternal life, and in the power of Jesus to bestow it, than to contrast the earnestness of their efforts for the things of time with the feebleness of their endeavours after the blessings of eternity.

2. Another case is that of the blind man in the 9th chapter of John. He had received his sight; he had stood up boldly for Jesus in the synagogue; for this he had been expelled; and after his expulsion Jesus met him. Though our Lord had restored his sight, he was not done with him. He put the question to him: "Dost thou believe on the Son of God?" When he asked, Who is he? Jesus answered: He who now speaks to you. We know not precisely through what process the man's mind passed; but he comes out very decidedly with an acknowledgment of his faith, and this he follows up very devoutly with an act of worship. Though we cannot trace the process in detail, we see what it must have been essentially. Evidently Jesus wished him to know that there were far higher blessings to be received from Him than the recovery of sight, and to excite in his bosom a desire for these. Speaking of Himself as the Son of God, He conveyed the thought that as the Son He had control over all the stores of heaven—the Father had committed them to His hand. The poor man understood the suggestion, grasped the thought that all spiritual bless-

ings were in Christ's hands, felt it to be especially refreshing when he had just been expelled from the synagogue, professed his faith in Jesus, and fell at His feet to worship Him. This was a case far more successful than the last: a new subject was gained for the kingdom of heaven.

3. Next let us glance at the case of Zaccheus. We cannot tell all his motives for wishing to get a sight of Jesus; but, on the face of the narrative, curiosity would seem to have had a leading share. But this curiosity may have had something substantial at its root; he may have heard Jesus spoken of as the friend of publicans and sinners, and his conscience may have testified very loudly that he stood greatly in need of such a friend. Because he was little of stature he ran before and climbed up into a sycamore tree; and as Jesus passed the tree he looked up and saw him, and said, " Zaccheus, come down; for to-day I must abide at thy house." If Zaccheus had heard of Christ as the friend of publicans and sinners, nothing could have better illustrated His character. The very summons must have thrilled his soul. For him to be selected from among all the men of Jericho as the host of Jesus; for him to come into such close contact with the Lord of the kingdom of heaven; what significance was there in this! What grace was there in selecting him; but what need of a great reformation in his heart and in his house, if he was to be worthy to entertain Jesus! The curiosity that had sought to see Jesus was changed into a far higher feeling; the elevation gained by climbing into the sycamore tree became the symbol of a far greater elevation. The change

in Zaccheus showed itself in the new life he purposed to lead: the very sight of Christ, poor, simple, beneficent, and self-denied, seems to have made his old life look black and hideous, and to have made him most sincere and cordial in the new ways and habits he was resolved to follow.

4. Going a step higher, we come to the case of Nicodemus. The ruler in Israel, when he came to Jesus by night, was moved by something higher than curiosity: he longed for heavenly light; and he believed he should get it from this teacher sent from God. But Nicodemus has hardly uttered his introductory word when he is at once transported by Jesus to a far higher level than that which he had proposed to occupy : " Verily, verily, I say unto thee, Except a man be born again, he cannot see the kingdom of God." All are familiar with the course of thought along which our Lord now conducted him. It is a striking example of the practice we speak of—taking hold of the actual feeling of the inquirer in order to make it the stepping-stone to something far higher and better.

5. The last case we notice under this head is that of the Greeks who had come up to the Passover, and who had expressed the desire to see Jesus. But in this case, as in some of the rest, we can but guess the motive that prompted the desire. Nor are we told whether Jesus had any actual communication with these Greeks, nor whether their desire terminated in faith. All that we are told is, that somehow the fact made a deep impression on Him, and led Him into a very solemn and lofty region of contemplation. He seems to have regarded the desire

of these Greeks as symbolical of that feeling which would thereafter be directed by men of all nations toward the Cross and Him who was nailed to it. He almost fancied Himself already dead, and by His death bringing life and salvation to the widespread family of man. He introduced that beautiful and significant figure—the corn of wheat, which, if it lives, abides alone, but if it dies, bears much fruit. In this way He improved the occasion of some strangers desiring to see Him by elevating the views of the disciples, and leading them to feel that an event was about to take place which to the end of time would draw eyes and hearts from all parts of the world, and draw them, not from any motive of curiosity, but because in Christ crucified they would see by faith the death of sin and the triumph of grace; and thus, " believing, rejoice with joy unspeakable and full of glory."

IV. A fourth and very important feature of our Lord's method of dealing with those on the borders of the kingdom was, His constantly pressing the duty of faith, and associating with it the highest blessings.

Matthew is the Evangelist who calls attention most systematically to this feature of His ministry. About a dozen instances may be gathered from his Gospel in which it is said that the presence of faith procured, or its absence hindered, the communication of some Divine blessing. The faith which was most commonly called for was the faith of healing. "Believest thou that I am able to do this?" was a common question before the cure took place. It seemed right to our Lord not to bestow cures unless

there was evidence of a respectful sense of His power and willingness to effect them. But the faith which Christ rewarded was sometimes of a higher and more spiritual kind. In such cases it was faith in His power to forgive sin—faith in His power to save. These two kinds of faith had a relation to each other, corresponding to the relation of the two kinds of blessings. As the temporal blessing of healing was typical of the spiritual blessing of salvation, so the faith that received the lower blessing was typical of that which received the higher. The essential quality of the faith which our Lord recognised in all cases was its *receptivity*—its capacity of receiving: but when this capacity extended only to the typical good it received only the typical blessing; when it extended to the higher good, it received the blessing of salvation. Sometimes there was a double receptivity, as in the case of the paralytic let down from the roof. In his case the common order was reversed; faith first received the higher blessing—
" Son, be of good cheer, thy sins are forgiven thee;"
and thereafter it got the lower, " Take up thy bed and walk." It is plain enough that there were cases in which men had the lower but not the higher receptive faculty. Of the ten lepers who on one occasion were healed together, there is no reason to suppose that the nine who did not come to give thanks cared for anything more than the bodily cure. The one who returned to give glory to God seems to have had another spirit. In the case of the blind man we have seen that the lower faith became a stepping-stone to the higher. The exercise of a receptive faith on a lower level seemed to

prepare the way for its exercise on a higher: in accordance with our Lord's saying, "To him that hath shall be given, and he shall have abundantly."

Receptivity, therefore,—a readiness to receive from Christ, was the attribute of that faith that, when turned toward the higher blessings of salvation, made one a member of the kingdom of heaven. But this receptivity was based on previous lessons and convictions that must not be overlooked. It was not like the feeling that impels a crowd, when they hear of some one flinging about handfuls of gold and silver, to rush for a share, no matter from whom the dole may come. It was not in this way that our Lord bestowed His gifts, at least in the case of individuals. The spirit that was rewarded in the Gospels was a faith based on a becoming, reverential attitude of soul toward Jesus, as a Higher Being: a certain deferential feeling, a lowly sense of their need, in presence of the august heavenly Power that was to confer the blessing they desired. It was the feeling appropriate in persons on whose behalf the great storehouse of the kingdom of God was about to be thrown open. It was something like the feeling with which the Israelites in the wilderness would gather the manna at first, or drink of the water from the rock, before the wonder became too common to excite their awe. Thus, before the resurrection of Lazarus, our Lord offered the prayer, "Father, I thank thee that thou hast heard me: and I knew that thou hearest me always; but because of the people which stand by I said it, that they may believe that thou hast sent me." Our Lord in His miracles had a purpose of edification. On occasion of the raising of Lazarus He desired most earnestly that this purpose might be fulfilled. By offering prayer He sought to produce a solemn sense of direct communication with the Father: to excite the feeling that the blessing was to come through Him straight from the One Fountain of all life and blessing—that it was a special gift from the God of heaven. There were some of His miracles that conveyed the sense of fellowship between Jesus and the Father with overpowering strength. At the miraculous draught of fishes Peter was seized with a strange emotion of awe: "Depart from me, for I am a sinful man, O Lord!" The glory of the Holy One shone so powerfully through the miracle, the sense of the Divine Presence was so bright, that that feeling of unworthiness and dread of destruction seemed to fall on Peter which sinful mortals have when they seem to see God—*that* God, who, as to sin, is a consuming fire.

So also in conferring the higher or spiritual blessings our Lord always desired to excite the feeling that a glorious communication was about to be made from the great Divine Fountain of grace and blessing. Thus, in the case of Nicodemus, our Lord's conversation was designed to make him look up, high up, as it were, to the very heavens,—to look up as a needy and empty sinner, that in this way all the wants of his soul might be abundantly supplied. He sought first to empty him—to make him feel that he had wants which earth could never supply, and to give him such a large conception of, the grace of God that he might look up to Him through Christ in the full belief that all that he required would be freely bestowed. There was in Nicodemus a sense of need, and a measure of receptivity, but far too small. Our Lord's dealings were designed in the first instance to increase both. It was not a few touches of improvement Nicodemus needed—he needed a new birth. You must be born ἄνωθεν, from above. You must be made a partaker of the Divine nature, having escaped the corruption that is in the world through lust. Nor need Nicodemus be thrown into despair by the impossibility of his reaching to such blessings: it is to bestow them that Christ has come. "God so loved the world, that he gave his only begotten Son, that whosoever believeth in him should not perish, but should have everlasting life." And He whom God has sent for this purpose is not merely a teacher sent from God: for "no man hath ascended up to heaven, but he that came down from heaven, even the Son of man which is in heaven." It seems likely that Nicodemus learned the lesson, and left Christ's chamber with a profounder sense of his own need on the one hand, but a sublimer faith on the other of the glory of Christ, as the ladder between earth and heaven by whom all blessings came.

The faith then that Christ rewarded was the faith that looked up to Him as the great channel of blessing, temporal and spiritual, for the needy children of men. It had in it a wistful, respectful, expecting element. It was trust in a person as well as belief in a doctrine. It was an attitude of the soul as well as an exercise of the intellect. It looked up to Christ as a Being exalted above the children of men, the messenger of God, the medium of His power, and the channel of His grace.

With this view of the faith that Jesus recognised and rewarded agree many expressions bearing on the reception of the blessings of the kingdom. "Blessed are the poor in spirit: for theirs is the kingdom of heaven." "Blessed are they that hunger and thirst after righteousness: for they shall be filled." "Except ye be converted, and become as little children, ye shall in no wise enter into the kingdom of heaven." To become as little children is to feel our emptiness and dependence. Not to feel emptiness and dependence is to be in a spiritual condition that excludes us from the blessings of the kingdom. Our Lord thanked the Father on one occasion because He had hid the things of salvation from the wise and prudent, and revealed them unto babes. In other words, because the law of the kingdom was such that the hungry were filled with good things, while the rich were sent empty away. It is a wholesome law, tending to good on both sides, and for that Jesus was thankful.

It is impossible to calculate the amount of blessed effect which has come out of this method of dealing with persons at the gate of the kingdom—out of the direction thus given to the thoughts and feelings of those who more or less consciously seek blessing at His hands. "Believest thou that I am able to do this?"—is the question still to be dealt with by all who come seeking pardon and life from Christ. The sense of personal emptiness, and an upward honouring look directed to Christ, as Him in whom "it hath pleased the Father that all fulness should dwell," are still essential elements of that faith which receives the blessings of salvation. It is a faith that make us partners with Christ, and that procures for us all needed grace:—not because it is itself a meritorious virtue, but simply because it is the link of connection with our Lord, the means of making us one with Him "in whom dwelleth all the fulness of the Godhead bodily."

Would we in this matter follow in the footsteps of Christ? We must endeavour to foster among our people a sense of emptiness, and the spirit that looks up with wonder and homage to Christ as God's gift, laden with all the blessings of heaven, to sinful men. We must encourage the quality of receptivity. The most receptive of all things is a vacuum. Thoroughly expel the air from a retort whose mouth is placed in a jar of water, and the water will immediately rush in, but no water will enter till the vacuum is complete. We must try to make a vacuum in the hearts of our people. We must teach them to look above, far above themselves, for righteousness and salvation. "I will lift up mine eyes unto the hills, whence cometh my help." The successful preacher is careful to lay the moral foundation for faith as well as the intellectual. He will stimulate feeling as well as thought. He will seek to subdue men into faith as well as to reason them into it. You may expound justification by faith very clearly, and defend the doctrine triumphantly, yet not bring your hearers any nearer to Christ. For mere reasoning goes but a little way in producing the vacuum. It is seldom by mere reasoning that you bring sinners to their knees.

We may see, too, how much a right tone in prayer may contribute to the gendering of faith. When our confessions of emptiness and helplessness before God, our wrestlings with the Angel of the covenant, and our appeals to Him who alone can save us, are marked by the true tone of contrition and pathetic earnestness, they both help to bring our people into the best frame, and they prevail with God to give the desired blessing. The very songs one gives out, and one's tone in reading them, will help the impression. What must be the effect of words like these said or sung with all the pathos of intense personal longing?—

> " My hands to thee I stretch ; my soul
> Thirsts, as dry land, for thee.
> Haste, Lord, to hear, my spirit fails :
> Hide not thy face from me ;
> Lest like to them I do become
> That go down to the dust.
> At morn let me Thy kindness hear ;
> For in Thee do I trust."

It may be observed that the psalms and hymns and spiritual songs that touch our hearts most, and come nearest home to our feelings, are those which start with the expression of want and dependence, but rise to a triumphant key as the grace and love of Christ are unfolded and realised.

> " Nothing in my hand I bring,
> Simply to Thy cross I cling ;
> Naked, come to Thee for dress,
> Helpless, look to Thee for grace ;
> Foul, I to the fountain fly,
> Wash me, Saviour, or I die !"

In such ways is fulfilled that first recorded prediction of Jesus—" Hereafter ye shall see heaven open, and the angels of God ascending and descending on the Son of man." In getting salvation you look up to heaven as the source of the blessing, and receive it as the gift of God through Jesus Christ. Faith is no mercantile transaction between debtor and creditor performed coldly under the conditions of an earthly contract. The soul of the recipient gets a heavenward attitude, and this attitude is maintained during the rest of his life. In nothing is the quiet but mighty influence of Jesus more apparent than in giving this upward direction to the soul. Henceforth it has real communion with the upper world. He who holds himself to be a believer, and whose soul is yet bent on the earth, must be self deceived. Those who have received Christ have their treasure in heaven, their conversation in heaven, their home in heaven. And no exhortation is felt to be more appropriate than this—"If ye then be risen with Christ, seek those things which are above, where Christ sitteth on the right hand of God."

CHAPTER XVII.

DEALINGS WITH DIFFERENT CLASSES.

III.—THOSE INSIDE THE KINGDOM.

1. In our Lord's dealings with those who had become deliberately and decidedly members of His kingdom, the first thing that arrests our attention is His great concern for the stability and increase of their faith.

Faith, as we have seen, was the vital test of discipleship; faith in Him as the Christ, the Divine channel of all saving blessings to man; and through Him, faith or trust in God as a Father, disposed to deal kindly with His children, and concerned for their every want. But faith was not a stationary, but a growing quality; it was subject to decay through neglect, and to increase through cultivation; and what our Lord was constantly aiming at was its growth and increase,—He longed to see it like a flower covered with blossoms, like a tree bending under its load of fruit.

A man with faith is a man who acts on his spiritual convictions; who feels that, resting alone on the Word of God, he has solid ground under his feet; who is not easily shaken by outward forces, as long as he can cling to his God and Saviour; and who can be stimulated to great undertakings and enabled to bear great sufferings, because God is at his right hand, and he shall not be moved.

It was one of our Lord's chief delights to witness commanding manifestations of such faith. His delight could not be restrained when these came from unexpected quarters. "I have not seen so great faith, no, not in Israel," was His exclamation when the centurion asked Him to speak the word that his servant might be healed. The faith of those who let down the paralytic through the roof was especially welcome to Him. His intuitive perception of deep faith in the Syrophenician mother was what led Him to delay the blessing she craved, for He saw that her faith was vigorous enough to remove mountains, and would but show itself in greater strength the more it was tried. The faith of the woman who poured on Him her box of very precious ointment was too beautiful in His eyes to allow her act to be exposed to carping criticism. The last act of mercy He performed was an acknowledgment of a very striking act of faith on the part of the thief: only a commanding exercise of faith could have drawn the promise, "Verily, I say unto thee, To-day shalt thou be with me in paradise."

If our Lord was thus delighted with strong faith, so He was distressed for little faith, and especially when it sunk so low as to be a case of doubt. Doubt was something which He could not away with. His treatment of it is one of the most marked features of His pastoral method. It will be worth our while to make this the subject of a careful examination.

Four cases present themselves of our Lord's dealings with doubt. (1.) The message from John the Baptist. (2.) The incident of Peter's coming to Him on the waters, and beginning to sink. (3.) The case of the disciples after the resurrection supposing they had seen a spirit, doubting whether the resurrection was real. (4.) The case of Thomas—although this was a case in which doubt had all but passed into disbelief—refusing to believe in the identity of the risen Jesus, unless he should handle His hands and His side.

In reviewing our Lord's treatment of these cases, we may remark these three things:—1. His patience toward the persons doubting; 2. His dislike of the thing itself; and 3. His way of removing it, viz., by presenting in the strongest manner the evidence that justified and even demanded faith.

1. As to our Lord's patience towards doubters. First, in the case of John the Baptist, no feeling of irritation is expressed at the strange break-down on the part of one whose faith had once been so strong, and who, in his new attitude of doubt, was doing no small disservice to Christ. A gentle reproof is contained in the closing warning: "Blessed is he whosoever shall not be offended in me;" but the reproof is not the fruit of impatience, it is the least that could serve the purpose for which it was needed, to warn others against the unfortunate attitude of John.

The words to Peter, after he had begun to sink, are perhaps in appearance the sharpest: "O thou of little faith, wherefore didst thou doubt?" Yet, in view of the intimate relations of Jesus and Peter, the words are consistent with the greatest kindliness; and, in view of the forwardness that had been shown by Peter, they are not a whit sharper than the occasion required. To the disciples who doubted whether they really saw the risen Saviour nothing could have been milder than His remonstrance: "Why are ye troubled, and why do thoughts arise in your hearts?" unless, indeed, it were His infinitely condescending words to Thomas: "Reach hither thy finger, and behold my hands; and reach hither thy hand, and thrust it into my side; and be not faithless, but believing."

2. But, amid all this gentleness of manner, it was made apparent what a serious evil He regarded doubt. Let us observe that what our Lord had such dislike for was, *doubt in the presence of strong evidence calling for faith*. The only excuse that could be made for such doubt was, that the mind was slow of apprehending the evidence and giving to it its due force. Faith being opposed to sight, sight is bound to give way the moment the claims of faith are established; but the mind is often sluggish, the senses are obstinate, and they linger about the scene like an obstinate child when ordered to leave the room, trying to keep their ground as long as possible. But our Lord would not have allowed more than this to be said for doubt in the face of evidence. Doubt, as a permanent state of mind, is not allowable; Doubting Castle is not the home of a friend, but the prison of a foe. There never was a more unreasonable or a more insolent question than that put to Christ by the Jews: "How long dost thou make us to doubt?" It certainly was not Jesus that made any to doubt. On the

great questions of the faith He held that there was light sufficient for all honest souls. " I am the light of the world ; he that followeth me shall not walk in darkness, but shall have the light of life."

3. But even where there was little or no excuse for doubt, our Lord showed His gentle patience with doubters by bringing a new stream of light to bear on the object, in order that, before such overwhelming evidence, doubt might be scattered for ever. "Go, tell John the things which ye do see and hear"— bring new light to bear on the question—light that cannot be resisted. " Behold my hands and my feet," He said to the doubting disciples, " that it is I myself; handle me and see, for a spirit hath not flesh and bones as ye see me have." We have already referred to His way of removing the doubts of Thomas. His method, as we thus see, was to meet the doubters on their own ground, and conquer them by their own weapons. He had patience for all their unreasonableness, and He provided light for all their darkness. There need be no want of light in the kingdom of heaven. If men were not satisfied with the good working light that was provided for them, it was easy to take a lens and concentrate it, so that all excuse of inability to see should be utterly removed. And being in earnest, and desirous above all things that faith should flourish, our Lord preferred to intensify the light that the blindest eye might see, and all shadow of excuse for doubt might vanish.

The treatment of doubt is no easy matter at the present day. Undoubtedly, if we would treat it successfully, it must be on the lines laid by our

Lord. But we must observe, in this connection, that what is commonly called doubt at the present time is not all of one quality. Some writers, instead of reproving doubt, praise it warmly as a philosophical virtue of the highest order, indicating a mind of honest and independent calibre. "Preliminary doubt," says Sir William Hamilton,[1] "is the fundamental condition of philosophy; and the necessity of such a doubt is no less apparent than its difficulty. We do not approach the study of philosophy ignorant but perverted. There is no one who has not grown up under a load of beliefs ... which may or may not be false, but which it is more probable may be a medley of truths and errors." Hence, he says, "philosophy requires a renunciation of prejudices—*præjudicata*—conclusions formed without a previous examination of the grounds." In this he maintains that philosophy and Christianity coincide. "What," he asks, "is the primary condition which our Saviour requires of His disciples? That they throw off their old prejudices, and come with hearts willing to receive knowledge, and understandings open to conviction: 'Unless ye become as little children, ye shall not enter into the kingdom of heaven.'" He refers to a chapter in Aristotle on the utility of doubt, and he maintains that the apostle was of the same mind. Did he not tell us to prove or test all things? And is not this just bidding us doubt all things?

It is obvious that much confusion is introduced here by the use of the term "doubt" in different senses, or, at least, in reference to different stages

[1] *Lectures on Metaphysics.*

of a process. While the philosopher commends doubt, the Saviour condemns it. But there is no real contradiction. What the philosopher commends is preliminary doubt; what the Saviour condemns is permanent doubt. The philosopher would have you doubt at the beginning, but this he would encourage in order that you may obtain reasonable certainty at the end. The philosopher commends doubt with reference to opinions that have been formed *without regard to the grounds on which they rest.* In the same sense our Lord would have had His disciples to doubt the propriety of the Korban, to doubt the propriety of swearing by the gold of the temple, to doubt the propriety of long repetitions in prayer, to doubt the whole body of tradition sought to be imposed upon them. To doubt in this sense is just to decline forming opinions until you see that the grounds for them are valid. It is unfortunate, however, that the term doubt should be applied to this process. To prove or test is a much more suitable word. A mule on the side of a Swiss mountain will not rest its weight on a projecting stone until it has first felt with its hoof whether it is firm enough to bear it. Here instinct is an example to intellect. And this process is just equivalent to the apostolic one—" Prove all things: hold fast that which is good." But this is very different from a permanent condition of doubt. Doubting, as a permanent condition of the mind, in presence of sufficient evidence, is alike contrary to the principles of philosophy and the claims of religion.

In the ordinary work of the Christian ministry

two kinds of doubt are to be met with, both calling for our best efforts to remove them. First, doubt as to whether the grounds for Christian faith are sufficient; whether it is one's duty to accept the Bible without hesitation as the inspired Word of God. In reference to this state, there are some religious guides who utter very strong warnings: who tell a young man that the moment he begins to doubt he is lost; that he never ought to suffer a doubt to enter his mind; that every doubt on such a subject is the vile suggestion of the devil.

But however well meant, this is foolish talk. Men ought to see that there are sufficient grounds for whatever they profess to believe, and if one has not from the beginning a convincing intuitive belief in the Bible as God's Word, it is right that he should carefully examine its credentials. The danger of doubt lies in beginning to doubt *against your own intuitive belief;* also, in remaining in a state of doubt as a permanent position; and, further, in demanding evidence for religious faith of a nature which the case does not admit of. What is demanded of the Christian minister in dealing with this is to follow his Master in being very patient, and in trying to increase the light and force of evidence, until it becomes overwhelming. But we must remember that the evidence sought is not always the evidence of logic. It is sometimes moral evidence,—the evidence of adaptation between the Bible and the needs of the soul,—the evidence of heavenliness, and love, and purity in the actual products of the Bible. And if in their own spirit and temper Christ's servants give ample proof of this, they will not be long of scattering doubt. It was the overpowering force of humble, gentle, condescending love on the part of Jesus that scattered the doubts of Thomas, and brought him to the feet of his Master, as trustful and guileless as a little child. The doubter has been known to say, I don't care for what you *say*; but I do mind what you *are* and what you *do*.

The other kind of doubt often met with by the Christian minister is that of those who have no speculative difficulties, but who oscillate between the impressions of sense and the claims of faith, and are thus, in the language of popular theology, troubled with "doubts and fears." The trouble is not in the head but in the heart. The difficulty is to bring their whole nature into harmony in the acknowledgment of truth. There are various phases of this state of mind demanding discriminating study on the part of the Christian pastor. A knowledge of the cause will usually be the best guide to the remedy. Sometimes it is the fruit of a morbid humility—a sense of unworthiness which thinks it would be presumption to appropriate to itself the tidings of the Gospel in all their glorious freeness. Sometimes it arises from contracted views of God, from measuring the Divine generosity by a human standard, limiting the Holy One of Israel. Often it arises from sluggishness of mind where there ought to be activity—from backwardness in acknowledging the sovereign claims of truth, or from spiritual dulness, cowardice, and timidity. In other cases, it is the result of moral laxity, of a habit of tampering with conscience, the eye ceasing to be single, and being unable to apprehend the simplicity of truth. The faithful pastor must do his best to understand the feeling, and the source from which it springs. But in this process of spiritual diagnosis and cure he will often find, as physicians find, that local ailments are healed best by quickening and strengthening the system generally. Looking away from self, having regard to the objective declarations of God, trembling at His word, be it promise or threatening, are the characteristics of a healthy spiritual condition; and where this wholesome state of mind is cultivated doubts and fears will retire, as owls and other creatures of the night hide themselves before the rays of the morning sun.

2. Another very characteristic trait of our Lord's treatment of those inside the kingdom was His encouraging among them a warm, simple, *family feeling*: encouraging them to think of God as their Father, of Jesus Himself as their friend and elder brother, and of the whole Church as a community of brethren. To soften the hard relations of the world, to sweeten all intercourse by love and confidence, to neutralise as it were the acids of sin and selfishness by the alkalis of forbearing and forgiving kindness, was one of the chief aims of His pastoral labours. The predominating thought in this course of influence was the fatherhood of God. "Our Father, which art in heaven." A serene trust in God as the Father, interested in all that concerns us; most certain not to think of us less than He thinks of the ravens and the lilies; most certain not to be behind earthly fathers in giving good things to them that ask Him: numbering the very hairs of our

heads; able to deliver us from them that kill the body; knowing what things we have need of before we ask Him:—this is the spirit He ever sought to foster. And a fruit of this spirit is calmness of mind, serenity of temper, freedom from fluster and excitement, like the tone of the little child in the storm at sea who felt so untroubled because her father was at the helm. This saintliness and serenity of soul is a high element in the religion of Christ. " Let not your heart be troubled, ye believe in God, believe also in me." If the spirit of serenity achieves its greatest visible triumphs in times of great excitement, it triumphs none the less in ordinary times, when in calm, untroubled trustfulness it bears the burdens and endures the worries by which others are overborne. Our Lord's calls to prayer connect themselves with the maintenance of this spirit. Prayer, besides its direct influence, recalls the thought of the Father, and to the trustful spirit the thought of the Father is the thought of one who will withhold no good thing from them that walk uprightly.

In the same spirit in which they were called to trust the Father, Jesus called on His people to trust in Him. While among them He had given all encouragement to this spirit. " Henceforth I call you not servants, for the servant knoweth not what his lord doeth; but I have called you friends: for all things whatsoever I have heard of the Father I have made known unto you." The call for trust in Jesus was more immediately connected with the administration of the kingdom. While among them, He had treated them in a friendly, brotherly way: encouraging familiarity, encouraging frank and easy intercourse; not holding them at a distance from Him, but allowing them to come very near to Him, and in this way inspiring them with confidence in His absolute friendliness, and encouraging the most thorough reliance on His sympathy and interest. It is in this way that Jesus would have His followers regard Him. He is not an high priest that cannot be touched with the feeling of their infirmities, but the real brother of His Church. Whether the matter in concern be their personal spiritual wellbeing, or the wellbeing of the Church of which some of them are the earthly guardians and guides, it is in this spirit of brotherly trust they are invited and expected to deal with Him. The two things react on each other; the sense of Christ's brotherhood inspires a happy, trustful feeling amid all Christian duty and service, and the exercise of this feeling deepens the sense of His brotherhood. And in the play of these feelings there is gendered a serene happy spirit, peculiar to the Christian life, making burdens light and trials easy, and ever kindling the hope and expectation of that nearer fellowship, when the Lamb in the midst of the throne shall feed them, and lead them to living fountains of water, and God shall wipe away all tears from their eyes.

And as Jesus encouraged the spirit of brotherhood from His disciples toward Himself, so He encouraged it likewise in their dealings one toward another. It was as brethren that they were to consult and decide about the affairs of His Church. The washing of their feet was a brotherly example—"that ye should do to one another as I have done to you." Forgiveness towards a brother, and especially a brother in Christ, was practically to have no limit. It is not without a purpose that the gospel history informs us how, even close on the crucifixion, these lessons had made so little impression that the disciples were contending with one another which of them should be greatest. Lessons of this kind require the spirit to be chastened by sore trial ere it receives the impression. The awful experience of the crucifixion-tragedy, and the further mellowing that took place when Jesus left them to go into heaven, softened the soil of their hearts. And no picture of brotherly unity and loving fellowship could be more beautiful than that presented in the first days of the Christian Church. The meetings for praise and prayer, the union in doctrine and fellowship, the holy meetings for breaking of bread, and the cheerful contribution of their goods to a common fund for mutual relief, showed how profound a hold the spirit of brotherhood had taken, and constituted a spectacle too rare, alas! in the history of the Christian Church, but very delightful to the Church as often as it has been realised, and very blessed and impressive in its influence on the world.

3. It may vary somewhat the tenor of these somewhat general statements to notice, thirdly, our Lord's method of dealing with the afflicted. And as the case of Mary and Martha, in connection with the death of their beloved brother, and the demolition of the structure of family love and joy in whose shadow they had lived, is the most conspicuous and striking of this class of cases, it may be well to confine our attention to it. What strikes us at once

in our Lord's procedure on this occasion is, that He gave Himself up entirely to relieve the trouble that had settled down on His friends. No doubt there was at first an appearance of indifference. It is one of those cases in which we should have expected Jesus to act otherwise than He did—in which we should have expected Him to hurry to His friends the moment He heard of their sorrow. But he that believeth shall not make haste. It was one of the proofs of our Lord's greatness that He could hold in complete command those strong impulses of the heart to which weak natures are constrained to yield, let the purpose of them be what it may. We must bear in mind the multiplicity and great importance of our Lord's engagements and duties, and the possibility that in the place where He was, there was important work doing, which could not be left suddenly, especially as the time of His death was now so near that He could not have returned to finish what He had begun.

This we say may have been; but undoubtedly our Lord's delay was caused mainly by a feeling similar to that which appeared at first to trifle with the Syrophenician woman, but which sprang from a conviction of the profundity of her faith, and the glorious triumph it was sure to achieve. So when our Lord abstained from going to Bethany it was with a view to final results: with a view to a more profound trial and reward of the faith of the sisters, and the performance of a miracle which, close on His own death, would yet show clearly that He had the keys of hell and of death. And for all time this great work was designed to carry the lesson that there is no sorrow too profound for Jesus to heal, and no calamity too irremediable for Him to change into a blessing.

It is very certain that when our Lord did go to Bethany, He gave His whole heart, His undivided attention and thought to the afflicted family there. He did not embrace this with other objects to be attended to; but for the time allowed this case to absorb Him wholly. It has been remarked by Dean Vaughan that one visit of true sympathy is pastoral work enough for one day. To bring the heart into thorough accord with friends plunged into the depths of grief is to place it in a condition which unfits it for the time for lighter and livelier duty. To make one's-self truly one with a profoundly afflicted family is in a manner to share their grief, and place one's self for the time wholly out of tune for the bustle of ordinary life. It is not very often that a bereavement happens of so overwhelming a character as that of Bethany, but with some such cases every minister is familiar. If other duties admit of it, and the relations of the minister to the family are near and cordial, by all means let him act as Jesus acted, give himself up for the time to sympathy and Christian help. This were to bring, as it were, his alabaster box of very precious ointment, and pour it upon the wounded heart; and in such a case it holds true that, " inasmuch as ye did it to the least of these my brethren, ye did it unto me." The tears of Jesus, as He sat with Mary, evinced the depth and thoroughness of His sympathy. In the view of what was about to happen, there was little call for tears; but Jesus was so identified with His friend in sympathy, that when He saw Mary "weeping, and the Jews also weeping who came with her," and thought perchance how often such scenes would be renewed in the earthly history of His people,— "Jesus wept."

To go over all that Jesus urged upon those within His kingdom would be to summarise His whole teaching on the Christian life,—its duties and temptations, its joys and sorrows, its difficulties and its triumphs. We should have to tarry over the Beatitudes, ponder each part of the Sermon on the Mount, ascertain the lessons of the parables, and weigh each discourse and each conversation. Into so wide a field the study of His pastoral methods hardly carries us.

4. But there is one great pastoral lesson which our Lord was accustomed to urge on His people with special earnestness, and to the due consideration of which He ever attached the deepest importance—namely, the duty of their bearing in mind His coming back, and of their ordering their whole life and service by a regard to that event. This great lesson is urged in two ways: first, on their consciences, as a stimulus to faithful, constant, zealous service; and secondly, on their hearts, as a blessed solace, a glorious hope, the climax and crown of all spiritual joy.

It is urged on their consciences. If the parable be that of the Talents, the duty of improving is urged not merely by the general sense of duty and the general hope of reward, but very specially by the consideration that the lord of the servants is to return, that he will look carefully into the matter, and will welcome the good and faithful servant into the joy of his lord. If it is the parable of the household over whom the lord has appointed one to be overseer, it is well for him to remember the temptations in his lord's absence to self-indulgence and injustice, and to think how these things will look when his lord returns and examines all that he has been about. If it be the parable of the Virgins, the slumber of all the ten denotes the danger of neglecting to watch, but the case of those who slumbered while there was no oil in their lamps indicates a profounder danger, only to be averted by remembering that at some moment to us unknown the cry may go forth, Behold, the bridegroom cometh!

If it should seem to any that this method of stimulating men to watchfulness is not the highest method: that if men were really conscientious, the fact that a thing is right, is required of them, is part of their indefeasible duty—ought to be sufficient, and that it is an inferior part of their nature that is appealed to, when they are warned to beware of a surprise, to take care lest they be caught, to consider how their lives must appear when the Lord comes to judge—we reply, that even granting this to be true, we are never in such a condition of confirmed goodness as to be able to dispense with the aid of even inferior considerations in favour of it. In fact, it is a principle in God's method of training us, to prop us up, to quicken and encourage us in His service by many considerations that would not be needed in a more perfect state. One of the most important of these influences is that of attachment to a person, and regard for his opinion. It is a great help in training a young person if among those about him there be some one of great excellence to whose person he is attached, and for whose opinion he has respect. The silent influence of that friend, the thought that what one does will come under his review, will prove a great help on the side of virtue, and against temptation. It is the same principle, but with far loftier application and stronger force, that our Lord brought to bear on the vigilance and faithfulness of His people, when He taught them to be constantly looking for His return, and to do all their work and service as in the great Taskmaster's eye.

But while He brought this truth to bear on their consciences to stimulate fidelity and vigilance, He brought it also to bear on their hearts as a source of hope and joy unspeakable. In this connection, He dwelt chiefly on two considerations. The first was, that the rewards to be given for faithful service would be on a most generous scale. To forsake the world for Christ would bring manifold more in this life, and in the world to come, life everlasting. The apostles would sit on twelve thrones, judging the twelve tribes of Israel. A cup of cold water given to a disciple would in no wise lose its reward. Those who had been faithful in a few things would be made rulers over many things. Services done to His little ones would be rewarded as done to Himself. The whole bountifulness of the Divine nature would be shown at Christ's coming in the recognition of faithful service. Just as there are occasions in the history of rich men,—perhaps a marriage festivity, or a royal visit, when they do their hospitality on a more than usually lordly scale, finding a pride and a pleasure in princely munificence, so, it would seem, the return of Jesus to earth is to be celebrated by the manifestation of the exceeding riches of His grace, by gifts of unexampled munificence, by the lustre of the distinctions to be heaped on the men whom the King delighteth to honour. "When Christ, who is our life, shall appear, then shall ye also appear with him in glory." "To him that overcometh will I grant to sit with me on my throne, even as I also overcame, and am set down with my Father on his throne."

The other consideration that Christ dwelt on to magnify the privilege of His servants at His second coming was, the closeness of the relation in which they were to be toward Him, and the warmth of the complacency of which they were to be the objects. "In my Father's house are many mansions: if it were not so, I would have told you. I go to prepare a place for you. And if I go and prepare a place for you, I will come again, and receive you unto myself; *that where I am, there ye may be also.*" In these words it was implied both that their presence with Him would go to complete His happiness, and that His presence with them would go to complete theirs. It is not possible for us to conceive what a bright and blessed influence Christ's presence had been among His disciples during His earthly sojourn. Though the distance every way between the fisher lads and the Divine Saviour of the world was so vast, yet all the time Christ was with them His presence must have been like a sunbeam, brightening and refreshing their whole life, and giving them many of the sensations of heaven. What a privilege it was to look forward to the same presence again, and to think of it not as a transitory but an abiding enjoyment; and not as a joy for which they had hardly begun to be fitted, but as one which their transformed natures would make infinitely deeper, infinitely sweeter, nearer to that mysterious joy which the Father had when the Son lay in His bosom, and was daily His delight, rejoicing continually before Him.

The history of Christ's dealings with those who were inside the kingdom is just the history of the process described by the apostle—" Christ also loved the church, and gave himself for it, that he might sanctify it with the washing of water by the word, that he might present it to himself a glorious church, not having spot or wrinkle or any such thing, but that it should be holy and without blemish." Does it not greatly elevate the scope and objects of the Christian ministry when it is regarded as the instrument ordained by Christ to achieve this glorious consummation? Not a magical or mechanical apparatus for saving souls; but an instrument adapted in every quality, intellectual, moral, and spiritual, for spiritual work:—the instrument by which the New Jerusalem is to be prepared as a bride adorned for her husband, so that seeing the great transformation, men are to ask, " Who is she that looketh forth as the morning, fair as the moon, clear as the sun, and terrible as an army with banners?"

CHAPTER XVIII.

HIS FAREWELL.

It is easy to see from the tenor of our Lord's last discourses, whether in the synoptic Gospels, or in St. John, that His ministry was drawing to a close. To the multitude, to the rulers, and to the twelve alike, He spoke as one whose voice was not much longer to be heard among them. In His words to all the three we mark that increase of frankness and earnestness, and that greater outflow of affection which we find so often in the bearing of friends conscious of the near approach of death. Like Samson gathering his strength for a last effort, many a person under the shadow of death has shown a frankness and a fervour in impressing his views on his family and friends, of which, in his more ordinary moods, no one would have supposed him capable. Full though our Lord's ministry had all along been of frankness and earnestness, yet even He could feel the quickening influence of the valley of the shadow, and even His voice could gather fresh pathos from the thought—" Yet a little while and ye shall see me no more."

1. In His addresses to the *multitude*, His consciousness of the night coming is shown in the

special prominence which He gives to the dread fact of *retribution*. Nearly all His parables of this period bear on the great winding up. The parable of the Wicked Husbandmen (Matt. xxi. 33) ends with the coming of the householder, miserably to destroy those wicked men. The parable of the Wedding Garment (Matt. xxii.) ends with the expulsion of the man who has no wedding garment into outer darkness, where there is weeping and wailing and gnashing of teeth. The discourse over the temple from the Mount of Olives (Matt. xxiv.) ends with another vision of judgment, where the faithful servant is rewarded, and the careless consigned to his final doom. The last group of parables (Matt. xxv.), embracing the Ten Virgins, the Talents, and the Sheep and the Goats, lead up, in every case, to the solemn retribution of the end. What more appropriate truth could our Lord have left ringing in the ears and consciences of the multitude? or what more tender appeal, in the view of that truth, could He have made than in the tearful lamentation which He poured out when He beheld the city, or in the figure of the hen gathering her chickens under her wings? It was His knowledge of the certainty and terribleness of the retribution that made His feelings so earnest, and His appeals so tender. Would that *our* hearts thrilled more to these solemn appeals, where in form after form our Lord surrounds us with the dread solemnities of the judgment, and the unchangeable retributions of that great day!

2. Again, in His dealings with the *rulers*, His consciousness of the coming end shows itself in His

frank and fearless exposure and denunciation of their wickedness. The breach between Him and them is now evidently final. They had rejected Him the first time He came to the temple claiming His own (John ii.); to give them another chance, He cleanses the temple a second time (Luke xix. 45-48); but the result is a more determined and malignant rejection than before. In numberless other ways they have shown their enmity. The day for mild remonstrance and gracious invitation is now past. They can no longer be classed with those whom He may hope to gain by the cords of love; they must be separated from the rest of the nation, treated as the incorrigible enemies of God and man, and so arraigned and rebuked that their influence with the people may be broken, and their authority annulled. This exposure must be made in the most startling and scathing words that language can supply (Matt. xxiii.). It is only in this way that their evil influence can be destroyed; or if it be possible in any case to pierce the hardened heart, it is these sharp arrows alone that will do it. That our Lord should have resorted to such a style of speech to gratify a personal feeling is utterly incredible. Towards His bitterest foe, He had no other feeling personally than—" Father, forgive them, for they know not what they do."

3. While the influence of the shadow of death is thus seen both in our Lord's dealings with the multitude and with the rulers, it is still more manifest in His farewell words to *the twelve*. Ever since His transfiguration He had been opening up to them the terrible tragedy that was about to be enacted.

His whole demeanour, during the intervening weeks, was in keeping with the situation thus disclosed. But in the closing discourses, and especially in the farewell address, as recorded in John xiv.-xvi., He throws Himself more fully into the situation. We notice a special frankness, a special warmth of affection, and a special graciousness of condescension. Never before did He tell them so plainly of their weaknesses—the coming treachery of Judas, the denial of Peter, the forsaking of them all. Never did He give them such tokens of His love as in the holy supper, followed by the washing of their feet. But this was not all. We mark in all His farewell dealings an earnest desire to prepare them for their new position. He seeks to counteract the natural feeling of loneliness and helplessness by which they were liable to be overwhelmed when He should leave them, and to fit them for the high duties and responsibilities under which they were to come.

More especially, what our Lord emphatically sought, was to keep up their faith in Him after He should leave them, *so that He should be as much a reality to them as He had been before.* He wished them to continue to do His work just as if He were at their head and in their midst; to believe that His care over them was as real as when He arose and rebuked the winds and the waves, and His help as effectual as when He filled their net with the miraculous draught of fishes. A blessed faith this, surely, not only for the twelve, but for all who are called to do Christ's work in the world! What courage and power would it give every servant of Christ's in the thickest dangers and most arduous undertakings, to have an unfailing reliance on the promise, "Lo, I am with you alway, even to the end of the world."

May it not have been in some degree with a view to this result in the case of the twelve, that so many rare and remarkable testimonies to Christ were accumulated during the last few days,—the time when He was passing through the scenes of His deepest humiliation? Across the dark background of man's ineffable atrocity, there came ever and anon, flashes of glory, fitted to confirm the faith of every perplexed disciple, and give fresh confidence in the person of Him who, though now seemingly abandoned to the enmity of men and the rage of devils, was still shown to be the Son of God.

(1.) Thus, first, there was the testimony of the woman who brought her costly box of ointment to anoint Him. Even yet we may be disposed to ask, To what purpose was this waste? But the whole circumstances of the case, as well as our Lord's vindication of the woman, show how fitting a testimony it was to the glory of Him who was just about to be subjected to the cursed doom of a malefactor.

(2.) Then came the testimony of the multitude that went out to meet Him as He came to the city, cutting down branches of palm-trees and strewing their garments in the way, and shouting Hosannah! And there was such heartiness in their shout, and the spirit that sought in this way to honour Him was so natural and so strong that, in the words of our Lord Himself, "If these had held their peace, the very stones would have cried out!"

(3.) There was also the testimony of the Greeks who came to Philip and said, "Sir, we would see

Jesus." It was a foreshadow, as Jesus expressed it, of what was to happen when He should be "lifted up." His exposure on the cross, meant as the crowning token of His disgrace, would prove the grandest occasion for the exercise of His royal power —" I, if I be lifted up from the earth, will draw all men to me."

(4.) There was next the testimony of the voice from heaven. When the prayer went from his lips, "Father, glorify thy name"—there came a voice which said, "I have both glorified it, and I will glorify it again."

(5.) Then there was the angel in Gethsemane that came to comfort Him.

(6.) There was the dream of Pilate's wife, and her earnest endeavour to save her husband from the guilt of His murder.

(7.) There was the testimony of the thief on the cross, bearing so emphatic witness to His kingly power, and the certainty of His coming in His kingdom.

(8.) There was the irrepressible testimony of the centurion, who could not but exclaim, "Truly this man was the Son of God."

(9.) And lastly, there was the testimony of nature,—earth and sun moved as it were by a common impulse,—the sun darkened, the earth quaking, the rocks rent, the graves opened,—all combining to testify that the sufferer on the cross was in very deed the Son of God!

All this, we say, was fitted to keep up the faith of the twelve in Jesus, even amid the awfully depressing influences of the crucifixion. True, it may be said, these testimonies were of little practical avail. All the disciples forsook Him and fled. A greater sign than any or all of them was needed—the resurrection from the dead. We grant it readily. They wavered till they saw the risen Lord. And what a proof of the reality of the resurrection we have in the fact that it did what all these testimonies had failed to do—made a complete revolution on the faith and courage of the apostles!

But the earlier testimonies were not in vain. In after times, they would all be gratefully recalled; they would be pieced together as parts of the manifold evidence that Jesus was the Son of God. All the memorials of Egypt which Jacob's sons presented to their father after their second visit,— the money in the sack's mouth, the return of Simeon, the narrow escape of Benjamin, failed to convince Jacob that his son was alive, till he saw the wagons that Joseph had sent; but after that, each of them would have its influence in deepening the impression. Even to us who have never known the crucifixion of Jesus as a depressing influence, it is a help to faith to remember how in the depth of His humiliation the very air was laden with testimonies to His glory. And they all serve to give effect to that conviction which our Lord was so eager to impress on His disciples,—that all that He was to them while He was in the midst of them, He is still to His servants, and will be to the end of the world. What a fearless attitude towards all the forces of evil may even the weakest man, or the feeblest church assume, if this truth be only held fast! If Jesus be among us, interested in our service, acquainted with all our difficulties, taking the burden of the enterprise on Himself, how calm and untroubled may the attitude of our souls be, and how firm our assurance of victory in the end!

To impress on His disciples the reality of His interest in them, and to induce them to think and act toward Him after He had gone as if He were still personally among them, our Lord had recourse to three things—acts, words, and prayer.

I. His *acts* were simple but very memorable—instituting the Supper, then washing their feet.

The Supper was at once instructive and touching. It was an everlasting memorial of what they owed to Him personally—of what all the Church owes to Him—deliverance through His sufferings and death. It was touching, because it was the last such meal they would ever have together; and likewise because of the holy tenderness by which the bearing of their Master was marked. It was like the soft light of the setting sun, when earth is bathed in the gentlest influences of heaven.

Apparently, it was a most unsuitable time for celebrating the old passover. The passover commemorated a great *deliverance.* Was it in grim irony that this feast was associated with the events that came immediately after, in the experience of Jesus and His followers,—the treachery of Judas, the arraignment of Jesus by the High Priest, the weak surrender of Pilate, and at last the shame and horrors of the crucifixion? What was there in such utter prostration of Him and His cause that could be linked with the joyous memories of that night when Israel, following the fiery pillar, marched safely through the depths of the sea? It is faith alone that can give a satisfactory answer; beneath the surface there lay a profound resemblance, but only faith could apprehend it. Through the breaking of His body and the shedding of His blood there was to come to His Church a deliverance far higher than the fathers had ever known. Death to Him meant life for them. The Supper was to keep alive the memory of His sacrifice and of His love. It was to be the token of the great Christian deliverance to the very end of time. What a triumphant faith our Lord must have had in the success and efficacy of His work, to institute this symbol of deliverance and eternal blessing on the very eve of His crucifixion! How well fitted was this act to lift their thoughts high above all the outer tokens of defeat and humiliation! Things were not as they seemed. The grain of wheat cast into the ground might seem to perish, but its apparent death would issue speedily in the multiplication of its life an hundred-fold.

The act in which the Supper was instituted was, moreover, as tender in manner as it was instructive in matter. A common meal has usually a kindly uniting influence; in a family circle, on the eve of some great bereavement, this is peculiarly found. Hearts saddened by a common sorrow are more disposed to love, and are more ready to appreciate love. The act of washing the disciples' feet, with which our Lord followed up the Supper, increased their tenderness of feeling, and sense of obligation. It was a new token of the gracious condescension of their Lord. It was an additional reason why their trust in Him should continue unabated. But it was more. "I have given you an example," He said, "that ye should do to one another as I have done to you." It was designed to foster among them the spirit that should keep their strength from being wasted in internal strifes, and bind them in a strong, united brotherhood. It was by brotherly counsel and united prayer that their work was to be carried on; while that spirit ruled among them, all would be well, but if they should begin to aim at lordly pre-eminence and seats of distinction, the very heart would be torn out of the body.

And this lesson is surely needed in our day, as much as it was needed in the apostles'. Alas! that in spite of all our Lord's efforts to the contrary, there has so often prevailed in the deliberations of Christian brethren the spirit of scorn and carping, bitterness and irony! Where are the forbearance and forgiveness, the love and confidence of brethren that the Master did so much to encourage? Why should the strife as to who should be greatest, which He did so much to suppress, start up again so often? By all the memories of that Upper Chamber,—by all the associations of that Holy Supper, let there prevail among us a habitual watchfulness against strife and bitterness, and an earnest endeavour to live and love as brethren!

II. Next, let us consider the bearing of our Lord's farewell *words*. We do not dream of surveying in all its length and breadth the wonderful discourse of the 14th, 15th, and 16th chapters of John. We confine ourselves to its *pastoral* aspect,—the influence it was designed to have in keeping up the spirit of the apostles as Christ's public servants, and especially in encouraging them to act and feel in their ministry as if Jesus Himself were still present among them.

In this point of view, the first words of the 14th chapter are the key-note of the whole. " Let not your heart be troubled: ye believe in God, BELIEVE ALSO IN ME." He wishes them to labour with untroubled hearts; hearts as calm as those of servants going on a simple errand, or of heralds carrying a plain proclamation. Terror, perplexity, gnawing anxiety, is not the right spirit of His ambassadors. It was not the spirit of the heroes even of the old dispensation. Moses knew it not when he followed the pillar through the sea; nor Gideon when he advanced with his three hundred on the hosts of Midian; nor David when, with sling and stone, he confronted the giant; nor Elijah when the word came to him, Go, show thyself to King Ahab; nor Nehemiah when he asked, Should such a man as I flee? Though we wrestle not against flesh and blood, but against principalities and powers, against the rulers of the darkness of this world, against spiritual wickedness in high places—our Master's Word to us is, " Let not your heart be troubled." Whatever else His servants may be obliged to carry about with them, they do not need to carry a troubled mind. It is not the restless eye and quivering lip that become them, but the child's look of confidence, and smooth unruffled brow.

Let us mark, further, the ground of this freedom from trouble. "Ye believe in God, believe also in me." Believe in me in like manner as ye believe in God. When the storm rages, you believe that it will soon be calm again, for you believe in a God that rides on the wind, and governs in the storm. Believe that in my government of the Church I have the same power as my Father has in the government of the world. Lean upon me as you lean on the Father, and you will say, as they said of old, "God is our refuge and strength, a very present help in time of trouble."

This being the key-note of the farewell address, its details to a large extent are just an expansion of this thought. Let us glance very briefly at some of the grounds on which the assurance should rest.

1. With reference to Jesus Himself, we are called to believe that He is now with the Father in His house, happy in His love, sharing His power, enjoying that oneness with Him which He had from eternity, and which He manifested so clearly in the work of redemption. He tells us that He abides in His Father's love, that He is in the Father, and the Father in Him, that they that have seen Him have seen the Father also. Partner of almighty strength, Jesus is abundantly able to succour His own. He is one with Him who doeth according to His will in the armies of heaven and among the inhabitants of earth. "The Lord said unto my Lord, Sit thou at my right hand, until I make thine enemies thy footstool."

2. Christ calls on His servants to believe in Him as still loving them and interested in them. He is

leaving them now only for a little time, to prepare a place for them in His Father's house, and He will come again to receive them to Himself, that where He is there they may also be. Though absent in one sense, He is with them in another. " I will not leave you orphans, I will come unto you." " If a man love me, he will keep my words, and my Father will love him, and we will come unto him, and make our abode with him." Did He not leave His peace with them just in order that their hearts should not be troubled? Did He not speak to them in order that His joy might remain in them, and that their joy might be full? Was He not giving them the strongest possible proof of His love in laying down His life for them? Had He not lived on confidential terms with them, making known to them all things that He had received of the Father? A relation like that could not be severed by His temporary absence. It was not a temporary but an abiding relation. "If I go and prepare a place for you, I will come again and receive you to myself; that where I am, there ye may be also." It was their privilege to cherish the sense of this changeless relation to the Prince of Heaven. The same privilege belongs to all whom He has called to serve Him still. Well may such servants hear Him say, " Let not your heart be troubled."

3. They were to believe on Him as still employing them in His service, fitting them for it, fitting them even for its greatest and most difficult achievements. " Verily, verily, I say unto you, he that believeth on me, the works that I do shall he do also; and greater works than these shall he do,

because I go unto my Father." His going to the Father was to bring in a dispensation not of less but of greater power. The ladder between earth and heaven of which He had spoken to Nathanael was to be a more wonderful medium than ever for the angels of God to ascend and descend. "Whatsoever ye shall ask in my name that will I do, that the Father may be glorified in the Son. If ye shall ask anything in my name, I will do it."

Again and again Christ returns to this privilege of ampler scope for prayer under the Gospel, and greater power in it to His people. "If ye abide in me, and my words abide in you, ye shall ask what ye will, and it shall be done unto you." Again, towards the end of the discourse, He says, " In that day ye shall ask me nothing [no question]. Verily, verily, I say unto you, Whatsoever ye shall ask the Father in my name, He will give it you. Hitherto have ye asked nothing in my name: ask, and ye shall receive, that your joy may be full." Prayer was to occupy a place of greater prominence and importance under the new economy. But it was to be prayer addressed to One who was waiting and watching for the cry of His children, and ready to act as Isaiah describes—"It shall come to pass that before they call, I will answer, and while they are yet speaking, I will hear." It was evidently a special aim of Christ's to encourage free, confidential fellowship between Him and His apostles by prayer. And those who entered most fully and cordially into this fellowship got from Him the largest amount of power. So it ever has been, so it ever shall be; for it is the rule of the kingdom: "Ask and ye shall receive."

4. But, perhaps, of all features of the farewell address, the most prominent is one that has yet to be noticed. Our Lord called on the apostles to believe in Him, because He was to pray the Father, and He would send them another Comforter, even the Spirit of Truth, to abide with them for ever. This was the consideration that turned the scale. Up to this point the considerations urged were undoubtedly powerful, but they could hardly suffice to show them that the balance of advantage was on the side of Christ's leaving them, or to induce them to go to work as if He were personally among them. But the glorious gift of the Spirit was to prove a real compensation for His personal absence.

The action of the Holy Spirit was to be twofold—on the apostles, and on the world. In His action on them He was to teach them all things; He was to bring all things to their remembrance that Christ had said to them ; to guide them into all the truth ; to show them things to come ; to receive of Christ's, and to show it to them. A glorious inward illumination and heavenly quickening was thus to come upon them.

In reference to the world, the Spirit was to convince it of sin, and of righteousness, and of judgment, and thus prepare it for receiving their words. He was at once to prepare the soil for the seed, and the seed for the soil. He was to save the apostles from the barren task of scattering seed on hard rocks, and to enable them to realise what they got in symbol in the miraculous draught of fishes. We know how this was fulfilled on the day of Pentecost. The figure of the ladder between earth and heaven was verified. For ten days of continuous prayer, the messengers went upward, and when the day of Pentecost was fully come the angels descended, the Spirit Himself came down in a mighty stream of blessing. The power came from heaven that was needed to turn men's hearts to God. Just as in nature it is the sun that draws up water from the earth to form the clouds of heaven, so in the kingdom of grace it is the Divine Spirit that draws human souls heavenward, by first drawing them to Christ.

The gift of the Spirit is like the gift of the sun. When our Lord promised this gift as an equivalent for His personal absence, the apostles would probably have deemed it impossible that it should be so. But when they witnessed the triumphs of the day of Pentecost they would be of a different mind. The power of heaven was exerted then in the spiritual world far beyond the measure of its exercise even in the personal ministry of Christ. Valleys were exalted and mountains laid low; the crooked became straight, and the rough places plain; the glory of the Lord was revealed, and all flesh saw His salvation.

The lesson thus taught respecting the value of the Holy Spirit, and His boundless power in the spiritual world, is most certainly a lesson for all time. The doctrine of the Holy Spirit, and His place in the process of redemption, is no mere question of theory, but a practical truth of supreme importance. Times when the doctrine of the Spirit has been neglected, or when the Spirit has been regarded as simply an influence from the Father, have always been times of lifeless desolation in the

Church. Seasons of spiritual awakening, and of great accessions to the kingdom of God, have as certainly been times when the Church has believed profoundly in the Holy Ghost, sought His presence most earnestly, and watched against all that was fitted to resist, or vex, or quench Him. And just in proportion as the ministers of the Gospel have felt that spiritual power was not in them, have sought to be simply instruments of the Holy Ghost, and have placed themselves at His disposal that through them He might carry on His work in the world : in the same proportion has spiritual power been given ; the devil, the world, and the flesh have been defeated; souls have been brought into the kingdom, and built up in the character and attainments of Christ's people.

III. We have yet to notice the third of the farewell influences which our Lord brought to bear on His apostles—His farewell *prayer*. But here, as in the case of the farewell address, we can but glance at those features of the prayer which bear on the public service of the apostles, and the relation in which they were to stand to Him after His departure.

In this respect, perhaps, the prayer is somewhat of a surprise to us. It hardly appears to recognise the position of the apostles. It does not seem from it that these feeble, ignorant fishermen are about to go forth to conquer the world. We do not find the petitions we might have expected to find on their behalf, for courage, for endurance in the prospect of all they have to suffer, for divine might to conquer their enemies, for grace to triumph over all the machinations of evil, for the wisdom that turns many to righteousness, or even for the tongue of the learned, that they might be able to speak a word in season to him that was weary.

Yet the Lord knew all their case. He did not care at such a time to launch out into all the details of petition that might be suitable on their behalf. He preferred to ask for them the very essence of blessing, the very elixir of life,—that which, if granted, would spread out in all necessary directions, and abundantly fit them for the highest service.

And that which He thus emphatically asks is, that the Father would keep them in His name, *that they might be one, as He and the Father were* (ver. 11). Unity is the grand object of His petition. And when He extends His prayer beyond the apostles then living, to those who should afterwards believe on Him through their word, it is still "that they all may be one; as thou, Father, art in me, and I in thee" (ver. 21). And when He speaks of the consummation of His work, it is still in the same terms, "I in them, and thou in me, that they may be made perfect in one" (ver. 23). There are other petitions for them,—that they may be kept from the evil in the world, and that they may be sanctified through the truth; but this thrice-repeated prayer for unity is manifestly at the head of all: of all things that Christ besought the Father for His servants, on the eve of His leaving them, the greatest and the highest was, that through Christ in them they might be one, and that the unity might be such as to correspond in some measure with the oneness there had been from eternity between the Father and the Son.

It is often supposed that what our Lord prayed for was simply that His followers might be kept from quarrelling among themselves, and that they might not be split up into a multitude of separate organisations. But if we examine the petition with care we shall see that it goes far deeper than this. The essence of the unity sought is oneness with Christ—" I in them." That the apostles, and all who should thereafter believe on Him through their word, might be ever in vital union with Himself, as He was in vital union with the Father; that in this way they might draw out of His fulness, even grace for grace; that the Church might never become a lifeless corpse, separated from the fountain of life, but might ever be an incarnation of Himself, each member living by faith on the Son of God; that thus, in all circumstances, she might have access to the one source of spiritual life, and draw from Him in such manner that His grace might be sufficient for her, and His strength perfected in her weakness—such was the farewell prayer of our Lord. Virtually it was a prayer, that though He was to be absent from them in the flesh, they might have Him with them in the spirit; guiding all their steps, fulfilling all their desires, blessing all their work.

And this spiritual oneness with Christ is ever the supreme condition of a prospering Church. Whoever would be a successful minister must look to this far above any other condition of prosperity.

Only thus can he wield spiritual power, and become a dispenser of spiritual blessing. "I in them, and thou in me, that they may be made perfect in one; and that the world may believe that thou hast sent me, and that thou hast loved them as thou hast loved me." Whatever else we desire for our ministry, above all let us desire this spiritual oneness with our Lord. The good Lord pardon all our eagerness for less hallowed unions—our longings for the countenance of the great and wealthy, or the wise and prudent of the world; may we ever feel how trifling any good must be which they can do us, compared with that which comes from the indwelling and inworking in the Church of the blessed Spirit of our glorious Lord.

CHAPTER XIX.

HIS RE-APPEARANCE.

THE re-appearance of Jesus to His disciples after His resurrection had many glorious effects; it gave a new foundation to their faith; it filled them with hope and courage; it showed them how gloriously He had triumphed, and how acceptable His sacrifice had been in the Father's sight. But our subject does not lead us into the more general bearings of the resurrection. The one aspect of the event with which we have to do is its bearing on the work of the twelve. Did He give them any new instructions on the advancement of the kingdom? Did He bring any new influence to bear on them with a view to their work? Or did He intensify any of the views which He had formerly taught them, or deepen the spirit with which He had sought to inspire them?

1. One great pastoral lesson which He had already taught was intensified by the peculiar manner in which He presented Himself among them after the resurrection. It was the lesson which, as we have seen, was so prominent in His farewell words— encouraging them to carry on their work after He should leave them with the same reliance on Him,

and the same sense of His sympathy and guidance as if He were visibly present. His intercourse with them during the forty days of the resurrection period was such that He could not be said to be either present or absent. It was a transition period, during which He would now and again present Himself suddenly among them, while for the most part He was as far off as if He had been in a different world. They were getting weaned from the life of sense, and initiated into the life of faith—translated from a condition of sensible into a condition of spiritual intercourse. From time to time He would glide into their company, so that they could not but see that He was profoundly interested in them and bound up with them in their work; but they could not detain Him, they knew not whither He went, and there was no spot of earth where they might hope to find Him. He who had never been further away from them than the top of some neighbouring hill to which He had retired for prayer, and on whose return next day they could count so surely, was not now as He had been then: it was but glimpses of Him they could obtain. But the experience of these mysterious weeks prepared them for the next stage of their career, after He finally left them and sat down on the right hand of God. The sense of His interest in them and readiness to help them which the transition period had fostered, remained with them when the cloud received Him out of their sight. Their whole work was carried on in the firm belief that Jesus lived; that though their eyes beheld Him not, He was still in the midst of them, and that men and devils were as much under His control as when He was among them. And if this was the lesson for the apostles of this strange chapter of our Lord's life, it is not less the lesson for us. To all truly consecrated servants, to us if we have given ourselves up entirely to His service, He is as much a reality, His sympathy is as true, His help is as real, as if He were present at our side. Let us live and work as with a present Lord, and we may rely on wonders of spiritual power being done among us, as signs and wonders were done among the apostles, in the name of God's holy child Jesus.

The consciousness of the actual though unseen presence of Jesus may be readily traced in the procedure of the Church after His ascension. The prayer at the election of the successor to Judas, "Thou, Lord, which knowest the hearts of all men, show whether of these two thou hast chosen," was precisely such a request as they might have made had Jesus been sitting at their side. The gift of the Holy Spirit on the day of Pentecost was felt to be as really the doing of Jesus as the wine at the marriage feast of Cana, or the miraculous draught of fishes on the lake. "Being by the right hand of God exalted, and having received of the Father the promise of the Holy Ghost, he hath shed forth this which ye now see and hear." It was He that healed the lame man at the temple as truly as He had healed the paralytic, or the woman bowed down by infirmity. The dying Stephen got a glimpse with the bodily eye of that same Jesus whom he had seen so habitually with the eye of faith. And Saul of Tarsus, on the way to Damascus, got something more than a glimpse—had an actual personal interview with the living Jesus, and the most blessed personal communication ever experienced of His grace and power. This sense of the presence of their living Lord, so manifest in the early Church, lends a perpetual charm to its history, and goes far to explain its holy, tranquil atmosphere, and its wonderful spiritual power.

2. In the pastoral dealings of the risen Saviour with His servants we note the special pains which He took to open up to them the Scriptures. If it be asked why He left this to the very end, the answer is, that the lesson which He gave then could not have been given with success at any previous time. It was only in the light of His own death that these Scriptures could become so luminous and satisfactory as they were felt to be. No laboured expositions of Hillel or Gamaliel could have thrown on Moses or Isaiah one atom of the light that was poured on them on the way to Emmaus, when, beginning at Moses and all the prophets, the Stranger expounded to the two disciples, in all the Scriptures, the things concerning Himself. To the larger audience gathered the same evening in Jerusalem the same views were presented, when Jesus showed how all things that were written concerning Him in the law of Moses, and in the prophets, and in the psalms, were now fulfilled. What a wonderful revelation it must have been! In the law of Moses, the altar of burnt-offering, the scape-goat, the solemn entrance of the high priest into the holy of holies, and a thousand other ceremonies, would receive their explanation. In the prophets, the wail of

Isaiah over Him who bore our griefs and carried our sorrows; the mysterious prophecy of Daniel that after threescore and two weeks Messiah would be cut off, but not for Himself; the dark call in Zechariah for the sword to awake against God's shepherd, and against the man that was His fellow, would all be placed in the light of day. The terrible darkness in some of the psalms; the cry from the twenty-second that had been uttered on the cross; the wail of the sixty-ninth when the waters had come in unto His soul; the lamentation of the eighty-eighth over the fierce wrath that went over Him, would pass into a brightness unknown before. It is remarkable that while bringing the Old Testament dispensation to an end, our Lord inspired His apostles with more respect than ever for its institutions and its Scriptures. A flood of light was poured on both. The great purpose of the sacrificial system, vast and manifold as it was, was revealed. Instead of discarding the Old Testament ceremonies as an elaborate mistake, their significance, as well as their Divine origin, was more clearly shown. The Mosaic economy never seemed more Divine than at the moment of its departure. It shone out with a Divine glory, like the beautiful ice-crystals of a winter morning, that gleam like pearls and diamonds under the sunbeam that is to melt them away.

Can we reasonably doubt that our Lord's explanation of His sufferings set them forth as the propitiation, the penalty of man's sin borne by the substitute? What other view can be conceived that would make the hearts of hearers burn within them, that would be to them like the lifting of a cloud from the sides and summit of a mountain, revealing in clear form and bright colours what had only loomed like a dark mass before?

It is painful to see the shifts to which able men, who deny the sacrificial character of the sufferings of Christ, are put, by their efforts to find some other view of these sufferings at all worthy of the infinite importance ascribed to them in Scripture. We may well be grateful to any who have taught us to value the self-sacrifice of Christ, and have laid emphasis on the beautiful surrender of His will to the will of God, and on the patient, loving endurance which His desire to benefit men entailed on the great Sufferer. But was this enough to form the burden of a whole series of Divine writings? Was this enough to furnish the key to the main rites and ordinances of an elaborate dispensation, of which sacrifice by the shedding of blood was the chief feature? Was the whole result of fifteen hundred years of burnt-offering and incense, of all that Moses had instituted, of all that David had sung, of all that the prophets had foretold of Messiah, simply to make it more clear, that it is only through self-sacrifice and suffering that the highest benefits can accrue to men?

The prominence which, on the very day of His resurrection,—on the very birth-day of the Christian Church,—our blessed Lord thus gave to the doctrine of His sufferings, ought surely to find for it a corresponding place in the ministrations of all His servants and witnesses. It is certain that it obtained that place in the ministrations of the apostles, and that it was one of the great factors in the early success of the Gospel. Its occupying the central place imposes no necessity on the modern preacher to restrict himself to the mere iteration of evangelical first principles, or leave out of his teaching any topic that bears on the welfare either of the individual or of the society. In the centre of the solar system, the sun occupies the best position for influencing every planet, but his rays go forth quite readily to the furthest outskirts of the system. "Christ crucified" in the centre of the Gospel firmament, is fitted to irradiate the whole sphere of moral and spiritual truth, and increase the power of every motive, and elevate the aim of every project that seeks to advance the true welfare of man.

3. We come now to a point of very great practical interest in our Lord's dealings with His apostles after His resurrection—the instructions which He gave them regarding the setting up and extension of His kingdom.

Having already adverted to His special dealings with two of His apostles, Peter and Thomas, whose cases were peculiar, we do not need to dwell on these again. We simply remark how interesting it is to find Him thus occupied with the case of individuals, even when His mind was filled with so vast a scheme as the evangelisation of the world. But for that great work it was indispensable that the agents be well equipped, and inasmuch as love and faith were the two great qualities through which the conversion of the world was to be accomplished, care was taken to make sure of these qualities in two of the chief instruments. Alas for any church where no bright faith and no warm love move the hearts of its ministers!

It would seem that not a little was spoken by our Lord after His resurrection "concerning the kingdom of God" (Acts i. 3) which has not been formally recorded. It is certainly remarkable that Luke has given us no notes of these conversations, which could not have failed to be profoundly interesting. We must conclude that the substance of them was reproduced by the apostles in their subsequent discourses and proceedings. Though the conversations are not recorded in form, they are translated into fact; the actual church of Peter and John and the rest of the apostles must have been the transcript of our Lord's instructions.

That the chief thing of which our Lord would speak to them was the coming work of the Holy Ghost can hardly admit of reasonable doubt. In His farewell address this had been a prominent topic; and not a few things seem to indicate that it was not less so after He rose from the dead.

Thus, on the very first evening after His resurrection, we read that "he breathed on them and said, Receive ye the Holy Ghost: whose soever sins ye forgive, they are forgiven unto them; whose soever sins ye retain, they are retained" (John xx. 22, 23).

Few passages have given rise to more diversity of explanation. What was denoted by Christ's breathing on them? It seems plain that it was not on this occasion that the Holy Spirit was actually given to the apostles. The very men on whom Christ breathed at this time are called on afterwards to tarry at Jerusalem until they should be endued with power from on high. The act of Jesus was symbolical and prophetic. It foreshadowed the day of Pentecost, and His words denoted the awfully solemn issues with which the brethren were to be called to deal. They would encounter multitudes in great anxiety about their sins, and on their instructions and spirit it would depend to a large extent whether these multitudes should be guided to the fountain of forgiveness, or whether they would perish in their guilt. As they were to be the instruments of giving in the plainest terms God's message to men, and men were to be called by them to deal with that message, they would be able to assure those who accepted it that their sins were forgiven, and those who rejected it that they were as far from forgiveness as ever. There are doubtless difficulties connected with this interpretation; but there are far greater difficulties in any view that gives to the apostles an absolute power of forgiving and retaining sin. It is certain that they never claimed such a power; Peter pointed to the exalted Saviour as the only source of forgiveness (Acts v. 31), and they all were accustomed to urge sinners to deal directly with Him, if they would be forgiven (Acts viii. 22; xi. 43; xvi. 31). Our Lord's purpose seems to have been to convey to His apostles a becoming sense of the solemnity of the work in which they were to be engaged. Their ministry was not to be a ministry of shadows, like that of the Aaronitic priesthood; nor a ministry of promises, like John the Baptist's; it was to be a ministry of facts. Trembling souls would come under their care, agitated by all the agony of remorse and the terrible forebodings of coming retribution; to deal with such they were utterly incompetent, unless they enjoyed the guidance of a higher agency—the power of the Holy Ghost.

It was to the same doctrine of the Holy Ghost that our Lord directed their thoughts when they conveyed to Him their still lingering, yet wistful desire that even yet He would set up a visible kingdom in Israel (Acts i. 6). Fain would they have had Him confront in His own person the great forces of disorder in the world, and erect a visible kingdom that would have been a rallying ground for all His followers. They were still oppressed by the consciousness of their impotence, and the impotence of any force they knew of, to get up His kingdom and rectify the disorders of the world. But our Lord gave no encouragement to such views. "Ye shall receive power," He said, " after that the Holy Ghost is come upon you; and ye shall be witnesses unto me both in Jerusalem and in Judea, and in Samaria, and unto the uttermost parts of the earth." Here was the function of the apostles—"ye shall be witnesses unto me ; " and here was the power which would make their testimony effective—" after that the Holy Ghost is come upon you." Little did they know what moral force would be found in such testimony, when made effective by the power of the Holy Ghost!

The lesson is as suitable to us as it was to them. It may be a humble office—to be simply witnesses to Christ. Not priests, dispensing the awards of life and death; not philosophers, reasoning cleverly on the nature of things, and constructing theories of the universe; not princes, wielding the powers of this world. They were to be only witnesses; servants whose business is to tell about another,—His birth, His death, His atonement, His coming again; and to persuade men to believe on Him " who of God is made unto us wisdom, and righteousness, and sanctification, and redemption." It was a strange idea that the devil would be subdued and the world transformed by any such process—as strange as the notion that carrying the ark round the walls of Jericho would be followed by the overthrow of her fortresses. But at Jericho, the strange idea was realised; and at Jerusalem, too, the witness of the apostles to Christ became the means of a great moral revolution;—not only was Jesus of Nazareth received as the Son of God, but under Him night seemed to turn to day and winter to summer, and every moral wilderness there and elsewhere seemed to brighten with the hues of Paradise.

And now came out clearly the extent of our Lord's scheme, as committed to these twelve men. They were to be witnesses for Him " to the uttermost parts of the earth." " Go ye into all the world," He said, " and preach the gospel to every creature." " Go ye and teach all nations, baptizing them in the name of the Father, and of the Son, and of the Holy Ghost, teaching them to observe all things whatsoever I have commanded you." Now it was made clear what meaning He attached to the promise to Abraham—" In thee and in thy seed shall all the families of the earth be blessed." It was plain how He understood those expressions in the psalms that call on God "to inherit all nations," and that call on " all lands to make a joyful noise unto God." No shadow of restriction was to be placed on Isaiah's vision when "the mountain of the Lord's house should be exalted above the mountains, and all nations should flow unto it"— when Zion should "arise and shine, and the Gentiles should come to her light, and kings to the brightness of her rising." In His obscure workshop at Nazareth this Master of theirs had formed the scheme of a kingdom wider than the empire of the Cæsars, under which His name would not command the homage of one great continent only, but would stand alone, pre-eminent in honour and glory, over all the globe. All the glory of David or of Solomon was but child's play compared to the renown to which He aspired,—that is, compared to the amount of blessing which He aimed at diffusing. What a project to enter into the brain of a penniless and friendless young man, bred in the obscurity of a miserable village, and having for His companions and coadjutors a mere handful of fishermen! What a surprise it must have been to these fishermen to hear Him proclaim the boundless reach of His ambition, to announce His claim to kingdoms wider far than those of which the tempter at the outset of His ministry had offered to put Him in possession! And how much greater their surprise to learn that they were to be the instruments of carrying into effect this world-wide project—that "their sound was to go into all the earth, and their words unto the ends of the world!"

There was one thing, however, that made the scheme a feasible one, and that encouraged the apostles to address themselves to it in earnest. "All power," said Jesus, "is given unto me in heaven and on earth." His authority and His ability to carry out His schemes are beyond question. There is no power in heaven and earth which He is not able to control. However far He may allow men to encroach on His domain, He always keeps hold of the restrictive word: "Hitherto and no further." This fact is one of infinite importance for the faith of His servants to grasp. The apostles did grasp it, and hence their courage, their hope, and their success. By faith they heard the Divine voice proclaiming, as Jesus ascended, "Sit thou at my right hand, until I make thine enemies thy footstool;" and when the Spirit came, they went forth to their work without fear or misgiving. They knew that Jesus had only to choose the way in which He would exert the might which He possessed for the conquest of the world; and that the way which He had chosen was, to make the efforts of His servants effectual for the mighty end. They had a deep conviction that the work was His, not theirs; that they were but instruments in the hands of an almighty Captain, who had planned all the campaign, and who would arrange and direct the whole operations of His army, and at last crown them with success. They knew that the Holy Spirit whom He was to send would make their words quick and effectual for opening men's eyes, convicting their consciences, renewing their wills, and transforming their lives. In that attitude, and in that trust, "they went forth, and preached everywhere, the Lord working with them, and confirming the word by signs following."

Would only that the same view of the situation had prevailed ever since—the same faith, the same love, the same hope—for the world to-day would be in a very different condition. Would that even now, all Christ's public servants could be brought back to the same view of things that influenced the apostles; the same sense of personal emptiness, the same trust in the Divine Captain of our salvation, and in the efficacy of the means by which He is to achieve the conquest of the world! One might be willing to blot out the record of all the intervening centuries, if the Church could only be brought back to the attitude of that believing handful, who felt so certain of their Lord's omnipotent power, waited with such unfaltering faith for the promise of the Father, and, when the Spirit came, were so bold and earnest in calling on men to believe on Jesus. Like the archer on the white horse, they went forth conquering and to conquer. Triumph followed triumph, wherever they proclaimed the story of Jesus of Nazareth. What hinders *us* from doing the same, and achieving the like results, except that we have not the faith which they had in the Father, and in the Son, and in the Holy Ghost? If only we would take up the posture of servants, executing the designs of a heavenly Master, relying on the grace of His Holy Spirit, and giving ourselves soul, body, and spirit to His work, results not inferior to theirs would crown our labours, and of our work as of theirs it would be written,—" So mightily grew the word of the Lord, and prevailed."

THE END.